D0550270

TURKISH COAST

Bodrum to Marmaris

Michael Bussmann and Gabriele Tröger
with walks by
Brian and Eileen Anderson
and Dean Livesley

SUNFLOWER BOOKS

First edition © 2007
Sunflower Books™
PO Box 36160
London SW7 3WS, UK
www.sunflowerbooks.co.uk

Published in the USA by
Hunter Publishing Inc
130 Campus Drive
Edison, NJ 08818
www.hunterpublishing.com

ISBN 978-1-85691-329-4

Important note to the reader

Apart from the walks, this book is a translation from a series of *general* guides originally published in Germany (see Publisher's note on page 6). We have tried to ensure that the descriptions and maps are error-free at press date. The book will be updated, where necessary, whenever future printings permit. It will be very helpful for us to receive your comments (sent in care of Sunflower Books, please) for the updating of future printings.

We also rely on those who use this book — especially walkers — to take along a good supply of common sense when they explore. Conditions change very rapidly in this part of Turkey, and *storm damage or building works may make a route unsafe at any time*. If the route is not as we outline it here, and your way ahead is not secure, return to the point of departure. *Never attempt to complete a trip by car or on foot under hazardous conditions!*

If you would like to offset the carbon dioxide emissions for your trip to Turkey, go to www.climatecare.org.

Text (except the walks) translated and adapted from *Türkei — Lykische Küste* and *Türkei — Westküste;* text, town and site plans © 2005, 2006 Michael Müller Verlag, Erlangen, Germany; translation: Thomas Wilkes and Pat Underwood
Photograph credits
© Michael Bussmann: pages 9, 10, 12, 18, 26, 29, 31, 32, 43 (bottom), 59, 63, 86, 106, 122, 124, 138, 142, 155, 156, 160 (bottom), 162, 168 (top), 176
© Brian Anderson: pages 20, 48, 71, 84, 87, 92, 93, 95, 101, 114, 117, 131, 132, 148 (both), 160 (top)
© i-stockphoto: cover and pages 16, 23, 24, 30 (both), 36, 39, 43 (top), 44 (both), 46, 55, 60, 90, 137, 156, 164-5, 168 (bottom)
Walking maps: John Underwood; © Sunflower Books
Sunflower Books is a Registered Trademark.
A CIP catalogue record for this book is available from the British Library.
Printed and bound in England by J. H. Haynes & Co. Ltd.

⬤ Contents

● Preface

The Turkish poet and writer Cevat Şakir Kabaağaçli once described the area between Bodrum and Marmaris as 'terrifyingly' beautiful. Silver-leaved olive groves and wild inland mountains yield up the stone remains of ancient civilisations. The dazzling multi-coloured bays, framed by fissured cliffs and collared with golden sand, are the stuff of dreams. Snuggled into the coves are romantic fishing villages, where you will be greeted with genuine Turkish hospitality. And in Bodrum and Marmaris you can mix with the Turkish jet set.

The region has so much to offer that of couse there is a 'down' side: some dreadful over-development. Many of the once-idyllic fishing villages have changed substantially in recent years, some have even become centres of international mass tourism. But there is a new surge of ecological tourism afoot. In some old mountain villages and along isolated sections of the coast there are more and more small quiet places to stay — with the flair of 'Tuscany meets the East'.

This book covers the ground from the Bodrum Peninsula to Marmaris, 100km east of Dalaman Airport, and includes several excursions and walks in outlying areas. A companion guide, *Turkish Coast: Kaş to Dalyan*, explores the area between Marmaris and Kekova. When you've taken in all that, you might like to move further east to visit eastern Lycia and Antalya, covered in a third guide.

Bodrum and Marmaris highlights ...

... for lovers of beautiful beaches

There are hundred of kilometres of coast, and away from the large resorts plenty of still-peaceful coves and bays. Even more opportunties for sun, sand and sea are offered by the many boat trips to nearby islands. Here are a few of the top choices:

Gulf of Gökova — with the two bays of Mazıköy, this is one of the most beautiful stretches of coastline in Turkey.

Hayıtbükü Bay — a favourite with the yachting fraternity. There's Greek flair and not a trace of mass tourism in this small protected bay on the Reşadiye Peninsula west of Marmaris.

... for archaeology and culture freaks

Numerous ruined cities, among them some of the most imposing in Asia Minor, are evidence of the importance of this region in ancient times. Among the major sites covered in this book, the following stand out.

Knidos — a spellbinding combination of stone remains and the grandiose landscape of a dramatic coastline. This site lay undiscovered on westernmost tip of the Reşadiye Peninsula for two thousand years.

Ephesus and Aphrodisias — the former a major city before Rome was even founded, the latter with the best-preserved ancient stadium in the Mediterranean area. Both sites are among the most important in all Turkey and easily reached by bus or car.

... for nature and landscape enthusiasts

The tiny Bodrum Peninsula is full of contrasts, with a limestone west and volcanic east. The countryside around Marmaris is totally different, with swathes of green pine cloaking the hills like giant waves frozen in motion.

Reşadiye Peninsula — steep mountains, gorgeous bays. The sparsly populated peninsula, which separates the Aegean from the open Mediterranean, offers magnificent views to the Gulf of Gökova.

Pamukkale — Even if these white sinter terraces don't lie right in the Bodrum/Marmaris area, they are easily reached on a day trip. The sight is something special, even though you can no longer bathe in the travertines.

Publisher's note

A couple of decades ago, we published Brian and Eileen Anderson's 'Landscapes' walking and touring guides to the Antalya and Bodrum/Marmaris areas. Brian and Eileen are still Sunflower authors, but these guides eventually went out of print. There was so much building work going on from the 1990s that the books really needed revision annually, but because of the long distances involved, coupled with rising car hire, petrol and accommodation costs in Turkey, this was no longer practical for UK-based authors.

We've been able to remedy the situation by finding two German authors who have been visiting and writing about Turkey for many years, and an Englishman who has his own guiding business on the coast. So this book has five authors, all with different interests. The walks were originally devised and written by Brian and Eileen; all were checked and rewritten where necessary by Dean just prior to publication, and everything else is down to Michael and Gabi, the main authors. Naturally this can lead to slightly different writing styles, but we hope it won't be a case of 'too many cooks'. A few notes follow.

Keep in mind that if a hotel or restaurant entry says 'recommended by readers', this refers to recommendations by *German* users of the original guides (in print for decades and revised every two-three years). This does *not* mean, however, that the establishment is predominantly frequented by German clients; what Michael and Gabi always seek out is the place with a personal touch, whatever the price category or clientele. Just log on to some of the hundreds of web addresses they provide with their recommendations!

Dean was a find; he has lived in Turkey for 15 years and helped research and implement the famous 'Lycian Way' (covered in the *Antalya to Demre* and *Kaş to Dalyan* guides). He has been involved in conservation for many years and now runs his own company organising activity, nature and cultural/historical tours from his base in Kaş. Should you travel east to the Kaş area, you can contact him at Kekova Aktif, www.kekovaaktif.com; ☎ 0242 8361416.

One common thread binds all the authors: a shared love of Turkey's ancient history, landscapes and traditional hospitality. This shines through all the pages of the book — from the humorous boxed asides about mythological characters to their determination to retrace ancient walking routes despite the bulldozers and overgrown paths.

Key to the maps and plans

touring map
- motorway
- trunk road
- secondary road
- minor road
- track
- ▲ mountain peak
- ⅟ viewpoint
- Λ campsite
- ⁑ ancient site
- ⑨ location of walks

town plans
- 🅿 parking
- beach
- Ⓜ museum
- mosque
- 🅸 tourist office
- post office
- BUS bus stop
- taxi rank
- car hire
- ✚ hospital, clinic

walking maps
- dual carriageway/trunk road
- secondary road/motorable track
- jeep track/path or old trail
- main walk and direction
- alternative route and direction
- bus, *dolmuş* stop/petrol station
- *sarniç*/tank, tap, water source
- mosque/ancient site
- windmill/viewpoint
- building/castle, fort or tower

Country and people of the crescent moon — Turkey in facts and figures

Official name: Türkiye Cumhuriyeti (Republic of Turkey)

Geography: With a surface area of 779,452 square kilometres, Turkey is more than three times the area of the United Kingdom. Just three percent of the area is on the continent of Europe, with the remainder (generally called Anatolia) being in Asia. Turkey's highest mountain is Mount Ararat (5165m) in the easternmost part of the country. Turkey is one of the most seismically active continental regions of the world, with a long history of earthquakes due to tectonic activities in the fault line and the drifting together of the Eurasian and Arabian tectonic plates.

Political system: Turkey has been a parliamentary democracy since the constitution of 1982. The president (Ahmet Necdet Sezer since 2000) is selected for a seven-year term of office by parliament, which is also the law-making body. There will be new elections in 2007. The Turkish parliament has 550 seats and, after a five-year legislative period, is also due for new elections in 2007. At press date the conservative AKP party under Prime Minister Recep Tayyip Erdoğan (since 2003) holds power with 368 seats. Laicism (separation of church and state) is guaranteed in the constitution.

Economics: Thanks to the AKP, which brought in long-awaited and much-needed structural reforms (privatisation of unprofitable state enterprises, transparent tendering procedures, central bank autonomy, better terms for international investors, etc.) Turkey has recently experienced some boom years, with economic growth of 10% or more. But the overstretched budget is worrying. The national debt amounts to about 70% of GDP — and as long as only one out of ten people in employment pays tax, it's difficult to see how the deficit will be overcome.

The annual inflation rate has decreased strongly over the last few years; in 2001 it was 54%, in 2005 — for the first time in 30 years — it was below 10%. The latest figures show unemployment standing at around 9%, with annual income per head at between £2700-4500. (depending on the source consulted). Income in the Istanbul area runs at about double the national average, in the poor eastern provinces it's only about half the average. Countrywide, agriculture contributes only 13% towards GDP (although it employs 40% of the total workforce), industry brings in 25%, and the service sector 62%.

Military: The armed forces number 515,000 men and therefore are among the largest in the world (the second-largest in NATO). Military expenditure as a portion of gross national product is approximately a third higher than the world average. Two reasons for this are the long conflict with the Kurds in the east of the country and the ongoing test of strength with Greece. Soldiers are highly respected by the Turkish people.

Population structure: In 2006 Turkey had approximately 73 million inhabitants (1960: 28 million); the average age is 28 (UK: 38.6). The population density

is very varied. The administrative district of Istanbul with 1330 inhabitants per sq km is clearly the most dense. The lowest population density is in the underdeveloped provinces in eastern Anatolia with only 16 inhabitants per sq km.

Sub-populations: 85.7% Turks, 10.6% Kurd, 1.6% Arab, and 2.1% mixed (Armenians, Greeks, Laz, Circassian, Georgians and Muslim Bulgarians).

Health/social: one doctor per 825 inhabitants. The average life expectancy for women is 73 years and for men about 68 years. Old-age pensions do not exist, nor are there any unemployment benefits.

Education: Over the last few decades much has been done for education; over 50,000 schools have been built since 1950. The estimated illiteracy rate for women is approximately 28%, for men about 8%. However there is a strong contrast between east and west: in the western part, illiteracy is mostly confined to the older generation, whereas in the east (where child labour is still common) the figures include children as well. Since 1997 eight years' schooling has been compulsory.

Religion: 99% of the Turkish population are Muslims. The remainder are Jewish and either Syrian or Greek Orthodox Christians.

☀ Introduction

This book covers the Bodrum and Marmaris peninsulas and the area around the Gulf of Gökova — as well as three of the most popular excursion sites in southern Turkey: Pamukkale/Hierapolis, Aphrodisias and Ephesus. Most people using this book will be arriving at/departing from Bodrum's airport or Dalaman east of Marmaris. If you plan a longer stay, there is the option of moving east with *Turkish Coast: Kaş to Dalyan*, which covers the ground from here to Kaş and the Kekova/Simena area.

When to go

The Taurus mountain range (with heights of over 3000 m) prevents the cool air mass from off the Anatolian highlands penetrating to the south coast until late autumn. Thus long, hot summers alternate with short, mild winters. The hot season experiences low rainfall, while the winter months are wet.

The bathing season around the Aegean lasts from Easter until mid-October, and outside this period many hotels are closed. April, May, September and October are the best months to visit, when the daily maximum temperatures only rarely exceed 30 °C.

Getting to Bodrum and Marmaris

By air

Most people reach the area on **charter flights** — either into Milas-Bodrum Airport 35km northeast of Bodrum or Dalaman Airport 100km east of Marmaris. The area is so popular that at time of writing there were (charter) flights to both airports from Belfast International, Birmingham, Bristol, Cardiff, Doncaster Sheffield, East Midlands, Edinburgh, Exeter, Glasgow, Humberside, London Gatwick, London Luton, London Stansted, Manchester, Newcastle and Norwich. Additionally, there are flights to Bodrum from Bournemouth and to Dalaman from Leeds Bradford, Liverpool and Teeside.

Scheduled flights (with Turkish Airlines or BA) necessitate a changeover in Instanbul. From the United States it's rather a long haul, with flights by Turkish Airlines in cooperation with American Airlines and BA, stopping over in the UK.

Flight-only options are ideal for anyone who wants to make their own accommodation arrangements — or fly into Bodrum and return from Dalaman (or even Antalya). It's very easy to make your own arrangements on the internet, and perhaps book a **fly-drive** as well.

Prices are highest between April and October, when there are also more flights: expect to pay around £270 *including taxes*. But in 'off-season' there are some very economical deals — around £130 return or less *including taxes*. Obviously, booking well ahead (or at the last minute!) you may well be able to better these prices. The **travel documents** you'll need are listed on page 50 in the 'A-Z' section; for information about Milas-Bodrum Airport, transfers, etc, see page 61.

Package tours to the Bodrum/ Marmaris area are are offered by a huge number of companies and are perhaps the easiest option if you just want to stay in one place and haven't the time to make your own arrangements. All the major UK tour operators offer both resorts, but there are also specialists for Turkey. For a list of specialist Turkish tour operators, visit www.gototurkey.co.uk and click on 'Specialist Tour Operators' (in the USA/Canada see www.tourismturkey.org and click on 'Tour Operators'). The most popular resorts with the main tour operators in the area covered by this book are Bodrum itself, Bitez, Gümbet, Gündoğan, Ortakent, Torba, Turgutreis and Yalıkavak on the Bodrum Peninsula; Marmaris itself, and nearby İçmeler, Turunç and Hisarönü just to the south. Naturally all tour operators will be only too happy to book you excursions to tourist sights outside the region, *gulet* trips along the coast, or even hiking tours. Often these excursions are offered at time of booking, or you can ask your tour rep about them.

The **baggage** allowance is usually limited to 20kg on flights, but if you are flying with a Business Class or other seat upgrade, or are staying longer than 28 days, you may be able to get this lifted to 30kg. Otherwise you are likely to have to pay about £3-7 per kilo for excess baggage (although if you're just a few kilos over they are likely to turn a blind eye). For **sports equipment** the rules vary between airlines: golf clubs and diving equipment are usually carried free, but sometimes they are classed as extra baggage for a flat rate of between £20-40. Bicycles, paragliders and surfboards can be charged at anything between £20-£100. Naturally you will want to check all this in advance — in any case you are legally bound to give the airlines advance notice of oversize baggage.

By car

Driving to Bodrum/Marmaris is *possible* for those who have plenty of time (allow 4-5 days), especially if you want to tour and camp (campsite details are listed under 'Accommodation'). You will need an international driving licence, the vehicle's registration documents and valid Third Party insurance. On arrival, details of the vehicle will be logged in your passport, and you won't be able to leave the country without it. After crossing the Channel, you would make for one of the Italian ports: *Brindisi* for ferries to Çeşme in western Turkey (Marmara Lines; www.marmaralines.com) or *Ancona* or *Venice* for ferries to Igoumenitsa in Greece (Anek Lines, www.anek.gr). The option via Greece is cheaper, but it's still another 1000km to the Turkish south coast.

By train

This option is only for those really keen on rail travel; it is far more expensive than air. There are daily departures from London via Paris and Vienna to *Istanbul* (two different routes, each taking three nights). For details of this trip, see www.seat61.com. At the same web site there are links for onward travel in Turkey itself but, since no trains serve the coast, at some point you have to change to a bus.

Getting around Bodrum and Marmaris
By car or motorcycle

Having your own wheels makes travelling around the peninsulas uncomplicated, but some caution is required. Once warrior-like Turks hunted on their steppe horses; today their great-great-great-grandchildren handle themselves with equal prowess in traffic — the combat cry has simply been replaced by the horn. For many drivers there is only one lane — the middle of the road. Overtaking on blind corners, driving the wrong way on a one-way traffic lane or street, not stopping for red lights: these things happen all too frequently. You will see all this for yourself in time, but it pays to be aware of it from the start. If this is your first visit to Turkey or this area, consider renting a car once you get acclimatised at your base, rather than picking it up at the airport — especially if you are arriving at night.

You can **rent a car** in the tourist centres on nearly every corner whereas, in comparison, the number of places offering **mopeds, motorcycles** and **bicycles** is pretty modest. If you are interested in renting any sort of vehicle, you must of course have your driving licence and passport or ID card. Some rental

Driving on the Reşadiye Peninsula

companies require that the driver is at least 21 or even 23 years old and has had their driving licence for at least one year. The cheapest (but at the same time the thirstiest) rental car is the Fiat 131, called *Sahin* in Turkey. The large international rental companies usually forbid you from leaving asphalt roads so that, strictly speaking, you would not be allowed to drive to any bays or ancient sites only accessible via tracks.

Prices are usually substantially lower from local hire companies than from the large international chains. Depending on the season, you'll pay between £15-30 per day with the smaller companies. They offer this price advantage by having an older and usually less well-maintained fleet of vehicles. The prices of the better-known hire firms differ little — again, depending on the season, they charge about £35-55 per day for the cheaper models. Which-ever you choose, the mileage is usually free. The best value is to book by the week before leaving home, and can be cheaper still if booked straight away as a **fly/drive**. Prices for motorcycles begin at approximately £20/day, scooters start at £15/day and mopeds at £10/day.

Do read the **small print**: make a note of the **insurance cover** specified in the contract, and particularly personal liability in the event of a claim. Note for instance that even with fully comprehensive insurance, under-body damage and flat tyres are not covered. Various rental companies accept credit card payment; gold cards usually offer an additional insurance

Special advice for motorists

• Avoid driving at night if at all possible. Badly lit lorries and cars will be on the roads — to say nothing of completely unlit horse or donkey carts and farmers in dark clothing on their way back from work. The risks of an accident are also higher at night because you can't see the potholes and building works ahead, and they may only be marked off with some stones. Add to that carefree pedestrians of all ages — the road is regarded as a pavement, especially in the country areas.

• If you are in the first row at a red light when it changes to green, look right and left before going ahead — not all your fellow road-users are interested in the colour play of traffic lights…

• In Turkey it is common practice to sound your horn before a blind bend. If the oncoming traffic does not hear anything, they assume the road is free. It is also common practice to sound your horn when overtaking!

• Exercise special caution on loose chippings, particularly on newly built stretches of road. Thousands of windscreens are broken every year. Keep well back from lorries!

• In order to curtail speeding, frequent radar controls are in place (minimum fine £35), and speed bumps have been added in recent years at the entrances to built-up and populated areas. For those who don't yet know their way around, these speed bumps can be treacherous, because there are usually no signs to make you aware of them, nor are they marked in colour (apart from large oil marks!).

Traffic signs — what's what?

Bozuk satıh — bad stretch of road

Dikkat — be careful; caution

Dur — stop

Düşük banket — unfinished road

Kay gan yol — slippery surface

Park (yeri) — car park

Park yapılmaz — no parking

Şehir merkezi — city centre

Tamirat — roadworks

Taşıt geçemez — road closed (driving through prohibited)

Yavaş — drive slowly

Yasak — forbidden/no entry

---

protection/cover, which makes it unnecessary to take out passenger insurance or the like. If in doubt, ask your insurance broker.

Should you be unfortunate enough to be involved in an **accident**, you must *not* move the vehicle, but summon the police, no matter how remote your situation or seemingly minor the damage. A police report is mandatory for any insurance claim. *Do not sign any report which you cannot read* — or else make a note on the report that you could not read it. There are a few scare stories around about accidents involving personal injury to the effect that it's better to put your foot down and drive to the nearest police station as quickly as possible, lest you meet with summary justice at the scene. However well meant, this is totally irresponsible advice. You would be charged both for hit and run and for not giving aid, with far worse consequences than any possible reprisals at the scene of the accident.

Keep the following **traffic regu-**lations in mind: the **maximum speed** in built-up areas is 50km/h (with a trailer 40km/h); otherwise 90km/h (with a trailer 70km/h); motorcycles 80km/h. On motorways the limit for both cars and motorcycles is 120km/h. The **blood alcohol limit** for drivers of *cars without trailers* is 0.5mg/l (generally equivalent to two glasses of wine), for everyone else (including motorcyclists) there is *zero tolerance,* no alcohol permitted at all. **Mobile telephones** may only be used with a hands-free device while driving.

Petrol stations are frequent along the main roads and open seven days a week. Lead-free *(kurşunsuz)* petrol is readily available. Petrol prices in Turkey are slightly higher than those in Britain at time of writing, with a litre of normal unleaded costing approximately £1.

Don't worry if you have a **puncture**; the Turks are very helpful. Ask for the nearest *Oto Sanayi* — a group of workshops, usually on minor roads at the entrance to or exit from the larger communities.

By bus

The bus is the king of cross-country travel. The number of companies with networks serving the whole country is incredible, and the price differences are small.

The busiest companies use modern Mercedes or Mitsubishi buses, which are manufactured in Turkey under licence. Air-conditioning (take a jumper with you on the bus!) and video are standard; the majority of the buses also have toilets, tinted windows, special seat cushions, etc. Well-known companies are Metro, Ulusoy, Kamil Koç, Pamukkale and Varan. The better bus companies give you a token for your stowed luggage, so it's easily retrieved at the end of the trip. During the journey passengers are usually catered for by a young steward. Biscuits and drinks are distributed free of charge, as well as a Turkish eau de cologne *(kolonya)* for sticky and sweaty palms.

All the buses are non-smoking (but they stop for breaks approximately every two hours). The departure times listed in this book serve only as a rough indication and refer to data from the larger bus companies. Journeys with the smaller (predominantly local) bus companies invariably take longer, since they make so many stops along the route. Further information about bus travel can be found with introductory details about the towns and villages covered.

Bus fares vary little; on average one pays 2-3 pence/km, with the up-market companies charging somewhat more. So a trip from Marmaris to Datça would cost about £2.75. Booking a ticket also includes a **seat reservation**, and you can choose your seat from a plan. Naturally the front seats are usually the best and most coveted, but wait: you may be exposed to the driver's cigarette smoke — unlike the passengers, the drivers *are* allowed to smoke on the bus!

Arrive well in advance of **departure time!** Buses leave punctually — and often up to five minutes early!

Turkish **bus stations** *(otogar, terminal* or *garaj)* are very like British and continental *railway* stations, with toilets, waiting rooms, kiosks, restaurants and shops. If there is no official 'left luggage', you can usually leave your things at the counter of your bus company. Bus stations are usually located several kilometres outside the city centres, so to get to them you often first have to take a service bus or *dolmuş*. But the well-known companies and local bus companies normally offer a feeder service with mini-buses from the centre of town. Smaller towns frequently only have a collection of simple bus company offices near the market, and the buses either leave from just outside the office or stop briefly on the town bypass.

At larger bus stations, **touts** working for different bus companies will try to persuade you to one ticket counter or other. Just ignore them, so that you can compare departure times and prices in peace.

By *Fez Bus*

The 'Fez Bus' (www.fezbus.co. uk) is a hop on-hop off service aimed at backpackers and independent travellers. From the end of April until the end of October a Fez Bus leaves Istanbul every two days and makes a circuit round half of Turkey before going back to the Bosphorus. With just one pass (which is valid for the whole season), you can get on and off as often as you want on whichever route you've booked, and you do not have to start at Istanbul. The basic route (Istanbul — Gallipoli

Gulets anchor in crystal-clear coves during the 'blue cruises'.

— Selçuk — Köyceğiz — Ölüdeniz — Kaş — Antalya — Cappadocia — Ankara — Istanbul) is called the 'Turkish Delight Pass' and costs about £135, including an English-speaking tour guide. There are a great many add-ons, too — from detour routes on the mainland to *gulet* cruises and trips to Greece and its islands.

By *dolmuş* (shared taxi)

Shared taxis are one of the most popular ways to get around in Turkey. *Dolmuş* means 'full up'; in practice, this means that they do not operate to a strict time-table, but instead set off when the driver is happy that he has enough people on board. A *dolmuş* (usually a mini-bus seating from 14-20 people) can be recognised by a sign on the roof or hanging in the window indicating the destination. In cities there are special *dolmuş* stations for connections to outlying parts of the region, otherwise they leave from the town markets. In large connurbations some routes will have intermediate stops. Moreover, you can stop a *dolmuş* anywhere along its route by waving it down. The *dolmuş* is a boon for walkers!

Dolmuş **prices** (specified by the city councils) are somewhat higher than bus prices in city traffic, but a bit less once outside the built-up areas. The fare is usually collected once you are underway. It's a good idea to take note of what your fellow (Turkish) travellers are paying, or you may end up paying an additional 'tourist fare'. The longer routes are broken down into sections, and you only pay for the stretch you travel.

By taxi

In the tourist centres you can find a taxi on every corner. The fares for longer journeys (for instance to some tourist attraction, site, etc.) are usually posted in the taxi in various currencies. For trips within the cities it's best to take a taxi with a meter or negotiate the price in advance. *Caution:* sometimes taxi drivers 'inadvertently' press their meter button, so as to make the fare higher. During the day *gündüz* must appear on the display (*gün* = day, *gündüz* = daytime; *gece* = night).

By train

Railways are not, so far, a significant element in Turkey's transportation network, and there are no trains operating in the Bodrum/Marmaris area.

By ferry

Ferries no longer ply the west or south coasts of Turkey. The only regular connections are from Marmaris and Fethiye to Rhodes. All the other Greek islands off the coast are served by excursion boats.

By chartered boat

The Lycian coast and the southern Aegean are among the most popular sailing waters of the Mediterranean, as you can tell from just one look at all the top yachting magazines on sale in the area. Boats can be chartered locally, with or without a skipper. Bodrum and Marmaris are both major yachting centres. Or you can anchor in many secluded ports and bays.

By organised tour

Take a helicopter to Pamukkale, a bus to Ephesus or a boat to one of the offshore islands: whether by air, land or sea, all the tourist centres offer innumerable half-day, full-day and two- or three-day excursions to local and

'Blue cruises'

The 'blue cruise' business is booming on the Turkish coast. A blue cruise is an all-inclusive holiday on a *gulet*, a beautiful, broad-beamed wooden yacht. While they do have masts and sails, they are usually motor-powered, and the only sail which is always raised is the protective awning. *Gulets* are usually very comfortably equipped, since blue cruises don't cater for yachtsmen but for tourists who enjoy seeing the coast from the water, bathing in isolated coves … and sharing the 'on-board' experience with others. The only disadvantage is that, once the initial excitement has worn off, sharing a confined space with strangers can be trying. Backpackers will be used to this kind of accommodation and have the right attitude, but for more mature travellers it's a good idea to book as a group and charter your own *gulet*.

Blue cruises are named after trips made by a famous circle of philosopher friends who gathered round the bohemian journalist Cevat Şakir Kabaağaçlı. This 'Turkish Jean-Paul Sartre' published his work under the alias 'Fisherman of Halicarnassus', after he had been exiled to Bodrum because of his anti-militaristic stance. He fell in love with the area and stayed on. In the early 1960s a group of his disciples joined him in Bodrum, where they all sailed along the Aegean coast on sponge-diving boats, trying to live as close to nature as possible and surviving primarily on fish and *rakı*. They called their soul-cleansing travels 'mavi yolculuk', or 'blue journeys'.

Tetrapylon at Aphrodisias, a popular destination on organised tours

surrounding sights. If you haven't time to plan an independent excursion or you prefer not to travel on your own, these organised trips are an enjoyable way to learn more about Turkey. From the price point of view, they are most economical for those travelling on their own, since a couple could probably hire a car for the same money. Even better value are the boat trips to secluded bays which you cannot reach by car.

The big catch with many bus tours and boat trips, of course, is that most of the routes are nearly identical, so many bays and tourist attractions are inundated with huge crowds for a just few hours of the day. What's on offer, and where, is listed for each area in the section 'Practicalities A-Z' under 'Boat trips' and 'Organised tours'.

Prices for these excursions do not vary greatly between tour operators. If you *do* find a tour that is substantially cheaper than that offered by the majority of operators … then you can expect far more shopping breaks for carpets than are normally in the programme! The tour guides of course earn commission on everything you buy.

By bicycle
It's rare to find bicyles for hire — and when you do, they are usually poor quality. Cycling here is still in its infancy so, if you want to tour this area by bicycle, take your own bike — and a helmet as well (you must wear one by law). Combined moped/bicycle workshops offer help with punctures and repairs — provided no exotic spare parts are needed.

By hitchhiking
It's not common to hitchhike in Turkey, since public transport is so inexpensive, but in principle

it's possible everywhere and once in a while is the best option at the end of a walk. But unaccompanied female travellers should *not* hitchhike on their own.

Walking

In recent years the development of the Lycian Way, Turkey's first long-distance trail, has been widely publicised. If you hadn't read that this is one of the world's top walks, you might never have thought of Turkey as a destination for walkers.

But you are in for a pleasant surprise! While you won't be following any of the Lycian Way (it ends well to the east of Marmaris and is covered in the *Kaş to Dalyan* and *Antalya to Demre* guides), in spring and autumn there is no more beautiful way to discover the Bodrum/Marmaris area than on foot. The countryside around each offers spectacular and unexpected walking opportunities. The scenic variety is awe-inspiring in the rugged open volcanic regions near Bodrum, while the green-cloaked hills of Marmaris rolling into an azure-blue sea present images certain to stop you in your tracks. This book describes **20 day walks**, with many variations, using local transport — or a car if suitable. There are walks for all ages and abilities, and all are graded.

Seasons: The best months for walking in this part of Turkey are those either side of summer: **April, May, September and October** (although early September can still be hot). The two walking seasons, spring and autumn, present different opportunities, but **spring** is loveliest, with a freshness in the air and flowers at their best. By April the temperature is rising and, given average conditions, sunny days are plentiful, but there can still be showers around or short unsettled periods. (Equally, temperatures can rise to 30° and more.) May sees a steady transition to the hotter, drier conditions of summer. As the temperatures continue to climb throughout June, the walking season ends. In high **summer** walking is *not* advisable, owing to the constant dangers of heat exhaustion and dehydration.

At some time in September, a short unsettled spell brings a change and, although the fine weather usually continues well into the **autumn** and often to the end of the year, the temperatures fall back into the 20s°C. This autumn rain brings on a new spring: cyclamen suddenly brighten the woodlands and olive groves, the crocus are persuaded into flower, and it is a delight to walk again.

Winter rains can be heavy, but there are many fine days, and the cool, clear conditions are ideal for walking. February is the earliest month that can be considered, although March is a better choice, with the real possibility of some gently warm weather.

Guidelines: The **time checks** given at certain points always refer to the total walking time from the starting point, based on an average walking rate of 4km per hour and allowing an extra 20 minutes for each 100m/330ft of ascent. These time checks are not intended to pre-determine your own pace but are meant to be useful reference points. Do bear in mind that they do not include any protracted breaks. Before tackling one of the longer hikes, compare your pace with the authors' on one of the shorter walks. Depending on your level of fitness, you may also consider some of their 'easy' walks to be 'easy-moderate' — or even 'moderate'.

Walk 20 begins and ends here at Datça.

Please accept some words of caution: keep to the routes described and do not try to make your own way in this vast, rugged and difficult terrain. Points that may look close can sometimes take many hours to reach. There is virtually no signposting or waymarking, nor are there any accurate large-scale topographical maps. For any walks except those graded 'easy', it will help to have some walking experience, a good sense of direction, perseverance, stamina *and a little good will!* This last is particularly true for Bodrum and Marmaris, where there is so much ongoing building work. All these walks were checked a few months before press date by an *experienced route-finder* (see page 7), but even Dean got lost at times in the new developments which spring up overnight. Be sure to add ample extra time for this kind of problem.

If you are an **beginner walker** or you are just looking for a gentle ramble, look for walks graded 'easy', and be sure to check all the short and alternative walks. Where there is some point of interest part-way along a walk, it is suggested as a turning-back point, but there is no reason why you shouldn't turn back even sooner.

Experienced walkers should be able to tackle all the walks in this book, taking into account the season and weather conditions of course. Quite a few are very long, so be sure of your fitness before you attempt them.

It is never advisable to walk alone, and this is especially true for women. If you must go alone, carry a mobile and a loud whistle to use as a distress signal in case of an accident. Whether you are alone or in a group, *do* inform a responsible person where you are going and what time you plan to be back.

Maps: The **maps** in this book have been drawn up from a wide variety of base maps — all very different, none of them accurate. Detailed large-scale maps for Turkey are not yet available, and it remains an area of some sensitivity. (Do *not* try to obtain large-scale maps in Turkey; at the very least you will be regarded with suspicion.) If anyone sends in GPS tracks for these routes, we will post them on our web site and use them to improve our maps (if a reliable government map becomes available).

Equipment: Give careful thought to **basic gear** before you go. Many footpaths are steep and stony; comfortable **walking boots** with ankle protection and good grip are strongly recommended. Long (and fairly thick) **trousers**, tucked into **long socks**, will help you avoid being scratched by prickly bushes and will keep ticks at bay too. **Sun protection** is crucial: sunhat, suncream, sunglasses, and a long-sleeved shirt. Always carry **plenty of fluid and food**: depending on the length of the walk you will need 1-3 litres of liquid per person. Your day **rucksack** should of course contain a **first-aid kit**, small **torch** and **mobile phone** (see page 48 for emergency numbers). You may also want to take an **anti-venom kit** (available from specialist camping stockists); see 'snakes' below. Between October and May, you should also take a

windcheat and **waterproofs**; in winter a **fleece** or two, **woollen hat** and **gloves**. In summer, don't forget **swimming things** where appropriate. Any other special gear will be listed under 'Equipment' at the top of each walk (Walk 18, for example, suggests **secateurs!**).

Nuisances: Dogs are generally no bother, as the Turks tend not to keep them as pets, and any stray dogs are usually harmless. (If dogs worry you, take a 'Dog Dazer', an ultrasonic device which persuades aggressive dogs to back off; they are available from the Sunflower website, www. sunflowerbooks.co.uk.) But you will have to be on your guard against **snakes**. Most are harmless and will move out of your way rapidly but, if they don't, the best advice is to quietly move out of their way. There are **vipers** around and, since it would be dangerous to step on a viper, it is *imperative* that you do not walk in the countryside in open sandals. Always have your feet and ankles well covered and, as a sensible precaution, wear your long trousers tucked into your long socks. Take special care near water, when you are about to sit down, or when you rest your hand, so unthinkingly, on a drystone wall. If you do have the misfortune to be bitten by a snake, seek medical help urgently — and if you cannot identify the species, kill it and take it with you!

In comparison with snakebite, the sting of the **scorpion** is painful, but not dangerous to most people. Again, as a precaution, don't leave any of your clothes on the ground. **Wild boar** forage for food in the mountains, but they are nocturnal creatures, and unlikely to be seen.

You can avoid **ticks** by keeping your body covered. If a tick does get to your skin, it is necessary to make it withdraw before taking it off; an easy way to do this is to touch them with a solvent such as methylated spirits or alcohol. **Bees** and **wasps** are around in summer, so make sure you carry the necessary medications if you are allergic to insect bites. In any case, always give beehives a wide berth!

Accommodation

Accommodation in the area varies from up-market resorts where you will be handed cocktails in the jacuzzi down to places where you wouldn't go into the toilets without shoes. Most hotels and guest houses are located along the coast. There is a very welcome increase in the number of '**boutique hotels**' — small stylish places to stay (some marketed as guest houses), which are often housed in old, restored natural stone buildings. *This book places particular emphasis on this type of accommodation.* The standard of most hotels is in direct relation to the price; Turkey is still an inexpensive destination. During the Turkish holiday period, July and August, reserving in advance is recommended, particularly in larger tourist centres. But outside these months you should have no problem finding a place to stay on-the-spot — on the contrary, your problem will be choosing from the large selection on offer.

In principle, bartering is possible in small cheap hotels and guest houses, but fortunately this is not usually seen.

All recommendations in this book mention facilities like air-conditioning or telephones only in establishments where you would not expect to find them.

All-inclusive resorts

The bulk of all-inclusive resorts in the area is clustered around Marmaris. These places, often behind high-security fences and with up to 2500 beds, are not geared up to receive individual travellers at short notice, so booking is either impossible or very difficult. If you do manage it, the walk-in rate is often well above double the normal rate that you would have paid booking through a brochure. Note, too, that the term 'all-inclusive' is not clearly defined, and some hotels give themselves this accolade without actually earning it. So make sure in advance whether for example the drinks or the sports facilities on offer are included in the price. At many hotels where 'all-inclusive' doesn't mean what it says, some crafty tour operators will advise you never to eat or drink anywhere other than at your base, to prevent being ill or even attacked. Rubbish! The advice is only intended to bind you to the hotel bar, where beer costs four or five times more than it would outside the resort.

Prices for the all-inclusives depend on equipment, service, size of the buffet, sports facilities, number of hosts and hostesses, etc. and range from £50-£165 per night for a double room.

Hotels

All hotels are registered with the Ministry for Culture and Tourism and are assigned categories. If you choose your accommodation depending on the number of stars, be aware that the classification is based on *equipment* (mini-bar, television, lift, restaurant, air-conditioning, etc.); criteria like location, architecture, friendliness of the staff, and the like are not considered. Moreover the rating is often out of date, because many Turkish hotels were built 'on the cheap', so the equipment often wears out quickly. This applies particularly to three-star hotels. Luxury boutique hotels are not categorised by stars. In hotels at the bottom end of the market and in many guest houses you will just have to accept the fact that there isn't always hot water and the amenities are often unreliable.

Prices: The larger, sophisticated hotels charge from £35 for a

Getting ready for the sunbathers at Marmaris

Bodrum: view from the old harbour to the new one

double, international chains from £70 for a double in peak season. Prices are up to 50% lower between September and May. Small hotels offer double rooms with shower or bath from about £17. A room in really cheap accommodation, without bath or WC, starts from £5.50 per person.

Pansiyonlar (guest houses)

When comparing simpler hotels and small *pansiyonlar*, the latter are usually the better choice, since their operators usually care more about the well-being of their guests. Even when compared with some of the top hotels, the *pansiyon* may be preferable, because the friendliness of the owners makes up for the (rarely missed) luxuries. *Aile pansiyonları* (guest houses for families) aren't everyone's cup of tea; these are often very simple places where everyone eats

together — and you may not want to share your evening meal with people with whom you have little in common.

Many campsites (see below) also let rooms — the equipment is spartan, but the rooms (often in bungalows) are usually quite well done.

Prices for *pansiyonlar*: a double room with shower/WC ranges from £10-25. Singles are usually given a double room at a reduced price.

Aparthotels

The number of aparthotels has been rising constantly in recent years. Basic equipment includes a kitchenette or small kitchen, a living room with a sofabed and TV and — depending on size — one or more bedrooms. Naturally the **prices** of aparthotels vary substantially depending on size, equipment and location. You should be able to get a good apartment for 4 people from about £30/day.

Youth hostels

In the whole of Turkey there are very few youth hostels, not least because many private *pansiyonlar* offer inexpensive rooms. There is only one youth hostel in the area covered by this book — in Marmaris (see page 123).

Campsites

The **official, licenced campsites** are, like the hotels, under the control of the Ministry for Culture and Tourism. The normal amenities include showers (not always warm), camper kitchens and power sockets, restaurants and (usually) supermarkets. Prices here are commonly around double the price of **unlicenced campsites**, where the ameneties leave something to be desired. Many campsites also let bungalows and parking bays for tents and camper vans. The 'bungalows' are usually simple wooden huts without much in the way of creature comforts, but they usually have tiled floors, bath and WC, terrace, etc.

'**Wild camping**' isn't a problem in Turkey's mountains (where there is no other option), but not otherwise recommended: between curious villagers and police checks it can be a very unnerving experience.

Prices: For two people and a tent, reckon on paying £4-8 — the price is the same whether you have a tent or camper van.

Opening times: Many campsites are only open from May to October. They are only crowded in high summer. By the end of September you may be the only guest on the site … and find that the bar, restaurant and super-market have closed.

Food and drink

'The Iman fainted', when asked to taste 'women's thighs' and the 'lady's navel'. 'The ruler was pleased' when served the 'vizier's finger'… Whole dramas can be performed based on the names of Turkish dishes! They also hint at which tradition the recipe falls back on and how much fantasy the chef puts into his creations.

'Life comes from the stomach' is a Turkish proverb. And in fact Turkish cuisine can claim to be of as high a standard as French. The basis for the dishes is usually fresh vegetables, including some that are either unknown or seldom used in Britain and Europe (like chick peas, broad beans, okra, rocket and purslane). It's different with spices: they virtually never use Eastern exotica, but rather trusted classics like pepper, paprika or parsley. Garlic is also used, but not as much as you might imagine.

Where to eat

In Bodrum and Marmaris you can of course find anything from Chinese restaurants to Italian pizzerias, Bavarian beer gardens, and cuisine from around the world. For Turkish specialities the choice is primarily between *lokantas* and *restorans*.

Lokanta: You eat in a *lokanta* to get a meal under your belt rather than to enjoy the 'dining out' experience. *Lokantas* are found on

A bit like Disneyland — an evening at Bodrum's Moonlight Bar

on every street corner; they are simple, good and cheap (prices start at £1.30). The décor — tiled walls and cold neon lighting — is spartan to say the least. The pre-cooked meals are kept warm in glass cases, and you select from meat and vegetable dishes, soups and stews. The busier the *lokanta*, the fresher the meals usually are. There are many variations on the *lokanta*, too:

depending on what the speciality of the house is, it may be called a *kebapçı, köfteci* or *pideci*. At an *işkembeci* they serve soup with entrails and other innards. Most *lokantas* do not have an alcohol licence.

Restoran: Restaurants normally have an alcohol licence, more tasteful décor, better service and of course higher prices. But the menu does not always differ from that of the simpler *lokantas*; this applies in particular to mid-range restaurants. A full meal with a beverage starts at about £4. For the better restaurants there is no set limit: if you want to enjoy a candlelit dinner at an elegant restaurant by the water's edge, expect to pay £15 or so per person (without wine).

Fish restaurants rank price-wise with the more expensive restaurants, and for a three-course set menu you can expect to pay £15-20 per person.

Tipping

In simple lokantas no tip is expected, but in restaurants it is. If the service is *not* included in the total (note that quite often it *is* included), about 10% of the total bill is expected (15% in more expensive restaurants). In restaurants where they have no menus and prices on boards, it is advisable to enquire about the prices before ordering — some waiters are sly foxes...

Breakfast

In the larger hotels in tourist areas, an 'international' breakfast is nearly always served as a buffet; how sumptuous or otherwise depends on the grade of hotel. Even in the less expensive establishments, you can expect coffee, jam, cheese spread and eggs.

But try a traditional Turkish breakfast (kahvaltı)! You will be served fresh white bread, jam, eggs (usually hard boiled), olives, cucumbers/gherkins, tomatoes, butter and sheeps' cheese. Turks enjoy sheeps' cheese on bread with honey. With all this, tea is the drink of choice. Filter coffee is not usually available; those who want it will have to settle for neskafe or something similar. Turks also eat pekmez (thickened grape juice) as a spread with tahini (sesame paste) on bread for breakfast — and it's delicious!

Starters

You can choose from things like piquant creamy yogurt (haydari), spicy vegetable purée (ezme), cold vegetables in plenty of olive oil (zeytinyağlı), stuffed vine leaves (yaprak dolması), melon with sheeps' cheese (peynirli karpuz) and similar delicacies. The Turks call such starters **meze**, and display them in glass cabinets for you to take your pick. It's also fairly common to do without the main course altogether and select only starters; in many restaurants it's no problem. Fresh white bread (ekmek) is always served on the side.

Turks rarely choose **soup** as a starter. They have soup as a replacement for breakfast, occasionally in between meals … or to nurse a hangover. Many Turks swear by the Alka Seltzer effect of entrail soup (işkembe çorbası) … but this may not be to your taste! If you would like some hot soup as starter, try the hearty lentil soup (merçimek çorbası) — another speciality.

> **Caution:** Avoid having starters in small beach-side restaurants which are not connected to mains electricity. Dishes with fish and mayonnaise that have been out in the heat for some time can lead to a bad stomach upset or food poisoning.

Meat

The most popular meat dishes are kebaps and köfte. **Kebap** is the generic term for meat dishes of any kind (usually lamb, sometimes poultry), which can be baked, grilled, or roasted. There is probably no need to dwell on döner kebaps. Şiş kebap is a tender meat dish roasted on charcoal, served with rice or bulgar (cracked wheat). Patlıcan kebaps are skewered minced meat with aubergine. If the meat is arranged with yogurt and tomato sauce on roasted round flat bread its known as a bursa kebap (or ıskender kebap). Also try the adana kebap, a strongly peppered mince meat kebab. Or güveç, a tender pot roast with vegetables cooked in a clay pot.

Köfte are essentially meat patties or meatballs made from minced mutton, lamb or beef; they can be roasted or grilled. The tasty 'women's thighs' (kadınbudu), with added rice and a coating of breadcrumbs, get their name from the elongated shape of the meatball.

Turks love offal — like roasted liver (ciğer) or kidneys (böbrek). Kokoreç is a snack on offer at many street corners — grilled intestines with onions and tomato in bread. There are many, many other curiosities to try, like grilled sheep testicles (koç yumurtası), stewed sheep heads (kelle) or feet (paça).

Vegetables

Vegetables (sebze) are used as the base of Turkish dishes rather than as a supplement to a meal. The choice of pot-roasted, baked, and stewed vegetables is enormous. A particularly popular dish is dolma: this consists of stuffed vegetables, like zucchini (kabak dolması) or aubergines (karnıyarık) filled with minced meat or bite-sized pieces of lamb. It is usually eaten with yogurt. Various stews are also tasty; try kıymalı ıspanak (spinach with minced meat). Chick peas (etli nohut) or okra with lamb (etli bamya) are also delicious. Caution: Take it easy, at least to start. The food is often swimming in olive oil — on stomachs unaccustomed to this diet, this can have the same effect as a dose of castor oil.

Fish

Salt-water fish frequently on offer are sea perch (levrek), turbot (kalkan), Mediterranean mackerel (kolyos), plaice (pisi balığı), mackerel (uskumru) and freshly-caught sardines (sardalya). Tuna (palamut) features on many

Turkey for vegetarians

A tired smile is all that most Turks can offer a vegetarian — because those who voluntarily choose to do without delicacies like şiş kebap, köfte or entrail soup must be either ill or mad. Don't worry: even without meat one can enjoy delicacies in Turkey. The bulk of the starters are purely vegetarian, and there are plenty of tasty vegetable stews, creamy soups, salads and filled pastry dishes awaiting discovery. In order to avoid any nasty surprises, make sure by asking 'Etsiz mi?' ('Is it without meat?', pronounced 'Aytsis mee?') and follow this up by saying 'Et yemiyorum' ('I do not eat meat', pronounced 'Ayt yaymeeyorum').

menus, too, prepared in several different ways. Trout is a particular fresh-water favourite, and there are several trout restaurants in the countryside.

Sweets and fruit

One of the most popular **sweets** (tatlı) is baklava, a pastry made from several layers of dough, interspersed with almonds and pistachios. The small rectangles have a syrup of sugar, lemon juice and honey poured over them. Helva is just as sweet and sticky, a calorific 'bomb' made of white flour, sesame oil, honey and sugar. Easier perhaps on the British stomach (and conscience) are almond pudding (keşkül) or rice pudding (sütlaç).

Those who enjoy experimenting should try aşure at least once — a jelly-like dessert: when prepared properly in a top-quality restaurant, this contains more

Aphrodisias is one of the most popular excursion sites.

than 40 ingredients, including rose water, nuts, cinnamon and even beans! It was inspired by the legend of Noah's ark — you mix all the left-overs together and boil them up.

The recipe for *tavuk göğüsü* is equally unusual — a mixture of chicken breast chopped into small pieces, rice flour, milk and sugar. All these and many others are on offer at the *muhallebici*, snack bars specialising in sweets. If you are happiest ending your meal with **fruit** *(meyve)*, there is a wide choice. Depending on the season, melons, figs, grapes, peaches, cherries, strawberries, pomegranates or citrus fruits are available. Washing all fruit thoroughly is good, but peeling it is better!

Soft drinks

Pepsi, Coke and all well-known brands are on sale everywhere. Water *(su)* is often placed on the table with the meal. If it comes from the tap, you should *avoid* drinking it. Freshly squeezed fruit juices *(meyve suyu)* are recommended. Delicious fruit juices are also sold everywhere in cans. *Ayran* is a refreshing drink made from yogurt, salt and cold water — a little like buttermilk.

Hot drinks

The Turkish national drink is *çay*. This good black tea from plantations on the Black Sea coast is drunk at every opportunity. Whether at breakfast, business meetings, in carpet shops or at the hairdressers, the small bulbous glasses are found everywhere. Tourists seem to have taken a shine to *elma çayı*, apple tea. Turkish mocha *(Türk kahvesi)*, which can de ordered either sweet *(şekerli)*, slightly sweet *(orta şekerli)* or without sugar *(sade)*, is usually taken

Making a Turkish pizza (top) and döner kebab (bottom)

each year in the interests of keeping the population healthy. 'Tekirdağ' is the brand most highly recommended. You can tell good quality *rakı* from inferior brands because it makes a film on the glass.

Beer *(bira)* is also a popular drink with meals, the Efes brand being the most common. You can also find Danish Tuborg (brewed in Turkey); it's somewhat drier than Efes.

Less known are Turkish wines (*şarap*). The better varieties are normally excellent — especially the Dolucas and Kavaklideres. Turkish wines are stomach-friendly due to their modest acid content.

Snacks

Snacking is an art form in Turkey, and *börek* can almost replace a complete meal; this speciality is a filo dough triangle filled with minced meat, spinach or sheeps' cheese. Similarly delicious fillings are hidden in *pide*, a crispy flat bread. Also worth sampling is *lahmacun*, the Turkish pizza topped with minced meat and herbs.

Mantı is known as the Turkish ravioli — so small that 30 fit on a single spoon; you eat it with garlic-flavoured yogurt, melted paprika butter and mint.

Simit salesmen are always around; their sesame rings are at their crispiest early in the morning. One often sees women in traditional dress beside them, preparing *gözleme*, a kind of pancake filled with different kinds of sweet or hearty ingredients. And try *kumpir*, if you get the chance, giant stuffed potatoes.

after a rich meal. Those who don't mind grit in their teeth order *neskafe*. In chic cafés you can of course also get cappuccinos, espressos or macchiatos.

Alcohol

Rakı is the favoured tipple — about 45 percent aniseed liquor — and tasting rather like the Greek *ouzo*. The Turks prefer to drink it diluted with ice and water from high, narrow 0,2 litre glasses. It then takes on a milky colouring and so is also called 'lion's-milk'. *Rakı* counts as a digestive and medicinal aid against all possible ailments, and 70 million litres are consumed

Practicalities A-Z

Ancient sites — the most important terms

Acropolis: castle hill, also the upper part of town

Agora: market and meeting place in ancient Greece; the major part of a colonnade, surrounded by shops

Architrave: a main beam (usually stone) resting across the top of columns

Basilica: central Roman hall, in which the side aisles are lower than the main aisle (only later was the term used for churches)

Bouleuterion: council hall of the senate in Greek and Roman times

Cavea: auditorium of an ancient theatre, in Roman times usually semi-circular, in Greek times usually facing outwards

Cella: main hall of a temple, usually with one or several religious statues

Gymnasium: centre for athletic training, originally part of a school

Heroon: religious building in honour of a hero or dignitary

Capital: uppermost end of a column

Necropolis: graveyard

Nymphaeum: fountain

Odeon: theatre-like building for small cultural events

Orchestra: performance area of the theatre

Pantheon: a temple for all gods

Peristyle: a space surrounded by columns

Propylon: gate building

Stoa: roofed colonnade or portico

Beaches

The search for sun, sand and sea attracts millions to the Bodrum/Marmaris area every year. Some of the most beautiful and best-

The local young people prefer this sort of scene to the isolated cove.

known beaches lie along the coast, but there is a multitude of idyllic 'hidden' bays as well.

Naturism is forbidden in Turkey (although it is quite usual to see Turkish men bathing in their underpants). There have been quite a few police raids on beaches frequented by naturists.

Average water temperatures			
January	15°C	July	24°C
February	14°C	August	25°C
March	15°C	September	24°C
April	16°C	October	22°C
May	18°C	November	19°C
June	21°C	December	17°C

Books for background reading

John Julius Norwich, *A Short History of Byzantium* (Penguin, 1998)

George E Bean, *Turkey Beyond the Maeander* (John Murray, 1989), available from Amazon if your bookseller cannot obtain it

Freya Stark, *Ionia, a Quest* (John Murray, 1954), also available through Amazon

Chemists

Turkish pharmacies (*eczane*; open Mon.-Sat. 09.00-19.00) have more or less everything you would find at home. Many medicines are called by a different name, however, and are often available without prescription (for instance, antibiotics) — and they are cheaper too.

The nearest **24-hour chemist** (*nöbetçi*) will be shown in the window of the *eczane*.

Children

Turkey is paradise for those travelling with children. If your offspring plays sailboats with plates in the restaurant or cries out from world-weariness on a long bus trip, nobody will get worked up over it, the pieces of broken glass will be removed with a smile, your child will even be comforted and probably given sweets. You will be welcomed with children wherever you stay — whether in a simple *pansiyon* or a luxury hotel. The latter often provide babysitters who arrange an interesting children's programme, the former will welcome you with unbelievable warmth — with the host even taking the little ones fishing on his boat.

Camel Beach

For alternatives to building sand castles there are camel rides on the beach, aquaparks with giant water slides, dolphin shows, etc. The best nappy brand in Turkey, by the way, is Ultra Prima, available in pharmacies.

Climate and weather

See 'When to go' on page 10 and the detailed information for walkers on page 19. Below some statistics.

Monthly averages		
air temperature*	hours of sun	rainy days
Jan. 10°C (7/16)	5	11
Feb. 11°C (7/17)	6	10
Mar. 13°C (8/18)	7	7
Apr. 16°C (11/21)	8.5	4
May 20°C (15/25)	10	3
Jun. 25°C (19/30)	12	0
Jul. 28°C (23/34)	13	0
Aug. 28°C (23/34)	12	0
Sep. 25°C (19/31)	10	1
Oct. 20°C (15/26)	8.5	5
Nov. 15°C (11/21)	6	7
Dec. 12°C (8/18)	4.5	11
*followed by minimum/maximum		

Consulates/embassies

Embassies for the English-speaking countries are located either in Istanbul (**(** prefix 0212) or Ankara (**(** prefix 0312).

UK (0212 334 6400
Ireland (0212 259 6979
USA (0212 335 9000
Australia (0312 447 2391
New Zealand (0212 244 0272

In case of emergencies, there are also British honorary consuls in Bodrum and Marmaris:

Bodrum
(: 0252 319 0093
(: 0252 319 0095
Marmaris
(: 0252 412 6486/36
(: 0252 412 4565

Crime

Thefts and robberies are relatively rare in Turkey. The country's worst crime is corruption, but that's another story and not a problem for tourists. Nevertheless, do be aware that, like everywhere else, there are cheats and con artists around — especially in the big cities and tourist centres. If you have a problem, contact the nearest police or tourist information office. They will help you because tourism is critical for the economy.

Of course it is a good idea to take the usual precautions of leaving valuables (including unneeded credit cards) in a hotel safe (*never on view in a car or on the beach*), carrying no more cash than you need, and keeping to well-lit streets at night.

Illegal drugs are on sale in Turkey: marijuana, hashish, opium and heroin. The punishments for bringing drugs into or out of the country, or drug use

are severe — and Turkish prisons are known the world over for their dreadful conditions. *Never take a package out of the country without knowing what is in it.* (By the way, many drug dealers co-operate closely with the police!)

Currency

The Turkish lira was devalued in 2005, when the new Turkish lira (*yeni Türk lirasi,* abbreviated YTL) was introduced. Thanks to this, the number of millionaires in the country was reduced to a manageable number, with the simple eradication of six zeros (10,000,000 TL became 10 YTL). *When you get change, check that you haven't been given old money — it's almost identical in appearance.*

Notes to the value of 1, 5, 10, 20, 50 and 100 YTL are in circulation. One new Turkish lira comprises 100 *kurus,* and **coins** have been issued for 1, 5, 10, 25 and 50 kurus as well as 1 lira.

The prices quoted in this book were as accurate as possible at the time of writing (late autumn 2006), but may differ substantially from the prices you find on the spot. Naturally the conversion to the new Turkish lira in 2005 (a boom year for Turkish tourism) led to a huge increase in prices, but by June 2006 the YTL had lost about 20% of its (over-)valuation. **At the time of writing £1 = 2.80 YTL.**

Turkey's **foreign exchange control regulations** require you to declare cash amounts to the value of US $5000 (about £2700) or more on arrival and departure. You can **exchange currency** at banks (normally open Mon.-Fri. from 09.00-12.00 and 13.30-18.00) or the many exchange bureaus in the area (Turks keep their savings in hard foreign currencies, thus the multiplicity of exchange bureaus). The difference in rates between the two is generally small. Always remember to keep a record, as proof that you exchanged your money legally.

Cash machines (ATMs) are thick on the ground, too, and the exchange rate on withdrawals using a debit card is often better than in an exchange bureau.

Credit cards are accepted in all of the better restaurants, hotels and shops.

Not every branch of a bank is authorised to redeem **travellers' cheques**. American Express Travellers' Cheques can be cashed free of charge (as long as it's by the person who signed them) at branches of Akbank.

Tipping: in restaurants the rule is generally 10% of the bill; hair-dressers, masseurs, chamber-maids (per day) around 2YTL. You needn't tip taxi drivers, but rather round up the fare. In bars and cloakrooms just leave some small change.

Students reductions and other **concessionary prices** are shown with the relevant entry fees.

Dress

Away from the holiday centres in Turkey, great importance is attached to cleanliness and proper dress. For what to pack check the table of monthly averages on page 32. For a bathing/beach holiday on the coast, light clothes — preferably cotton — are enough, but remember that in the spring a cool breeze blows off the water in the evening.

Shave ... or lose out

Whether bushy and magnificent or fine and delicate, they are always well trimmed: only a moustache makes a Turk a man — at least in Anatolia and in conservative circles. Even today village men who have worn moustaches for years keep an eye on the younger generation, to make sure that no young rascal grows a moustaches before the 'proper' age.

But in many places on the south coast the young don't want to know about such antiquated traditions, so they are smoothly shaved or sport designer stubble. To them, the classical mousta-chioed male, with his standard grey department store jacket, has all the status of the village nincompoop from the Anatolian countryside. Even the young women see them as sleazy perverts with x-ray eyes. In some trendy clubs, the bouncers make sure that anyone with a moustache is barred.

Those who wear full beards also remain outsiders, at least when it comes to public offices and universities. In secular Turkey (see page 42) the full beard is seen as a symbol of the wearer's Islamic faith — the equivalent of women covering their heads.

For visits to mosques see the panel 'Mosque etiquette' on page 41.

Electricity

The power supply is 230 volts as in continental Europe, and two round-pin plugs are the norm, so take your continental or international adapter.

Festivals and holidays

The tourist centres on the coast have surprisingly little information about national holidays — probably because it's always holiday time (but only for the tourist, not for them!).

1st January: New Year's Day

January or February: Kurban Bayramı (movable dates, four days); see page 41.

23 April: Independence Day, commemorating the first time the parliament sat in Ankara (on 23 April 1920). Is also celebrated today as 'Children's Day'.

1 May: Spring Festival (an unofficial holiday replacing the former Labour Day).

19 May: Youth and Sports Day; it marks the start of the Turkish War of Independence in 1919.

30 August: Victory Day, commemorating victory over the Greeks in 1922.

29 October: Republic Day; Turkey was proclaimed a republic on 29 April 1923. This festival is celebrated with parades.

October or November: Kadir Gecesi (movable dates); see page 41 and Şeker Bayramı (moveable dates); see page 41.

10 November: while not an official holiday, the day of Atatürk's death (1938) is 'semi-official', since a large part of the population stays away from work.

See also 'religious holidays' on page 41.

Flora and fauna

The coast is characterised by typical Mediterranean vegetation, with forests of pine and cypress as well as bushy macchia

comprised of oleander, holly, kermes oaks, box trees, myrtles, lavender, carob trees, etc. On the higher elevations, the prevailing tree is the Turkish pine *(Pinus brutia)*, but you will also find isolated firs and cedars. Uncontrolled hunting of wild game has led to the decimation of animal numbers roaming free. Stags and roe deer once played in the forests; today one only sees them rarely. With a bit of luck, in the mountains you can still come across foxes, wild boar, badgers, polecats, tree martens, stone martens and the almost-extinct porcupines or rodents like the cute ground squirrel. Wolves, bears, jackals and leopards are found only extremely rarely in distant eastern Turkey.

Fauna with 'lower profiles' can be seen darting or waddling along on the ground — lizards, geckos and turtles. When you're out hiking, you will also see snakes once in a while. Most are not dangerous but, if you are going out walking, read more about snakes on page 22.

Of the birds, the storks (under protection in Turkey) are

fascinating. There are also many birds of prey such as eagles, falcons and buzzards. Further east (see the *Kaş to Dalyan* guide) ornithologists will be in their element on the beach at Patara and by the Dalyan Delta, where they can see grey and purple herons, kingfishers, white storks, songbirds, night swallows, and many more.

Finally, just another piece of advice regarding 'animal pests': mosquitoes, fleas and cockroaches don't only see the forests as their habitat!

Gays and lesbians

Homosexuality is frowned on in Turkey; being outed leads to merciless descrimination. A decree by the Ministry of the Interior even forbids organised groups of homosexuals to gather on Turkish streets. Some years ago 800 participants on a gay cruise were prohibited from docking at Kuşadası. Turkish gays and lesbians can only avoid discrimination in the anonymity of very large cities.

Greeks and Turks

At the beginning of the 20th century the Greeks were the largest non-Muslim minority in the Ottoman Empire. Many places on the Mediterranean and Aegean coasts were in Greek hands. Over centuries they had lived together peacefully with the Turks; tensions were the exception, not the norm. But after the First World War and the attempt by Greece to seize Asia Minor, the situation changed. The Turkish War of Independence followed, at the end of which came the so-called 'population

exchange' — a driving out and/or ethnical cleansing: some 1.4 million Greeks had to leave Turkey, while about 350,000 Turks moved back from Greece. A Greek-Turkish 'Ice Age' began, which reached its peak with the Cyprus conflict. For many years NATO partners worried at the behaviour of its two warring 'allies'. The improvement in relations between the two nations has only come about in recent times with, for instance, each offering the other help with severe earthquakes and wildfires. Greece is now a proponent of Turkish entry into the EU.

Import and export regulations

You are allowed the following **duty-frees** for personal consumption when entering Turkey:
200 cigarettes (400 if bought in a Turkish duty-free shop before going through customs)
50 cigars or 200g of tobacco
0.7 litre spirits
gifts to the value of £165.
If you come into the country with anything extremely valuable (a high-carat diamond for example), it must be registered in your passport by the Turkish customs on entry.

To **export antique objects** from Turkey, one needs the written permission of a museum director. This also applies to old seals, medals, carpets, etc. Offenders are threatened with harsh punishments. The export of **minerals** also needs written permission (from MTA in Ankara, (0312 2873430). To take or ship out **carpets**, you must produce a receipt.

When you leave the country,

items bought for private use (clothing, for instance) up to a value of £145 can be brought back into the UK tax free (at time of writing). Check with the airlines before leaving about the latest regulations on bringing back duty frees.

Information about Turkey

All the international branches of the Turkish Ministry of Tourism (www.gototurkey.co.uk or, in the USA, www.tourismturkey.org) have mouth-watering brochures that they will send on request (direct from their web sites). Otherwise you can contact:

UK
Turkish Culture and Tourism Office
First Floor, 170-173 Piccadilly
London W1V 9DD
(020 7355 4207 or 020 7629 7771
(020 7491 0773

USA (Los Angeles)
Turkish Culture and Tourism Office
5055 Wiltshire Boulevard, Suite 850
Los Angeles CA 90036
(323 937 8066 or 323 937 4961
(323 937 1271

USA (New York)
Turkish Embassy Information Counselor's Office
821 United Nations Plaza
New York, NY 10017
(212 687 2194/5/6
(212 599 7568

USA (Washington)
Turkish Embassy Information Counselor's Office
2525 Massachusetts Avenue, Suite 306
Washington DC 20008
(202 612 6800/01
(202 319 7446

Tip on info
Compared with many other destinations, there's relatively little information on Turkey's 'official' web pages, so it's worth surfing the names of places in this book — from hotels to sites. For practicalities, a brilliant site is www.turkeytravelplanner.com

---

Inoculations

No inoculations are *required*, but it is advisable to be vaccinated against tetanus, diphtheria and hepatitis A before your trip. Double-check with your airline, tour operator or the Department of Health (www.dh.gov.uk), to see if there are any changes.
By the way, if you are plagued by a cold during your stay: blowing your nose in public is considered very unrefined in Turkey!

Internet access

There are plenty of internet cafés in Turkey for those who want to surf the web or send e-mails during their stay. The more stylish the café, the more expensive it is to be on-line: half an hour costs £0.45-0.80. The addresses of internet cafés have *not* been listed in this book, because they change so frequently. Many hotels and even *pansiyonlar* also offer internet access.

Invitations

The Turks are extremely hospitable. Those who enjoy mixing with the locals, whether on bus journeys or on visits to simple restaurants, are frequently spontaneously approached or even invited to tea. Invitations to their homes, on the other hand, for example for the evening meal, are much more rarely extended, because of the sanctity of the family. If you are ever invited into anyone's home, you can take it as a sign of special esteem. Because of this, it is important to remember some of the host's customs and conventions (although small breaches of etiquette will obviously be forgiven).

Guests usually bring a **gift** — nothing lavish, just something simple that would please the host or family.

Shoes are removed at the entrance. If there are no indoor shoes ready, socks will do.

For a hearty welcome, one traditionaly exchanges a double **kiss** (right cheek, then left cheek) — this is more common between people of the same gender than the opposite gender. If you are uncertain, just politely offer your hand and let your Turkish host take the initiative before committing a *faux pas*.

Speaking loudly in the presence of older people is considered poor manners. Seniors are treated very courteously. In traditional families it is even usual to stand when the head of the family appears.

To refuse something offered is impolite. The hosts have undoubtedle made a great effort to please you, possibly spending well beyond their means.

Islam

Islam (in English 'submission' or 'surrender') is the youngest of the major world religions. Like Judaism and Christianity, it is a strictly monotheistic religion; its followers believing in one omnipotent God. According to Islamic belief, Allah is the creator and guardian of all things and all life. He cares for, guides and judges human beings; on the day of the Last Judgement, 'the saved' enter paradise, while 'the condemned' descend to hell.

The religion's founder was Mohammed (around 570-632), who grew up as an orphan in Mecca. His religious and political work began around 610, after the Archangel Gabriel appeared to him in a vision, but his first sermons were received with scepticism in his home city. It was only when Mohammed moved to Medina in 622 (the start of the Islamic calendar) that he became established as a world and religious authority, generally accepted as a legislator and prophet. Some of Mohammed's messages were revolutionary for the times — for instance the condemnation of slavery in the name of God.

The role played by the Islamic faith in Turkey varies from region to region. For many inhabitants of the Westernised coastal towns, it means almost nothing. For the Turkish state, the swirling currents of fundamentalist religion are a thorn in the side. But the more vehemently they try to supress fundamentalism, recent years have seen an enormous upsurge, fuelled by the lack of prospects and discontent with the economic and political situation in the country.

The Koran and *Sunna* are the fundamental teachings of the Islamic faith. The **Koran** (Holy Book of Islam), which consists of 114 *suren* (chapters), is believed

Koran, with translation into modern Turkish (see page 51).

The Five Pillars of Islam
The Koran dictates five obligations for all Muslims:
— profession of faith *(kelimei şahadet)*: 'I testify that there is no God except Allah, and Mohammed is His prophet...')
— prayers *(namaz)* five times a day, washing before you pray
— extending charity to those in need *(zekat)*
— fasting during daylight hours during the month of Ramadan *(oruç)*
— a pilgrimage to Mecca *(hac)*
With some of the duties there is a bit of flexibility. Thus the Muslim need only make his pilgrimage to Mecca if he is healthy and can afford it; washing before prayer can be just done as a ritual, if no water is available; pregnant woman, the sick, and young children can postpone fasting.

to be the true word of God, as told to Mohammed by the Archangel Gabriel. This explains the infallibility attributed to the Koran. The Sunna ('Tradition') is a collection of 9th-century stories *(hadith)* about the life of Mohammed and his followers, giving an insight into how some of the Koran's more obscure chapters can be put into practice. In contrast to the Koran, the Sunna is *not* considered infallible.

Islam teaches that since human beings are morally weak and fallible, God sends **prophets** to them, who teach them how they should live. In Islam, Jesus also ranks among these prophets, beside Abraham and Moses. The Christian view, in which Jesus is seen as the son of God, is not shared by Islam. Muslims believe that the long line of prophets came to an end with Mohammed, and that the Koran is the final true word of God.

Disputes after Mohammed's death about who should succeed him led to **a splitting of Muslims into two main groups: Sunnis and Shiites**. Over 70 per cent of Turks are Sunni. The Sunni saw the caliph as Mohammed's legal successor and the head of the Muslim world. For the Shiites (the name comes from the Arabic word *schia,* or 'party'), however, only a blood relative of the prophet could stake their claim to leadership. Since Mohammed left no surviving sons, the Shiites saw Ali (Mohammed's cousin and son-in-law) and his descendants as the legitimate successors *(imams).*

Around 25 per cent of Turks (including many Kurds) are

Laicism: separation of religion and state

'Islam will one day govern Turkey, the question is only whether the transition will be easy or hard, sweet or bloody.' Statements like this, from the former party chief Necmettin Erbakan, were one of the reasons for the banning of the Islamic Welfare Party (1998) and the Virtue Party that succeeded it (2001). From the broken pieces of the latter, the Party for Justice and Development (AKP) was formed, winner of the parliamentary elections in 2002. The banning of religious parties was justified on the grounds that Turkey had been a secular state, with a strict separation of state and religion, since Atatürk founded the republic ('any politician who needs the help of religion to run the government is an idiot').

For the revolutionary modernisers, supported by the military and Western-orientated politicians, Islam was the largest obstacle in the way of modernising the country. Atatürk rejected the Islamic calendar and withdrew Islam from its position as state religion. The Turkish experiment was the first and most successful example in the world of the secularisation of an Islamic state.

But even after all these years laicism is still exposed to many dangers, as was pointed out by the former Turkish President Süleyman Demirel (1993-2000): 'Our state is laical, but its population is not'. The secular way presents a constant potential for conflict, insofar as the basic Islamic social philosophy is the principle that all spheres of life form an inseparable unit, whether spiritual, social, political or economic. While radical forces militate for a religious state, moderates look for ways to preserve traditional Islamic values in today's secularised world and not play off one side against the other. A popular advocate of this approach is Yaşar Nuri Öztürk, Dean of the Islamic Faculty at Istanbul University. His publications rank among Turkish best-sellers.

Alevis, who are Shias. But the only thing Alevis have in common with Iranian Shias is the belief in blood-line succession. For example Alevis reject the strict Islamic *Sharia* law: unchanged for more than 1000 years, this interpretation of the Koran and Sunna sets out the rights and obligations of individuals in the community and covers every conceivable aspect of life.

Mosques (*cami*) are not only intended for prayer; they are also used for community meetings, theological lessons, political meetings and temporary accommodation for pilgrims and the homeless.

Usually one enters a mosque via a forecourt (*avlu*), where the ritual washing is done at the cleansing well (*şadırvan*) before prayer. The prayer hall, spread with carpets, consists of a prayer niche (*mihrab*) which always points toward Mecca, a pulpit for the Friday sermon (*minbar*) and a chair or kind of throne (*kürsü*), from which the prayer leader (*imam*) reads out passages from

---

Mosque etiquette

Turkish mosques can be visited by non-Muslims at any time, but follow some simple guidelines:
— non-Muslims should not visit during prayers
— men should wear long trousers and long-sleeved shirts
— women should cover their heads and shoulders, and their skirts should be at least knee length
— shoes must be removed
— maintain a respectful silence
— those at prayer should not be photographed

---

the Koran. Men and women pray separately, always however in the direction of Mecca. By kneeling and bending the head to the ground, one shows Allah humility and respect.

The muezzin calls followers to prayer five times a day from the mosque's minaret. Minarets were only introduced in the 8th century — before that the muezzins climbed onto the roof. But today the call to prayer, so alluring and 'Eastern-sounding' to the European ear, usually only comes from loudspeakers.

The exact timing of **religious holidays** (see also 'Festivals and holidays' on page 35) is determined each year according to the Islamic moon calendar. In Islamic convention a holiday begins at sunset the evening before. When it comes to important holidays, all shops, offices, etc. will close at noon the day before. The following holidays are of particular importance.

Kadir Gecesi (Night of Power) falls on the 27th night of the fasting month of Ramadan. This holy night celebrates the Revelation of the Koran to Mohammed through the Archangel Gabriel. People believe that wishes and prayers expressed on this night will be granted.

Şeker Bayramı, the Sugar Festival, is the feast marking the end of Ramadan, the month of fasting. One visits relatives, and children go from house to house asking for sweets — hence the name. All businesses and public offices are closed for this three-day holiday.

Kurban Bayramı, the Sacrifice Festival, is the most important Islamic holy time and a four-day public holiday. This festival is rooted in the story of Abraham, who was willing to sacrifice his son Isaac, in order to prove his loyalty to God. At the last moment God provides a ram instead. The Turks follow in this tradition, with a lavish meal of newly slaughtered sheep for family and friends. All left-overs are donated to charity.

This is the time of year when pilgrims travel to Mecca, so that

---

Ramazan

This is the name the Turks give the Islamic month of fasting, which is called Ramadan in most other Islamic countries. Followers may not eat, drink, smoke or have sexual intercourse between sunrise and sunset for 30 days. After darkness falls however ... everything is possible. In conservative rural areas, you may find many restaurants closed during Ramadan, but of course in the holiday centres on the coast one hardly notices any difference.

both domestic and international travel in Turkey is at a peak — be aware of this and try to avoid travelling on the first or last day. Remember, too, that banks will be closed and some ATMs will run out of money.

Medical care

There is no reciprocal health agreement between Turkey and the UK (or any other English-speaking country); it is strongly recommended that you take out **private health insurance** and read the conditions carefully if you intend to take part in any potentially dangerous sports like paragliding or rafting.

For minor ailments, it often suffices to visit one of the many chemists' shops and describe your symptoms to the pharmacist. Although they are very unlikely to speak English (use gestures), they have been dispensing remedies for the usual tourist problems for years. If by chance you are suffering from 'tourist tummy', straight away you might try drinking some black tea with a bit of salt in it.

Music and belly dance

To European ears, all Turkish music may sound the same, but there are different styles.

Folk music: In traditional Turkish folk music (*halk müziği* or *'Türkü'*) a *saz* (Turkish lute, usually with three strings) takes pride of place. Soloists or small combos sing about the simple things of countryside life — birth, love, death. After decades of absence, Kurdish folk music is also making a come-back. One hears this music mostly in a cosy oriental tavern (*Türkü-bar*).

Classical (art) music: In contrast to folk music, *fasıl* or 'art music' is performed in restaurants. It had its origins in Ottoman palace music, but there are traces of more modern influences. The singers are usually accompanied by the *kanun* (zither), *darbuka* (hand drum), *tef* (tambourine) and *ud* (lute). One of the most successful interpreters on the Turkish art music scene is busty Bülent Ersoy: gaudily made up and clothed in mink and glitter, this corpulent 50-year-old Barbie Doll was a man until 1979.

Turkish **pop music** addresses the same topic as most English hits: love. 'Türkpop' mixes traditional Turkish melodies with modern influences, so the interpreter has a wide-ranging palette — from top songwriters like Sezen Aksu ('the Madonna of the Bosphorus') to trendy teen stars and even schmaltz.

Arabesque music, as the name suggests, has its roots in Arabian music: the topic is unrequited love. This rather monotonous oriental 'wailing' is often heard on the TRTint TV station … or on the *dolmuş*. Top among performers is Müslüm Gürses, who comes across as a love-sick dachshund. There have been some notorious Arabesque concerts frequented by 50-year-olds (usually stoned) who fall about howling in ecstacy and cutting themselves with razor blades.

Many Europeans see **belly dancing** as the epitome of Turkish-oriental sensuality. But in Turkey itself, even today it is seen as somewhat indecent and is often attributed to other cultures. So for instance conservative

Belly dancers' costumes on sale; below: catching up on the news

Turks will tell you that these erotic shows originated in Egypt, whereas the Arabs are convinced that the dance was brought to Turkey by the Ottoman occupiers. Belly dance today is primarily put on for the tourist market.

Rock and electronic beats: Catchy guitar sounds are supplied by top rock bands like Duman, Kargo, and Manga or soloists Özlem Tekin, Şebnem Ferah and Teoman. Rashit's music is more punk. Since the Eurovision Song Contest in 2004, God and the world knows that Athena stands for Turkish ska-punk. Among the country's most popular DJs are Yunus Güvenen, Emre and Soulsonik. Arkın Allen, who lives abroad and is also known as Mercan Dede, pioneered links between Turkish Sufism and contemporary Western electronic music.

Newspapers and magazines

English newspapers and magazines are on sale in all the tourist centres along the coast, the papers usually being on sale the day after publication. The English-language *Turkish Daily News* prints background information and current news —politics, economics, sport and culture.

Opening times

The Islamic day of rest is Friday, but the legal day of rest in Turkey has been **Sunday** since Atatürk's reforms.

Banks: see 'Currency', page 33.
Government offices: Mon.-Fri. 08.30-12.00 and 13.00-17.30; closed Sat./Sun.

Shops: The retail trade has no standard opening times; usually shops open Mon.-Fri. from 09.00-13.00 and from 14.00-19.00 and on Sat. from 09.00-13.00 only. But in tourist centres every day is shopping day. Large shopping centres are also usually open every day until late in the evening.

Post office: Mon.-Fri. 08.00-12.00 and 13.00-17.00; closed Sat./Sun. In larger cities and in some tourist centres post offices are open for certain services (like the telephones) until midnight and from 09.00-19.00 on Sun.

Museums: Usually closed Mon., but see individual entries.
Restaurants: Usually open daily from 11.00 until at least 23.00. But small *lokantas* often close early in the evening.

Police

You'll see a lot of police about. Since they are very badly paid, they are usually bad tempered — except in their dealings with tourists, when they are generally very pleasant and courteous. In addition to the police (with blue uniforms) there are tourist police in the major resorts, many of whom speak some English. Yet another police force is the *jandarma*, a military unit in green uniforms, who ensure public order and security.

Everything from scarves to seeds is on sale at the weekly pazar.

Post offices

Post offices (and post boxes) are instantly recognisable by their yellow signs with the three black letters PTT. The main post office (*merkez postane*) in larger cities is usually located near the main square or the bank and/or shopping district. A **postcard** takes about a week to arrive in the UK. Post offices usually have **telephones** (see page 48).

Prices

Compared with the UK, Turkey is an inexpensive destination. Although prices rocketed with the introduction of the YTL in 2005 (and are of course higher in tourist centres than in the rest of the country), Turkey still offers extraordinary value for money.

What Turkish names can mean
Imagine your butcher being
called Etyemez ('he does not eat
meat') or the drinks salesman Eck
Suiçmez ('he does not drink
water'). This can happen in
Turkey.
The many strange, composite
surnames go back to a law
passed in 1934. In the course of
Atatürk's reforms the Turks, who
until that time had no surnames,
had to give themselves one. Some
could select a name, others were
appointed one. Some made
perhaps a suitable choice for their
circumstances at that time, but
didn't consider the legacy that
would be left to their sons and
daughters. And so the piano
player at the hotel bar may be
called Parmaksız ('without
fingers')...
Unfortunately, today only the
choice of first names remains. But
these are in no way lacking in
imagination either: the joy felt at
the birth of a first child may be
expressed by the name Devletgeldi
('the luck came') or Gündoğu
('the sun rose'). On the other
hand, sometimes when the family
is too large, they hope to be able
to stop by naming the last-born
(whether a boy or girl) Yeter ('this
one's enough') or Dursun ('it
ought to stop').

According to economists, the
YTL was substantially over-
valued, and no one was
surprised when it suddenly (but
not unexpectedly) dropped about
20% in value by June 2006. What
a holiday will cost you depends
on your requirements, but there
is something for virtually every
budget. Living very simply, for
instance in a *pansiyon* with
breakfast provided, picnic lunch
and one restaurant meal, you
could get by on well under £25 a
day, including bus or *dolmuş*
travel.

Shopping and bargaining

Leather goods, carpets, gold
jewellery, ceramics, tea, spices,
onyx, and all the other purchases
that hint of the Orient are among
the most popular souvenirs. Not
forgetting T-shirts, jackets and
trousers from the top designer
labels — these are all imitations
of course, but at least they fulfil
their purpose: one can wear
them. On the other hand, take
care with the deceptively
packaged top-name perfumes,
which are just ghastly.
It's best to buy from boutiques
and shopping centres in the
larger cities, where items are
priced and you can compare
prices. Where there are **no fixed
prices**, you must **bargain**. To
bargain well, you must be able to
estimate value and authenticity.
Without wishing to get the better
of you, unfortunately just about
all Turkish dealers are sly as
foxes (like the waiters mentioned
earlier). So don't let them sell you
leather from pigs as fine napa
lambskin and only believe a
fraction of what you are told. If
you know, when you first plan
your trip to Turkey, that you will
be interested in buying gold
jewellery or carpets, check the
value of what you want to buy in
your own country before you
leave.
Turkish **weekly markets** with
stalls selling everything from
vegetables and cheese to clothing
and shoes are called *pazar*; **fixed**

Some tips for buying hand-knotted Turkish carpets are in the panel opposite ... forewarned is forearmed.

markets, like those at the market quarters, with proper shops, are *çarşi*.

VAT: If you buy anything to the value of around £60 or more from shops or boutiques with a tax-free symbol in the shop window, you can get the VAT of 18% refunded in the airport departure lounge at so-called 'Cash Refund Offices' (the counters are usually in the airport check-in hall). To claim the refund you need a completed tax-free receipt from the seller.

Sites and museums

Some of the most famous ancient sites in the world are covered in this book and the *Kaş to Dalyan* and *Antalya to Demre* guides. You will also come upon a multitude of other sites, all indicated by brown signs. The most important of these are described, usually with accompanying site plans.

Any site not described here is not worth the visit, unless you are a fanatic willing to walk a long, sweaty way through brambles just to stand next to a couple of weathered stones.

The **entrance prices** for ancient sites and museums are not uniform and are updated annually. Once in a while you find extreme jumps in price of 30-50% (up or down). However, as a rule of thumb, an entrance fee of up to £6.50 is demanded for the more expensive ones. At time of writing only rarely were **concessions** available for students (with ISC) or seniors — this may change in future. **Photography** or filming (video) occasionally costs extra and then usually *quite a bit extra* (up to £6.50!). On the other hand there is a multitude of sites offering free extrance.

A word to the wise: often self-appointed 'guides' try to take

Buying Turkish carpets

Turkey is well known for its low-priced carpets. But you have to know what you're doing and exactly what you want. Most tourists are talked into buying something on the spot — usually overpriced, too large, too small, or in unsuitable colours.

To negotiate a good price you must be able to distinguish high-quality workmanship from inferior goods. Forget everything you've ever heard about settling on one-third the asking price to guarantee a bargain; everyone gets two-thirds off after the tenth tea. The dealers know all about this rule of thumb, so who's to say that they don't start with a price magnified a hundredfold?

If you know next to nothing about carpets, by all means buy a small, cheap one as a souvenir (when you consign it to the loft the moths will be happy) — or go to a specialist back home, put up some security, and take a carpet home to try out.

If you must buy a carpet in Turkey, go with the advice of an expert: check the thickness of the knots and the number of knots per sq cm. Flex the carpet in natural light, dividing the pile with your fingers to make sure the colour goes straight through. Be careful not to burn a hole in the carpet with the infamous ciga-rette lighter test, or you'll fall straight through. Be sure to ask if the carpet can fly and, if not, immediately ask for a 50% dis-count. If you heed all this advice, the dealer won't take you for a fool. One more thing: never accept a dealer's offer to post your carpet home for you!

money from tourists. Don't let yourself be taken in; only officially-authorised guides can hand over an entrance ticket!

Sport and leisure

In places where the Turks themselves holiday, the sports on offer generally amount to nothing — after all, the precious holiday weeks are taken for recovery, which means lazing about. In the international tourist centres however, the trend is towards the European style of active holidays. More and more tour operators offer leisure and sports programmes in addition to the obligatory excursions to touristic highlights. Naturally water sports dominate along the coast.

Diving: You can snorkel with mask and fins almost anywhere along the coast, but underwater hunting with tanks is forbidden — as is removing any historical and/or antique articles.

Golf: There is a golf course in Bodrum and one is planned for Marmaris (2007-8). But Belek, about 45km east of Antalya, is the golfing centre of Turkey, with championship courses.

Paragliding: The flying centre is Kocadağ (640m) between Bodrum and Marmaris; see under 'Ören' on page 107.

Riding: There are riding stables at Bodrum offering treks in the highlands; you can usually book through local tour companies.

Sailing: see page 17.

Surfing: Bodrum is one of Turkey's top places to surf; the surfing schools also rent out surfboards.

Tennis: Many of the larger hotels have tennis courts, at which non-guests can also pay to play.

Water sports: In the international resorts on the coast, various water-based activities are offered — water skiing, banana- and speed-boating, paragliding off a boat, jet skiing, etc. The organisers are usually on the beaches.

Telephone

Making calls with a mobile phone is problem-free in nearly the entire area, but expensive. Those who don't have a mobile or want to save money should make calls using a card phone. You can telephone from post offices (you will be assigned a booth and pay at the counter when the call is completed), from kiosks or from shops with the sign *kontörlü telefon* (telephone counter).

International dialling codes: for the UK first dial 00 44, for the USA 00 1, for the Irish Republic 00 353. This is followed by the local code (without the initial zero, if there is one), then the number.

Calls to Turkey: From outside the country dial 00-90, then the local code (without the initial zero), then the number.

Telephone cards *(telefon kartı)* are available from post offices, kiosks and small roadside stands. A good choice for international calls is the Arakart (www.arakart.com.tr): 250 units for example (15 YTL) allows you to phone the UK for 83 minutes.

Internet: Many hotels and guest houses now offer wireless internet connections, whereby you can call free using Skype (www.skype.com).

Beware of making calls from your hotel room; these are often charged at extremely high rates. Better to make a brief call and ask to be called back (directly to your hotel room).

Emergency numbers
Police ℂ 155
Traffic police ℂ 154
Jandarma (see page 44) ℂ 156
Ambulance ℂ 112
Fire brigade ℂ 110
Forest fire watch ℂ 177

Günnücek Milli Parklar is a lovely green park bordering the sea about 1km east of Marmaris's bus station — a pleasant place to stretch your legs.

The *hamam* — cleansing body and soul

The saying goes that the Ottoman past lives on in the *hamams*, the traditional Turkish communal steam baths which cater for all classes. Once inside, you're in a different world ... enveloped by hot, moist air and the smell of soap, relaxing under the spell of splashing water and the murmurings of shining naked bodies lying on a huge marble slab.

The *hamam* is divided into three areas. The entrance hall *(camekân)*, usually with a decorative fountain, is surrounded by the reception and changing rooms. On entering, you will be given a small robe *(peştamal)* and sandals. While it's usual for men to wear a towel around the loins and for women to bathe naked, you can bring a swimsuit if you prefer.

After changing you move through a passageway *(soğukluk)* into the main part of the *hamam*, the steam room *(hararet)*. The huge marble slab in the centre, which is warmed from below, is the *göbek taşı* (navel stone).

First you are expected to wash all over at the basins along the wall, then rise thoroughly (taking care to leave no suds behind, in case the water is used for ritual washing at the mosque). Then you lie on the marble slab, first to sweat for 15 minutes or so, and then to be massaged.

Women are usually massaged by a hefty masseuse, men by wiry muscle-men. Before the massage begins, the *tellaks* soap you down, then use a very rough flannel for exfoliation (a procedure called the *kese*). By this time your limbs are soft and rubbery, ready for the massage. Be warned: you will be pulled, twisted, kneaded and pummelled like a lump of dough; the massage is intended to loosen tight muscles and joints. Afterwards you will feel totally drained, totally relaxed.

Most *hamams* have separate sections for men *(erkekler)* and women *(kadınlar)*. At smaller baths men and women bathe at different times or on different days, but in tourist centres mixed bathing is sometimes offered.

Time

Turkey is on Eastern European Time, two hours ahead of Greenwich Mean Time, in both summer and winter (clocks go forward or back on the same days). At noon in Turkey, it's 10am in the UK, 5am in New York.

Toilets

Men's toilets have the label 'Bay', women's 'Bayan'. In tourist centres the facilities are usually up to European standards; otherwise is it not uncommon to find the stand-up 'hole in the floor', and no paper will be provided. *Take your own!* If a small bucket is provided in the toilet cubicle, please throw any paper in there and do not try to flush it away — the old-style thin sewage pipes simply cannot cope (and besides, toilet paper in the cesspits delays decomposition).

Naturally there are toilets in museums and at sites (small charge), and in restaurants. Otherwise you can usually find public toilets near a mosque.

Travel documents

Travelling from the UK or any English-speaking country you will need a **passport** and a **visa**. Package tour operators will arrange visas for you, otherwise you can buy one on the spot *for cash* at the airport or border when you enter Turkey.

While not strictly required, it is suggested that you also have a **ticket** for return or onward travel.

At time of writing you do not need any **inoculations**, but see page 37. Private **health insurance** is strongly recommended; see page 42; **travel insurance** is mandatory.

If you plan to hire a car, you must have your **driver's licence**; if you are driving to Turkey in your own car, see pages 11-12.

Visiting or business cards

Turks seem to love them, and will sometimes honour you by handing you their card, or will ask for yours. Before a Turk hands you his card, he will usually make a squiggle on the back, thus 'invalidating' the card. This is because in the past people could go into a restaurant or shop, and it was understood that the bill would be settled by the person named on the card.

Turkish

In all the tourist centres you should be able to communicate in English with no difficulty. But in the countryside you may have problems if you don't know at least a few words of Turkish, since many schools there teach no foreign languages at all.

Turkish is a very logical language and, once you have mastered a few of the rules you can progress quite rapidly, especially with pronunciation. A number of the letters in the Turkish language are unfamiliar to English speakers, but are easy to pronounce; one or two 'normal' letters are pronounced differently. **In Turkish, *usually* the first syllable is stressed.**

C/c	pronounced like the 'j' in 'jet'; *cami* (mosque) is pronounced **dja**mee
Ç/ç	pronounced 'ch'; *çam* (pine) is pronounced **cham**
Ğ/ğ	just elongates the previous vowel; *dağ* (mountain) is pronounced **daah**
İ/i	pronounced 'ee'; *iki* (two) is pronounced ee**kee**
I/ı	pronounced 'eh'; *altı* (six) is pronounced al**teh**
Ö/ö	pronounced like the 'ea' in 'learn'; *köprü* (bridge) is pronounced kurh**prew**
Ş/ş	pronounced 'sh'; *şeker* (sugar) is pronounced **sh**eker
Ü/ü	pronounced like the 'u' in 'lure'; *köprü* (bridge) is pronounced kurh**prew**

Basic words and phrases

Evet/hayır	Yes/No
Lütfen	Please
Teşekkür ederim	Thank you
Affedersiniz	Excuse me
Merhaba	Hello
Allaha ısmarladık (said by the person leaving)	See you later
Güle güle (said by the person staying)	See you later
Hoşça kal	So long, cheers
Günaydın	Good morning

İyi günler (as a greeting or when leaving)	Good day
İyi akşamlar	Good evening
İyi geceler	Good night
Nasılsın?	How are you (singlular)?
Nasılsınız?	How are you (plural)?
İyiyim	I'm fine.
... var mı?	Do you have...?
Saat kaç?	What time is it?
Büyük/küçük	Big/little
İyi/kötü	Good/bad

In towns

Tren istasyonu	Railway station
Garaj/otogar	Bus station
Havalimanı/ havaalanı	Airport
İskele	Ferry dock
Saray	Palace
Sokak	Alley
Cadde	Road
Meydan	Square
Cami	Mosque
Hisar	Fort
Kule	Tower
Kilise	Church
Müze	Museum
Banka	Bank
Hastane	Hospital
Köprü	Bridge
Ada	Island

Modern Turkish

Originally Turkish contained many Arabic and Persian words written in Arabic script. Despite Atatürk's language reforms (the Roman alphabet has been used since 1928), these influences remain. In his attempts to make the language more 'Turkish', the old words had to be transliterated into the Roman alphabet, leading to some inconsistencies that remain today.

Kütüphane	Library
Kitabevi	Bookshop
Eczane	Chemist
Bakkal	Grocer
Süpermarket	Supermarket
Pazar	Weekly market
Çarşı	Market
Postane	Post
Seyahat acentası	Travel agency

Directions/getting around

Nerede ... ?	Where is ... ?
Ne zaman?	When?
Sağ/sol	Right/left
Doğru	Straight ahead
Otobüs	Bus
Tren	Train
Araba	Car
Taksi	Taxi
Vapur	Ferry
Yaya	On foot
Bilet	Ticket
Varış	Arrival
Kalkış	Departure
Giriş	Entrance
Çıkış	Exit
Tuvalet	Toilets
Bay/Bayan	Men's/Ladies'
Açık/kapalı	Open/closed
Polis	Police
Girilmez	No entry

Numbers

Bir	1	*On sekiz*	18
İki	2	*On dokuz*	19
Üç	3	*Yirmi*	20
Dört	4	*Yirmi bir*	21
Beş	5	*Otuz*	30
Altı	6	*Kırk*	40
Yedi	7	*Elli*	50
Sekiz	8	*Altmış*	60
Dokuz	9	*Yetmiş*	70
On	10	*Seksen*	80
On bir	11	*Doksan*	90
On iki	12	*Yüz*	100
On üç	13	*İki yüz*	200
On dört	14	*Bin*	1,000
On beş	15	*On bin*	10,000
On altı	16	*Bir milyon*	
On yedi	17		1,000,000

Eating and drinking — general

Şerefe!	Cheers!
Yemek listesi	Menu
Bunu ısmarlamadım	I didn't order that
Hesap, lütfen	The bill, please
Kahvaltı	Breakfast
Öğle yemeği	Lunch
Akşam yemeği	Dinner
Tabak/çatal	Plate/fork
Bıçak/kaşık	Knife/spoon

Breakfast

Beyaz peynir	Sheep's cheese
Bal	Honey
Reçel	Marmalade
Ekmek/tereyağı	Bread/butter
Yumurta	Egg
Seker/tuz	Sugar/salt

Drinks

Çay/kahve	Tea/coffee
Türk kahvesi	Turkish mocca
Neskafe	Instant coffee
Süt	Milk
Meşrubat	Non-alcoholic
Su	Water
Soda	Sparkling water
Meyve suyu	Fruit juice
Ayran	Drink made of yogurt, water and salt
İçki	Alcoholic drink
Bira	Beer
Fıçı bira	Draught beer
Şarap	Wine
Beyaz şarap	White wine
Kırmızı şarap	red wine
Viski/votka	Whisky/vodka

Starters

Meze	Turkish starters
Ezme	Vegetable or yogurt cream
Haydari	Yogurt dip with mint and garlic
Humus	Hummus
Patlıcan salatası	Aubergine salad
Zeytinyağlılar	Cold vegetables in olive oil (various types)

Piyaz	Salad of beans, olive oil and lemon
Sigara böreği	Elongated fried pastry filled with sheep's cheese
Çerkes tavuğu	Chicken in walnut sauce
Beyin salatası	Salad of calves brains
Çiğ köfte	raw meatballs
Çorba	soup
Mercimek çorbası	Lentil soup
Yayla çorbasi	Yogurt soup with mint and lemon
Domates çorbası	Tomato soup
Tavuk çorbası	Chicken soup
İşkembe çorbası	Entrail soup

Main courses

Dolma	Stuffed vegetables
Yaprak dolması	— vine leaves
Biber dolması	— peppers
Patlıcan dolması	— aubergines
Kabak dolması	— zucchini
İmam bayıldı	Baked aubergine with onions and tomatoes (literally 'the Iman fainted')
Güveç	Braised vegetables, often with bits of meat
Köfte	Meatballs
Hindi	Turkey
Tavuk	Chicken
Piliç	Small chicken
Sığır/dana	Beef/veal
Kuzu	Lamb
Pirzola	Cutlet
Karışık izgara	Mixed grill
Şiş kebap	Skewer
Adana kebap	Peppered mince kebab
Bursa kebap	Doner kebab/tomato sauce and yogurt

Tas kebap	Braised lamb
Arnavut çiğeri	Pieces of liver

Fish and seafood

Alabalık	Trout
Balık	Fish
Barbunya	Mullet
Levrek	Sea bass
Lüfer	Blue bass
Kılıç	Sword fish
Sardalya	Sardines
Kalkan	Turbot
Hamsi	Anchovy
Uskumru	Mackerel
Dil balığı	Sole
Midye/yengeç	Mussels/crabs

Vegetables and side dishes

Sebze	Vegetables
Bamya	Okra
Kuru fazulye	Dried beans
Taze fazulye	Green beans
Bezelye	Peas
Havuç	Carrots
Ispanak	Spinach
Karnıbahar	Cauliflower
Lahana	Cabbage
Domates	Tomatoes
Zeytin	Olives
Soğan	Onions
Salatalık	Cucumbers
Sarmısak	Garlic
Salata	Salad
Çoban salatası	Mixed salad with sheep's cheese
Yeşil salata	Green salad
Cacık	Yogurt/cucumber/garlic
Makarna	Noodles
Patates	Potatoes
Pilav	Rice
Bulgur	Cracked wheat
Yoğurt	Yogurt

Fruit

Meyve	Fruit
Armut/elma	Pear/apple
Karpuz	Watermelon
Kavun	Honeydew
Üzüm	Grapes
Muz	Banana
Portakal/limon	Orange/lemon
Çilek	Strawberries
İncir/kiraz	Figs/cherries
Şeftali/kayısı	Peach/apricots
Nar	Pomegranate

Desserts, sweet

Tatlı	Any sweet
Sütlaç	Rice pudding
Lokum	Turkish delight
Dondurma	Ice cream
Kek	Sweet biscuits
Pasta	Gâteau

Snacks

Börek	Stuffed filo triangle
Gözleme	'Turkish pan cake' (filled)
Lahmacun	Turkish pizza
Simit	Sesame rings
Turşu	Pickled vegetables

Women

Thanks to the reforms of Atatürk in the 1920s (and Turkey's ambitions to join the EU), the position of women is nothing like that in most other Islamic countries. Nevertheless there is a large discrepancy between their legal rights and reality in a country so long dominated by men. Naturally the divide is greatest between town and country. The increased literacy rate is mainly due to the education of women. On the Mediterranean coast and in the towns, over 50% of the female workforce has had some education, but only 5% continue beyond the compulsory eight years. In the countryside more than half the women are illiterate.

Just out of interest: one-third of all university graduates are women, and more women work at the Istanbul stock exchange than men…

History

From about 150,000 BC (palaeo-lithic): Nomadic hunter/gatherers roam across the Turkish Mediterranean coast according to finds from caves near Antalya; cave finds on the Aegean coast date from about 80,000 BC.

8,000-5500 BC (neolithic): In what is now southeastern Turkey town-like settlements spring up, which today rank among the oldest 'cities' in the world. Loam is used in the building of dwellings. With the establishing of settlements, agriculture and cattle breeding also begin. Pottery is developed at about the same time — during excavations close to Konya (about 150km northeast of Antalya as the crow flies), archaeologists discovered small sculptures of full-breasted goddesses, symbols of fertility.

5500-3200 BC (chalcolithic): More finely-worked pottery and simple tools come into use, wrought from copper. The first settlements on Turkey's west coast date from the end of this period.

3200-2000 BC: The Early Bronze Age sees the spread of spinning and weaving mills, as well as bronze jewellery work. Troy is founded, the oldest city on the Turkish coast. Traders from Assur (on the Tigris in what is today northern Iraq) meet with the central and eastern Anatolians, bringing them into contact with writing.

2000-1200 BC: The Hittites cross the Caucasus, and central Anatolia becomes part of the 'Old Kingdom', from which the 'Great Kingdom' is later formed.

Hattussas (some 170km east of Ankara) is made the capital. At the same time Mycenaeans expand their rule over the Aegean as far as Minoan Crete. Troy develops into a prosperous trading centre.

Around 1200 BC: The so-called 'Sea People', about whom little is known, invade from the north via Thrace. Among them are the Phrygians, who play a substantial role in the destruction of Troy and also put an end to the supremacy of the Hittites and Mycenaeans.

1200-700 BC: There is an increase in Greek colonisation (Aeolian, Ionian and Dorian) on the Mediterranean coast of Asia Minor. They come into direct competition with the local tribes (Lelegians, Carians, Lycians, and Lydians). By the 9th century BC many of these Greek settlements have grown into substantial ports.

690-550 BC: The Lydians found a large kingdom in the west of Asia Minor, with Sardis as its capital (about 90km east of İzmir); their king, Croesus, becomes legendary. They also conquer further parts of the south and west coasts. Art, culture and science begin to flourish in the cities.

From 545 BC: Under Cyrus the Great, the Persians penetrate as far as western Anatolia and destroy the Lydian Kingdom. They use satraps (colonial governors) for the administration of Asia Minor. Regular rebellions against the Persians follow.

From 479 BC: The Persians withdraw from the Aegean coast.

Cities and small towns come and go.

334-333 BC. Alexander the Great conquers Asia Minor. This is the beginning of the Hellenistic period, which lasts until the era of the Roman Caesars and brings enormous cultural development.

From 323 BC: After Alexander's death the Macedonian Kingdom disintegrates; its army leaders divide it among themselves. The most important of these Diadochian realms are those of Ptolemy (in Egypt), incorporating Lycia and other parts of the south coast, the Attalid Kingdom of Pergamon in western Anatolia,

and the Seleucid Empire — the largest part of Alexander's former kingdom, with Antioch (modern Antakya) as the capital.

From 133 BC: On the death of Attalus III, Pergamon passes to Rome and becomes the first capital of the new province of Asia; the capital later moves to Ephesus.

42 BC: With Caesar's murder, the eastern part of the Roman Empire falls to Mark Antony.

31 BC: Octavian (later Emperor Augustus) is victorious over Mark Antony's fleet in the battle of Actium. Beginning of the 'Pax Romana', lasting nearly 250

Hardly anything remains of the Artemision of Ephesus, one of the Seven Wonders of the Ancient World.

years. Roman culture penetrates all cities in Asia Minor. Temples, boulevards, theatres, aqueducts and the like still bear witness today to the glory of the age.

45-60 AD: St. Paul the Apostle stops off at Ephesus and visits different cities on the Lycian coast during his missionary journeys. The first Christian communities are formed.

330: Emperor Constantine (the Great) names the former Byzantium (Istanbul today) Nea Roma (New Rome) and makes it the new capital of the Roman Empire. Soon after his death, Constantinople becomes the generally accepted name.

380: Christianity becomes the state religion; all pagan cults are forbidden.

395: The final division of the Roman Empire into west and east. The latter, later known as the Byzantine Empire, becomes the heartland of Christianity, with Roman law and Greek as the language.

527-565: Under Emperor Justinian I, Byzantium expands and blooms. It extends from southern Italy over the Balkan Peninsula and the whole of Asia Minor to the edge of the Iranian highlands. All building activity is concentrated in Constantinople. The coastal towns play a subordinate role from now on, even though many of them are made diocesan towns.

622: Mohammed and his followers emigrate to Medina (the *Hijra,* or 'Flight'); this is later designated the first year of the Islamic calendar.

From 636: Eastern Byzantium is conquered by the Arabs. Trained by Syrian sailors, seaborne invaders plunder the Byzantine coastal towns. Coastal fortresses are rebuilt or strengthened for protection — often using ancient stonework for the building materials.

1054: Schism of the Roman Catholic and the Greek Orthodox churches.

From 1071: Seljuk Muslims penetrate west from the Kirgistan steppes and attack Byzantine troops in the battle of Manzikert. They bring Islam with them, and spread throughout central Anatolia, making Konya their capital and holding the remnants of the Byzantine Empire in fear.

From 1096: Help comes to Byzantium from the Occident: the Crusades begin, to free the lost holy cities from Islamic rule.

1204-1261: The Fourth Crusade is organised against Constantinople itself, with the intention of reviving the Roman Catholic faith. After taking the city, the Knights establish a Latin (Roman Catholic) Empire. The Greek Byzantines withdraw to Nicea (İznik); it is not until 1261 that, under Michael VIII Palaeologos, the Greeks take Constantinople back from the Latins.

1226: The Seljuks conquer further parts of the coastal region. Venetians and Genoese receive permission to establish future trade.

From 1243: The Seljuk Sultanate is crushed by the Mongols. In its place several small principalities are established in Anatolia by Turkmen dynasties.

From 1309: The Order of Knights of St. John found a sovereign state on Rhodes; in the following years they establish various fortresses in the Aegean.

1326: Osman I (1281-1326), army leader and chieftain of a Turkmen tribe, conquers the west Anatolian city of Bursa, later called the cradle of the Ottoman Empire. Since Mongolian armies control the east, Osman's successors look to the north and west.

1354: Gallipoli is conquered by the Ottomans, providing them with their first foothold in Europe.

1402-1406: The Mongolian ruler Timur Lenk (1365-1405; also known as Tamerlane) makes a short and bloody appearance in Anatolia, devastating many cities. This however has little effect on the ascent of the Ottoman Empire.

1453: The Ottomans conquer Constantinople, the only remaining stronghold of the Byzantine Empire, thereby wiping it off the map. From now on Constantiniya, the future Istanbul, is capital of the Ottoman Empire, and its sphere of influence grows steadily. Less than 20 years later the Ottomans take the Turkish south coast.

1517: Selim I (1512-1520) conquers Syria and Egypt, thus bringing the Caliphate to the Bosphorus.

1520-1566: Süleyman I, known as the Magnificent, conquers

Sultanate of Women

Süleyman the Magnificent (1520-1566) and his main wife Roxelane initiated the so-called 'Sultanate of Women' — a transfer of power from men to women and an explanation for the slow decline of the Ottoman Empire lasting over three centuries.

With her intrigues and murderous plots, Roxelane brought her own son Selim II (1566-1574) to the throne. He went down in history as 'Selim the Sot'. Even before he slipped and drowned in the bathtub, the Ottoman Empire lost its entire fleet.

Selim II had five sons, four of whom were murdered by his wife Nurbanu, so that her own offspring could be crowned Sultan Murat III (1574-1595). Like so many sultans, he proved to be more active in the harem than in politics. This rewarded him with over 100 children, of whom his wife Safiye contrived to have 19 murdered, so that their son took the throne as Sultan Mehmet III (1595-1603)…

One could go on and on about the history of female influence on the successors to the Ottoman throne. And the fact that the budding sultans grew up in the harems, pampered and spoilt, in a world completely out of touch with reality. Flattered by courtiers scheming to see their own interests satisfied, the regents were for the most part incapable of acting for themselves. Many were not even strong enough to govern to the natural end of their lives. They were either strangled, poisoned or so weak-willed that they were driven out of office.

Bagdad, Belgrade, Rhodes, Hungary, Georgia, Azerbajan and parts of North Africa. In 1529 he besieges Vienna for the first time. He leads the Ottomans to the zenith of their powers, when it takes 75 minutes for the sun to set over their Empire. Süleyman and his successors have little interest in the development of Asia Minor's coastal towns.

From 1683: Defeat after the second siege of Vienna means the end of expansion and heralds the gradual decline of the Ottoman Empire. There are repeated flashes of unrest on the domestic front.

From 1808: Under Mahmut II (1808-1839) the first attempts take place to gradually reform the Empire. He eliminates the Janissaries (an elite military unit who resist all progressive currents), probably by the ruse of inciting them to revolt, leading to their massacre or exile. He outlaws the turban and introduces the fez in its place.

1853-1856: The Crimean War; the alliance of the UK, France, Sardinia and the Ottoman Empire recaptures the Russian-occupied territories. Florence Nightingale gains fame for her nursing work in Istanbul.

1875: The 'Sick Man of the Bosphorus' receives the bill for its failure to join the Industrial Revolution and its many expensive wars: France and England cancel all credit; the consequence is national bankruptcy.

1908: At the start of the Young Turk movement, officers force the resignation of Sultan Abdül Hamit II in favor of his brother.

True power now lies in the hands of the military.

1912-13: The First Balkan War; the Ottoman Empire loses its remaining European territories.

1914-1918: During the First World War the Turks side with Germany and lose. The winners divide the spoils: Greek troops march on Ankara; Italy occupies the coastal strip around Antalya; France occupies Cilicia; English troops control the Bosphorus. The Ottoman Empire now only consists of central Anatolia.

1919-20: Istanbul is forced to accept the Treaty of Sèvres on behalf of the Ottoman Empire, however the nationalists do not. April 1920 sees the first meeting of the Grand National Assembly in Ankara and the formation of a new government under Mustafa Kemal, later Atatürk (see panel opposite). Military resistance is organised.

1921-22: Kemal's troops strike the Greek army at the Sakarya River. The Italians and French retreat.

1923: With the Treaty of Lausanne the Allies recognise the independence and sovereignty of the new Turkey. In Ankara, the new capital, the National Assembly proclaims the Republic and selects Mustafa Kemal as President. In the same year, the Norwegian Fritjof Nansen, working on behalf of the League of Nations, suggests a population exchange between Greeks and Turks. Ankara agrees immediately. This effectively ends the 3000 years' history of the Greeks in Asia Minor.

1924: A new constitution comes into force, which among other

things incorporates the separation of state and religion. Islamic Sharia law is replaced by Swiss civil law, Italian criminal law and German commercial law.

1925-1938: Up until Atatürk's death numerous reforms are brought in to Europeanise Turkey: education and writing reform (transition from Arabic script to the Roman alphabet), the introduction of surnames, changing of the rest day from Friday to Sunday, etc.

1945: Having remained neutral for most of the Second World War, Turkey declares war on Germany. In the same year it becomes a founding member of the United Nations.

1950: Atatürk's former political party loses the first free elections.

1952: Turkey joins NATO.

1960: Kemalistic officers stage a *coup d'état* and allow the execution of the Prime Minister Adnan Menderes. The military sees itself as the guardian of Laicism (see page 40) and guardian of Atatürk's legacy. It stands in clear opposition to Islamic fundamentalism and radical left-wing groups.

1971: Social unrest and strikes. The cabinet is forced to resign. But the following government is also faced with unemployment, inflation, foreign exchange debts and the rising militancy of left versus right, Kurds and Turks, Alevites and Sunnis.

1974: Turkish troops occupy northern Cyprus.

1980: The military take power again and dissolve Parliament.

1984-1999: The Kurdish fight for autonomy claims roughly 25,000 victims in the east and southeast. The situation eases in February 1999 with the arrest of Kurdish Workers' Party boss Abdullah Öcalan; a truce is agreed.

1995-1998: The pro-Islamic Welfare Party (RP) led by Necmettin Erbakan wins the forced elections, thus becoming the first Muslim overall winner in the 72 years since a republic was established. But the party is banned as anti-constitutional in 1998, and Erbakan himself is forced from the political arena.

1999: A devastating earthquake hits northwest Turkey; approximately 18,000 people die.

From 2002: The AKP emerge as clear winners in the government elections; many small parties lose seats due to a clause requiring a 10% minimum threshhold for a party to gain entry to Parliament. Party leader Recep Tayyip Erdoğan becomes the head of

government one year later. Under his leadership there is a full-on push for much-needed reforms. Laws are passed to meet the Copenhagen criteria for EU membership. But Islamic extremists do not want to see a successful democracy in an Islamic land: to destabilise the country and make Europe fear Turkish EU membership, a Turkish terrorist cell with supposed Al-Qaida connections commits several atrocities. The bloodiest of these shake Istanbul in November 2003: explosions at the British Consulate, two synagogues and the HSBC Bank kill 64 people (including the British Consul) and wound 750.

From 2005: The PKK brings more terror to the land, having ended their five-year armistice in 2004. Splinter groups cause atrocities in several Mediterranean tourist resorts, including Marmaris.

2006: The long-awaited EU negotiations begin. But any joy in finally getting to the table is quickly swept aside by the unwelcoming attitude of the EU member states. EU euphoria in Turkey decreases correspondingly: in 2004, 70% of the population were in favour of joining, by 2006 the figure is down to only 50%. Orhan Pamuk becomes the first Turk to win a Nobel Prize; his novels typically deal with the clashes of identity between East and West.

Outlook: 2007 brings new presidential and parliamentary elections. EU membership for Turkey is not expected before 2015, since the measuring stick for Turkey has been set higher than for any other EU aspirant.

1 BODRUM

*History • Accommodation/camping • Food and drink • Nightlife •
Beaches and diving • Sights • Practicalities A-Z*

Area code: 0252
Information: Tourist Office at the port in front of the castle; usually unfriendly and unhelpful staff who just give you a plan and brochure. In summer open daily from 08.30-18.00, in winter shorter hours and closed Sat./Sun. (3161091, 3167694.
Connections: The international airport, **DHMI Milas-Bodrum Hava Limanı**, lies about 35km northeast of Bodrum on the road to Milas. It has both national and international terminals. Before passing through customs you have another opportunity to buy **duty-frees** — at prices usually below what you would pay in the UK or on board. In the international arrivals terminal there are cash machines, a post office, tourist office (5230101, 5230288; usually only staffed when planes land), and a branch of **Avis** car hire. In high season there are daily flights to Turkish and many UK destinations.
Transfers to and from the airport are by **Havaş buses**, who

meet the incoming and outgoing flights of Turkish Airlines (THY); there are about 8 a day. These buses leave Bodrum from the bus station (fare about £5.50). You can buy tickets at the THY main office at the Oasis Shopping Centre (see 'Shopping', page 73; (3171203, bodrumsatis@thy. com) or in the many travel agencies in the centre. By taxi the trip costs £30. It's about 1.5km from the airport to the main Milas/Bodrum road, where there are *dolmuşes*.
Bus and *dolmuş*: The bus station is on Cevat Şakir Cad., just a couple of minutes on foot from the centre. There are several buses every day to Kuşadası (2 hours; £2.50), İzmir (4 hours; £4) and Pamukkale (5 hours; £4.75), as well as to all the holiday resorts along the coast and the major towns in western Turkey. *Dolmuşes* also operate out of this bus station, with good connections to all the places on the Bodrum Peninsula and Milas (45 minutes).

Bodrum has St. Tropez's glamour and Ibiza's nightlife. The small white 'sugar cube' town with its large marina ranks among the most popular motifs for photos of the Aegean. The city's main landmark is a castle built by the Knights of St. John on a peninsula in the middle of the picturesque twin bays.

Bodrum is the pearl of the Turkish west coast and much finer than its reputation suggests. The largely intact and well-kept centre, with its serried ranks of whitewashed houses and palm-lined promenades gives the place its charm. Winding alleyways with bougainvillea-draped mansions and magical gardens remind one of when Bodrum was still Greek. Fortunately it was recognised in time that building large hotels here would damage the image and attractiveness.

But this small town of 40,000 inhabitants is only tranquil in the shoulder seasons. Between June and September high-life prevails around the clock, and the population swells to 250,000. Tourists from all over join the hip Turkish youth to take part in the hottest parties of the year here. Even Istanbulites, with all the nightlife they are accustomed to, swarm to the Bodrum Peninsula during summer. Nowhere else in Turkey can you find more love of life, liberal attitudes and an 'anything goes' atmosphere.

Bodrum's popularity as a resort and place for a second home has resulted in the city expanding more and more: it has already merged with the neighbouring towns of İçmeler to the south and Gümbet to the west. Gümbet offers what Bodrum unfortunately (or fortunately?) lacks — a long sandy beach. As a result Bodrum itself is more often a destination for day trippers from the local resorts and the nearby Greek island of Kos than a holiday base.

History

It is assumed that ancient Halicarnassus, in what is today the Bay of Bodrum, goes back to a Dorian settlement from the 11th century BC. The city's first famous personality was Artemisia I, who in 480 BC fought so courageously on the side of the Persian King Xerxes that he is supposed to have commented 'My men have turned into women and my women into men!' Her compatriot Herodotus (about 485-425 BC), known as the 'Father of History', also features strongly in the city's past.

In the 4th century BC, the Persian satrap Mausolus (376-353 BC) moved the seat of government from Milas to Halicarnassus, and it blossomed into one of the most outstanding cities in the region. His monumental mausoleum, one of the Seven Wonders of the Ancient World, gave the city immortality (see under 'Sights'). In 334 BC Alexander the Great met with heavy resistance during the conquest of Halicarnassus. During the first half of the Hellenistic age, the city came under the control of several short-term foreign rulers, but it still maintained its position as an important centre. Only when Rome took control of Caria in 190 BC, did the city's star begin to sink. And once Gaius Verres, the governor of Cilicia, had robbed all the city's works of art, Halicarnassus slipped into obscurity.

The situation changed again in 1402, when the Ottomans were occupied with Timur Lenk. This gave the Knights of St. John of Rhodes the opportunity to move into Bodrum unimpaired and develop a fortress. Their rule lasted approximately 120 years before the Ottomans conquered Bodrum, and the small town once again disappeared from the history books.

At the beginning of the 20th century, Muslim refugees from

View over Bodrum

Crete brought boat-building and sponge-diving to Bodrum. And in 1923 the Greek inhabitants (the majority) were forced to abandon their homes during the population exchange, with a second wave of Muslim refugees from Greece taking over those houses that had become free.

People lived modestly here from traditional trades. The only 'visitors' were exiled dissident artists and journalists (see 'Blue cruises' on page 17). All that changed however in the 1980s, when tourism discovered Bodrum and the local peninsula. Within a few years, it went from being a simple fishing village to the most exclusive holiday destination in Turkey.

Accommodation/camping
(see plan overleaf)
Bodrum has approximately 60,000 hotel beds and accommodation in all categories. If you decide to stay in the centre, be prepared to share in the nightlife — there's little peace and quiet.

From July until the beginning of September reservations are recommended, and even the shabbiest rooms will be expensive in high season. In the shoulder seasons, however, prices tumble.

Majesty Hotel Marina (14), relaxed atmosphere by the port. 85 rooms divided among several buildings set around the pool. Very chic, bright lobby, Art Nouveau prints in the corridors, classical-modern rooms with marble washbasins — but unfortunately rather small windows. Fitness area, sauna. Double rooms £85, as singles £65. Neyzen Tevfik Cad. 226, ℂ 3162269, www.majesty.com.tr.

Antik Tiyatro Oteli (1), one of the most beautiful and elegant little luxury hotels in Turkey: 19 comfortable rooms and 1 suite, set among several terraces full of greenery. All rooms with superb view over the city. Pool. First-class restaurant (see 'Food and drink' on page 67). One bitter note is its location on the noisy

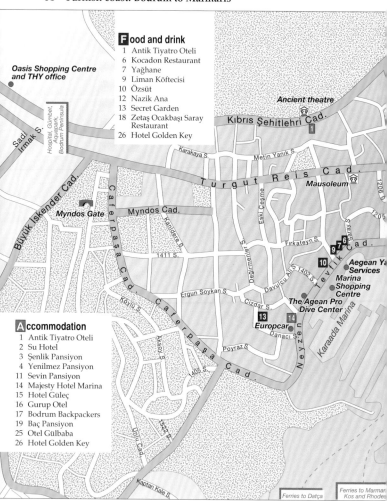

Oasis Shopping Centre and THY office

Food and drink
1 Antik Tiyatro Oteli
6 Kocadon Restaurant
7 Yağhane
9 Liman Köftecisi
10 Özsüt
12 Nazik Ana
13 Secret Garden
18 Zetaş Ocakbaşı Saray Restaurant
26 Hotel Golden Key

Accommodation
1 Antik Tiyatro Oteli
2 Su Hotel
3 Şenlik Pansiyon
4 Yenilmez Pansiyon
11 Sevin Pansiyon
14 Majesty Hotel Marina
15 Hotel Güleç
16 Gurup Otel
17 Bodrum Backpackers
19 Baç Pansiyon
25 Otel Gülbaba
26 Hotel Golden Key

ring road, but all rooms are on the side facing away from the road. Double rooms £80, singles £60. Kıbrıs Şehitlerı Cad. 243, (3166053, www.premierhotels. com.

Golden Key (26), on the far eastern side of Kumbahçe Bay, away from the crowds, but not totally out of earshot. Wonderful view from the terrace. Eight luxuriously decorated rooms and

one apartment with 2 bedrooms in the former summer home of the ex-Prime Minister Mesut Yılmaz. Private boat to take guests to nearby bays. Double rooms about £80. Şalvarağa Sok. 18, (3130304, www. goldenkeyhotels.com.

Su Hotel (2), is an idyllic little place only a short way from the centre and yet totally tranquil. 21 comfortable rooms with nice little

Walk 9 Walk 10

Mars Temple

s Mabedi Cad.

Sports stadium

Kıbrıs Sehitlehri Cad.

Milas

Hasan Reşat Cad.

Hüseyin Nafiz Özsoy Cad.

Cevat Şakir Cad.

Derviş Görgün Cad.

Kazman S.
Derne S.
Aftan S.
Panili S.
Dere S.
Meydan
Tirman
Yaka S.
Dere S.

Bus station
BUS

Kulcu S.

Üçkuyular Cad.

Yıllıkçı Cad.

Ali Yalı Galip Efendi

Bardakit S.

Türkkuyusu Cad.

Bodrum Hamamı

Flash Rental

Cevat Şakir Cad.

Paça S.

Fabrika S.

Küle S.

Bardakçı Hamamı

Dere Seçenler S.

Dr. Mumtaz Ataman Cad.

Rasattepe S.

Launderette

Helvacılar S. Adiye S.

Ahmet Hoc

Küle S.
Mandalin S.
Çıkmazı S.
Bahçe S.
2430 S.

Etham Efendi S.
Fevzi S.
Çakmak S.

Atatürk Cad.

Cad Meltem S.
Nazım Tnçl Cad.
Task S.
Üç Kuyular Cad.

EC

Meyhaneler S.

Dr. Alimbey Cad.
Kaynar S.
Ram S.
1017 S.
Adiye S.

Cumhuriyet Cad.

Orman S.
Yasemin S.
Avcı S.
Çiçek S.
Zambak S.
Resathane S.
Meltem S.
2420 S.

Begonvil S.

Police
İskele Meydanı

Sadko Tour

Merhaba Tour

Nightlife
5 Küba Bar
8 Fink
20 Moonlight Bar
21 Café del Mar
22 Bodrum Marine Club
23 Yettigari Bar
24 Club Hadigari
27 Club Halikarnas

Kumbahçe Bay

Bodrum

Akasya S.
Tepe S.

Atatürk Cad.

Deli Salih S.

Zeki Müren Museum

Peter's Castle, Museum of Under-er Archaeology

Halk Plajı, İçmeler

Zeki Müren Cad.

---

design touches, laid out around a small pool dripping with bougainvillea. All the rooms decorated with great attention to detail. Double room £55. Just nearby they also rent two comfortable and tastefully decorated stone cottages (one for 2 people, the other for up to 8; £65 for 2 people); these also have a pool. Turgutreis Cad. 1201 Sok., (3166906, www.suhotel.net.

Baç Pansiyon (19), small, well-kept and friendly guest house on the street facing Kumbahçe Bay. 10 excellent rooms with climate control and marble floors. Double rooms with balcony and sea view £42 (super); the same facing over the shopping area £4 cheaper (boring). Highly praised by readers. Not accessible by car. Cumhuriyet Cad. 14, (3161602, bacpansiyon@turk.net.

Gurup Otel (16), You couldn't find a more central location. Facing the harbour on Belediye Meydanı, above a shop. 12 small, simply furnished rooms with TV, climate control and stained carpets — but at least with narrow balconies from where you can watch the comings and goings down at the port. Double rooms £35, singles £19. (3161140, (3133151.

Otel Gülbaba (25), a three-story hotel opened in 2004; 18 tiny rooms, small pool and roof terrace. The big advantage here is that it's new and very clean. Double room with climate control £30. Somewhat hidden away on a narrow street, Papatya Sok 24. (3168027, www. otelgulbaba.com.

Hotel Güleç (15), a clean little guest house some way back off Kumbahçe Bay. Welcoming rooms with climate control and tiled floors. Breakfast served in a lovely garden, where birds twitter in the orange trees. Double room £30. Üçkuyular Cad. 18/A, (3165222, www. hotelgulec.7p.com.

Sevin Pansiyon (11), pleasant, budget guest house near the promenade with international guests. Welcoming rooms with tiled floors and good baths with shower cabinets, café, Internet connection, courtyard with hammocks. Double rooms with climate control £27, without £24. Türkkuyusu Cad. 5, (3167682.

Şenlik Pansiyon (3), another pleasant central address. 10 clean rooms with tiled floors and nice balconies; roof terrace. Relaxed, friendly atmosphere. Heating if needed. Per person £11. Books up quickly. Türkku-

yusu Cad. 115, (3166382.

Yenilmez Pansiyon (4), 9 simple, very clean rooms of varying sizes, all with private bath. 4 rooms have balconies. Friendly, family atmosphere. Double rooms £22. Menekşe Çıkmazı 30, (3162520.

Bodrum Backpackers (17), the local backpackers' meeting place. Turkish/British management. Popular with Brits/drinkers (despite the outrageously over-priced terrace bar) who can't bear to miss a Premier League game. Well-kept rooms; unfortunately the service is orientated to turn-over and nothing more. Bed in the dormitory £4.75; double room with bath £13. Atatürk Cad. 31 B, (3132762, www. bodrumbackpackers.com.

Camping: The nearest campsite is in **Gümbet** (see page 74); another lovely place is at Yahşi Beach (see page 76).

Food and drink

(see plan on pages 64-65)
Being hungry in Bodrum is expensive. Every evening in the summer Bodrum's waterfront esplanade transforms itself into an enticing display for the wealthy 'beautiful people'. There are top-class Italian, Indian, Vietnamese and Chinese restaurants, sushi-bars, exquisite fish restaurants, and … and … and — with the exception of Istanbul or Ankara, nowhere else in Turkey is the gastronomic palette broader or the prices for a cosy dinner higher. Travellers with thinner purses should make for the simple *lokantas* on the way out of town. But to avoid any unpleasant surprises, always ask about the prices whenever

they are not posted outside or the menu is only written in Turkish.

Antik Tiyatro Oteli (1). To have dinner at this hotel (see 'Accommodation' on page 63) can be a wonderful memory of your visit to Bodrum. There is fantastic Turkish/international cooking and an equally fantastic view, with wonderful service. A superb evening meal here will cost you £24 per person without drinks. ℂ 3166053. Another good hotel restaurant is the one at the **Golden Key (26)**. Mediterranean cooking with Italian overtomes; similar prices. ℂ 3130304.

Kocadon Restaurant (6), another of Bodrum's long-established gastronomic highlights, especially popular with foreigners who live in the city. Idyllic garden with decent lighting (!), hidden behing the promenade by a high old stone wall. A1 service. The small but well-chosen menu changes daily; international and Turkish cuisine. Main courses £8.50-13. Saray Sok. 1, ℂ 3163705.

Yağhane (7), with an atmosphere as pleasant as Kocadon's. Here you dine between the well-restored ruins of an old olive oil factory. Equally excellent cooking — try the octopus *güveç* or medaillons of calf with pineapple. Main courses £7-11. Neyzen Tevfik Cad. 170, ℂ 3134747.

Liman Köftecisi (9), just near Yağhane. A good value-for-money address for anyone who wants to eat on the promenade. Meze and meatballs in various versions (£2-3.50). Neyzen Tevfik Cad. 172, ℂ 3165060.

Secret Garden (13), a pleasant garden restaurant. French-inspired cooking — seafood soup with saffron or calamares in *rakı* sauce (each about £7) for starters, then stuffed breast of chicken or shoulder of lamb with rosemary (each about £8.50). Excellent wine list. Only open in the evenings. Danacı Sok. 20, ℂ 3131641.

Zetaş Ocakbaşı Saray Restaurant (18), equally popular with tourists and locals, with a large terrace. All prices (kebabs £2.20-4.50) are posted and the dishes explained in English. A large beer costs another £1.20. Aside from the speciality (grills), they also serve pizzas, pastas and breakfasts. Atatürk Cad. Eski Adliye Sok. 12/A.

Nazik Ana (12), a low-budget tip. Large self-service *lokanta* with top-quality home cooking. The dishes change daily. Friendly young staff and decent music; no rip-offs. A really satisfying meal for £3. Eski Hükümet Sok. (a small side-alley between Türkkuyusu Cad. und Cevat Şakir Cad.).

Sweets: Özsüt (10), part of a countrywide chain that is very popular for its huge variety of tasty cakes, rice and other puddings, etc. With terrace. Neyzen Tevfik Cad. 198.

Nightlife

(see the plan on pages 64-65)
Bodrum nights are long — not for nothing is it called the Ibiza of Turkey. Put on heavy make-up, take a fat wallet and off you go. But the dancing doesn't start till 1am. Until then you spend your time at the chic bar scene in Neyzen Tevfik Cad., at Salmakis Bay or in various locations on Cumhuriyet and Dr. Alim Bey Cad. in Kumbahçe Bay — where

you will find all sorts of cafés and bars. The change is enormous and what's 'in' today is 'out' by tomorrow (or has a completely different name) — so discover them for yourself! The most lighthearted drinking places are the many pubs in Meyhaneler Sok. (a side lane off the Kale Sok.).

Kumbahçe Bay: Halikarnas (27), an open-air night club for over 5000 people, in business for over 20 years. It ranks among the largest and (self-proclaimed) best discos in the world — in any case it could stick most large European city discos in its pocket. Various stages, many different music genres, laser show, parties, roof terrace and huge dance area. Dress code. Open till dawn. Entry £15 (includes a free drink). www.halikarnas.com.tr.

Bodrum Marine Club (22), on a catamaran moored at the foot of the castle. Apart from Halikarnas, *the* in place in the city — also with room for 5000 night owls. Huge dance floor (glass bottom (!), 8 bars. In summer prices like Halikarnas, in the shoulder season often free entry. Here too there is a wide range of music, themed parties, etc. Dress code. Also open till dawn. www.clubbodrum.com.

Club Hadigari (24), the smallest of the 'big three' clubs, with room for only 2000. One of the forerunners of Bodrum's hot club scene, in business since 1974. Mostly standard music, sometimes live performances. VIP lounge right on the water. Near the castle. With an entry fee of £11 somewhat cheaper than the other two. www.hadigari.com.

Yettigari Bar (23), just a few steps from the Bodrum Marine Club. Pleasant bar at the foot of the castle. DJs, garden, dancing. Chrome furniture, nice terrace. Dr. Alim Bey Cad. Nearby **Fora Bar (20)** has an equally lovely terrace and small dance floor.

The **Moonlight Bar (20)** will appeal to anyone looking for somewhere romantic. A lovely place to have a drink at sunset. A couple of tables right on the beach, with sea spray and a view of the boats anchored in the bay and the illuminated castle. Somewhat hidden, at Cumhuriyet Cad. 60.

Café del Mar (21), about 100m past the Moonlight Bar. Also a couple of tables on the beach, this time with jazz, really good coffee and all kinds of drinks. This place is less full at sunset than at sunrise, since it's a good 'after hours' bar, open 24 hours a day. Cumhuriyet Cad.

Salmakis Bay: There are several classy lounges and clubs on Neyzen Tevfik Cad. which runs along Salmakis Bay. Most have cosy gardens in front of old Greek houses. Without doubt the most chic is **Fink (8)**, with cool electro music and a lot of 'beautiful people'. Without the right gear (and what might that be?), you've no chance of getting in.

Küba Bar (5), a bit further along, also has a good ambience — with more sedate music.

Beaches and diving

Bodrum's public beach, the small Halk Plajı right at the southern end of Kumbahçe Bay, is not the most attractive of beaches, but those who want to see and be seen can rent a sunbed here. For swimming, the wonderful bays on the Gulf of Gökova (east of the city, see page 105) or the beaches on the Bodrum Peninsula (see page 74) are far better — especially Gümüşlük. Or you could take a boat trip with stops for swimming.

Diving: There are several options. They speak English at The Aegean Pro Dive Centre (diploma courses). Taster course including lunch £32. Two boat-diving courses for experienced divers (including equipment) are offered for the same price. Beginners course £180. Neyzen Tevfik Cad. 212, ℭ 3160737, www. aegeanprodive.com.

Aquapark: Dedeman Bodrum, an enormous aquapark with 'Kamikaze tube', 'Hydro-tube', etc. — a jamboree for families with children. Entrance fee: adults £11.50, children £7. On the Ortakent road; *dolmuşes* stop right in front.

Sights

There is no longer much to remind one of ancient Halicarnassus, and what *does* remain is scattered around the city is hardly spectacular. On Mars Mabedi Caddesi above Salmakis Bay there are the meagre remains of a **Mars Temple**; the **Myndos Gate**, which was once part of the city defences, is near Büyük İskender Caddesi on the way to Gümbet; the 3rd century BC **theatre** (*Antik Tiyatro*, still used for events today) is on busy Kıbrıs Şehitleri Caddesi high above Bodrum. Although the theatre has been quite well restored, the site is not very interesting (*open daily from 08.30-12:00 and 13.00-17.30; entry fee £2.20*). In any case, the most

important legacy from Halicarnassus is the mausoleum.

Mausoleum: The mausoleum of Halicarnassus, a monumental tomb, was considered one of the Seven Wonders of the Ancient World and gave its name to all burial places of this kind. During his lifetime (4th century BC) Prince Mausolus commissioned the architect Pytheos to do drawings for a tomb which he later had built from white marble; the work was completed after his death by Artemisia II, his sister and wife. It stood on a terrace 105 x 242 metres in size and was over 50 m high. A step-pyramid formed the top, at the apex of which was a statue of Artemisia and Mausolus riding a *quadriga* (a two-wheeled chariot drawn by two pairs of horses). The best artists and craftsman of the time took part in the decoration of the tomb. Earthquakes — and plundering of the stonework for the building of the castle — account for the fact that only the foundation walls remain today. Fortunately a few diagrams help one form a mental picture. The first excavations of the mausoleum were undertaken in the 19th century by Sir Charles Newton. Precious finds such as reliefs and tableaux were sent on to the British Museum, so only a few unspectacular column bases remain for visitors today. *Address/opening times: 100m inland from Salmakis Bay, Turgutreis Cad. Open daily (except Mon.) from 08.30-17.30; entry fee £1.65.*

Bodrum Castle/Museum of Underwater Archaeology: Also called the **Castle of St. Peter**, this powerful building was established on the foundations of an older Byzantine fortress by the Order of the Knights of St. John of Jerusalem during the first half of the 15th century. At that time the Order, which had founded a sovereign Knights' State on the island of Rhodes, possessed an enormous fleet, with which it plundered Islamic trading vessels. The Order was divided into several sections, known as 'tongues' (due to the different languages spoken). Each tongue had its own lodgings, and in the event of an attack had a section of the fortress to defend. The designation of the towers by nationality originates from that time.

In 1523 the knights were driven out of the Aegean, and a few years later established themselves on Malta. During the Ottoman era, the castle lost its importance, and at the end of the 19th century it was transformed into a prison. It came under attack for the last time during the First World War, when the French warship Dubleix sailed into the Bay of Bodrum. Today the castle accommodates a museum for underwater archaeology, the largest of its kind in the world, boasting finds from some of the more than 20,000 boats that have sunk off the Turkish coast. Frankly, it sounds grander than it is, unless you have a tremendous interest in amphorae…

The **entrance** to the castle is in Salmakis Bay. Just behind the ticket office you cross a small courtyard with a shady café. From there you walk along one of the outer bastions to a courtyard with a mulberry tree in the centre. On the right is a small

chapel from 1406, which has a minaret added by the Ottomans in 1523. Today the chapel houses the replica prow of a Byzantine ship which sank off the Bodrum Peninsula in 626. To the left in the courtyard is a large exhibition of **amphorae** (it is estimated that the oldest dates from 1400 BC).

Beside the chapel, steps lead to an upper courtyard covered in greenery, with some peacocks strutting about. Here you pass the **Glass Hall**. Inside are small vases, glasses, and bowls which sank to the seabed between the 14th century BC and the 11th century AD. A few steps further on is the entrance to the **Glass Shipwreck Hall** (with a separate admission fee and an exit in the lower courtyard). On view here is the skeleton of a trading vessel which sank close to Marmaris in the year 1025. Also on display are finds from the hold and personal possessions belonging to the crew.

Another few steps further along is the **Spanish Tower** — also known as the Snake Tower, since a relief of a snake is carved into the stone at the left of the entrance. Inside are — amphorae. The small exhibition in the upper part of the tower about 'birth, life and death', was closed at the time of our last research. It was a similar story in the nearby **German Tower**: on the ground floor are amphorae, while the exhibition above, with furniture in the style of the German Renaissance, was also closed. Opposite rise the **Italian** and **French towers**. The first houses a small collection of coins and decorations, the latter medieval

Bodrum Castle

weapons. From the terrace between these two towers there is a wonderful view over Bodrum.

Next is the **Carian Princess Hall** (which also demands a separate admission fee). Inside are the bones of the Carian 'princess' Ada from the 4th century BC. Her sarcophagus was found by construction workers close to Bodrum in 1989. On show are burial objects (including golden bracelets, a chain and a laurel ring) and — the pride of the museum — a life-size model of the lady herself. This was created at the University of Manchester with the help of the latest patho-logical knowledge (pity that science does not cheat a bit in favour of beauty).

From the Carian Princess Hall a pathway leads to the **English Tower** in the southeastern part of the castle. Its interior décor evokes the Order of the Knights of St. John of Jerusalem, with arms, flags and coats of arms. If you keep walking along the outer, eastern fortress wall, you pass a low building housing the remains of **Bronze Age ship-wrecks**, including the oldest known wreck (14th century BC), recovered from Ulu Burun near Kaş. A somewhat kitsch model shows the ship with a tableau. Further along, a sign enquires: 'Do you have a strong heart to walk into the dungeon?' Maybe the question refers to the many steps down to the **dungeon** (a dead end), because there is nothing shocking inside: what you see is a gloomy red colour and what you hear is some indistinct tape-recorded groaning.

If you leave the courtyard by the German Tower, you pass yet another exhibition hall with the skeletons of slaves who were condemned to row on the galleys. Their bones, still in iron chains, were not discovered until 1993 near the English Tower. *Opening times: daily from 09.00-12.00 and 13.00-18.30 (in winter till 17.00). Entry fee £4.50. Carian Princess Hall and Glass Shipwreck Hall (only Tue.-Fri. 10.00-12.00 and*

14.00-16.00) £1.65 extra for each attraction.

Zeki Müren Museum: Zeki Müren is hardly known outside the country, but in Turkey he had cult status (only surpassed by that of Atatürk) due to his many films and hit records. The rise of this charismatic sentimental singer and composer began in the 1950s, unhindered (even then) by his gay/transsexual appearance. In 1955 he received Turkey's first golden record. Up until his death in 1996 (when he had a heart attack during a live performance), he had brought millions to tears. He was buried in his hometown of Bursa. Müren's house in Bodrum is now open as a little museum. On view are fan letters, records and costumes full of fantasy.

Address/opening times: Zeki Müren Cad. Open daily (except Mon.) from 08.30-12.00 and 13.00-17.30; entry fee £0.90.

Practicalities A-Z

Boat trips: Several day trips are on offer to various places where boats lay anchor — for example to Karaada (Black Island) with hot springs, to Ortakent Beach (see page 76) or to the so-called 'Aquarium', a crystal-clear snorkelling bay. These boats leave from Salmakis Bay west of the castle, usually around 10.30, and return around 17.00. Per person with lunch £8.50. It's best to book at the last minute, so you can see how full (or overloaded) the boat is.

Car hire: Available everywhere. The cheapest car with local firms is about £25 per day, with the internationals about £37. **Avis**,

Neyzen Tevfik Cad. 92/A, ℂ 3161811; www.avis.com.tr.; **Europcar**, Neyzen Tevfik Cad. 232, ℂ 3160885, www.europcar. com.tr.

Consulate: see page 33.

Doctors and dentists, English-speaking: Universal Hospital Bodrum on Kavaklı Sarnıç Cad. high above Gümbet Bay, ℂ 3191515.

Events: In summer various events are held in the ancient **theatre**, from ballet festivals to pop concerts. Every year there is a *gulet* **regatta** at the end of October.

Ferries: There are ferries to **Kos** all year round. In high summer there are two a day: a hydrofoil (sailing time 25min., one-way £20, day return £22, open ticket £40) and a car ferry (sailing time 60min., one-way or day return £15, open ticket £29; motorbikes one-way £29, cars £70-105). In winter only the car ferry runs — and sporadically at that.

In summer there is also a daily ferry service to **Datça** (or, more precisely, to Körmen, from where a connecting bus takes you the 8km on to Datça. This is not a good idea for a day trip, as the journey time each way is about 2 hours (return ticket £12.50). Other ferry connections in summer (up to four times a week) are to **Marmaris** (sailing time about 1h30min, day return £20) and Rhodes (sailing time 2h30min, day return £40). Tickets and information about the ferries to Kos, Rhodes and Marmaris are available from **Bodrum Express Lines** (ℂ 3164067, www.bodrum-expresslines.com), and for Datça from the **Bodrum Ferryboat**

Association (☎ 3160882, www.
bodrumferryboat.com), both
located at the ferry docks by the
castle.

Launderette: There's a laundry
on almost every street corner, for
instance **Nesli Laundry** at
Türkkuyusu Cad. 27. Machine
wash and dry £2.25.

Money: Cash dispensers are
everywhere in the centre.
Exchange bureaus are mostly
located on Cevat Şakir Cad.

**Newspapers and magazines in
English:** These are available at
almost all kiosks in the centre.

Organised tours: The dozens of
tour operators arrange trips to
the hinterland as well as boat
trips. Choice and prices vary
little. **Hi Tour (Merhaba Tour)**
near the Tourist Office (İskele
Meydanı) has, for example, the
following — among much else —
on offer: excursion to Pamukkale
or Ephesus including lunch
£15.50; two-day tour to Ephesus
and Pamukkale with overnight
accommodation in a four-star
hotel £35; trip to Milas £5.50; jeep
safari around £17. ☎ 3169833,
☎ 3166518.

Police: Near the Tourist Office,
☎ 3168080.

Post: The post office is on Cevat
Şakir Cad.

Riding: Horse-riding and
trekking can be booked through
various tour organisers (like **Hi
Tour** mentioned under 'Organised tours' above). Two hours in
the saddle, including transfer,
costs about £26.

Shopping: Clothing, carpets,
leather jackets, jewellery, and
kitsch of all kinds — the choice is
huge, but in Bodrum it is not
inexpensive. If you can afford it,
the chic goods (Tommy
Hilfinger, Diesel, Paul & Shark
Yachting, etc.) are all on sale in
the **Shopping Center at the
Marina**. Another modern
shopping centre is the **Oasis** on
Kıbrıs Şehitleri Cad., the ring
road north of the centre. This has
many clothing shops and all
kinds of economical and good
restaurants. **Markets** are held on
Tuesdays (clothing) and Fridays
(food) at the bus station.

Turkish Bath (hamam): Bardakçı
Hamamı, over 250 years old, lies
on Omurca Dere Sok. at Kumbahçe Bay east of the castle.
Mixed bathing. Entry with
massage £13. Open until late in
the evening. The newer **Bodrum
Hamamı** (same prices/opening
times) is on Cevat Şakir Cad.
opposite the bus station. Separate
sections for men and women.

Two-wheel hire: There are a
couple of firms near the bus
station. **Flash Rental Service**
(Cevat Şakir Cad. 28, ☎ 3169636,
www.flashmoto.com) has
scooters from 50cc (£10/day) to
250cc (£30/day), as well as 600cc
Enduros (£40) and 800cc
Choppers (£55). At time of
writing there were no shops
renting bicycles.

Yacht charter: The coastal waters
around Bodrum are just perfect
for yachting trips lasting several
days, and there is a correspondingly good choice of boats
available for charter. Depending
on the season, outfitting and size
(maximum 12 people), reckon on
a boat with crew for between
£135-2000 per day. You can deal
direct with the captains at the
marina or go to an agency like
Aegean Yacht Services, Neyzen
Tevfik Cad. 198, ☎ 3161517,
www.aegeanyacht.com.

2 BODRUM PENSINSULA

Gümbet • Bitez • Ortakent and Yahşi • Kargıkoyu • Akyarlar • Turgutreis • Gümüşlük • Yalıkavak • Gündoğan • Türkbükü • Gölköy • Torba

Area code: ℂ 0252
Connections: The *dolmuş* connections between Bodrum and the places on the peninsula are very good, but connections between the villages themselves are not. To tour the whole peninsula, it's best to have your own transport.
Walks: 1-10

It's quite a long time now since the Bodrum Peninsula has been an idyll of undisturbed nature. Holiday villages and club resorts dominate most bays, and the 'Lego'-style building still continues apace although, fortunately, there are no six or seven-storey apartment blocks. But it seems to be only a question of time before the entire coast of the peninsula is forested with houses. Many once-romantic little places have been robbed of their charm — although not in the eyes of the country's high society. For them the Bodrum Peninsula in summer is still *the* place to be. So much so that many areas are very well-kept and ritzy-looking.

At sunset, the views from the inland hills over the coastline full of bays are lovely, especially with the silhouettes of the offshore islands adding a charming lattice-work backdrop.

In the farming villages you will often see a large white, semi-circular cistern called a *sarnıç;* these *sarnıçlar* feature on several walks (see photograph on page 87. Up until a few decades ago, rainwater was stored inside them during the winter, for watering thirsty cattle and dry fields in the summer. Today they are usually functionless.

Below is a tour of the peninsula in a clockwise direction.

Gümbet

This bay, 5km west of Bodrum, has been taken over by package holidaymakers, primarily from Britain and Germany. The beach, which is quite narrow, gets a new set of clothes in the spring, when several truckloads of sand are brought in. In the high season you can easily read the latest newspapers by glancing over at the next beach chair. Just behind the beach there's a row of bars (including a few nice beach clubs), restaurants, souvenir shops and well-maintained club resorts. In addition, all the usual fun water sport activities are on offer.

Accommodation/camping: For individual travellers (campers excluded) it's not a good scene. The guest houses only start three or four streets in from the beach, and better accommodation can be found elsewhere for the same price.

Zetaş Camping, however, is one of the best places on the peninsula. Large shady meadow, good

Bodrum Peninsula

3,5 km

and plentiful sanitary facilities, campers' kitchen, relaxed atmosphere. Restaurant. Camper van-friendly. Beach. Camping for 2 people with tent or van £8. Apr. to the end of Nov. (3162231, zetascamping@hotmail.com.

Bitez

In the next bay is Bitez, the calmer and more modest continuation of Gümbet. The crush of people on the narrow beach (in places more shingle than sand), with a mosque right by the sea, is manageable most of the time, and the water sports on offer are similarly good.

Accommodation: Most accom-modation is directly behind the beach and — in contrast to Gümbet — there are also a few guest houses.

Yalı Han, a friendly little hotel with 21 rooms, some of them around the green pool area behind the shore promenade, 16 with sea view. Diving and surfing. Double room with climate control £46. (3637772, www.yalihan.bitez.net.

Çömez Motel, a pleasant inn right next to Yalı Han, a short way back from the beach. 14 very clean, well-kept rooms with dark furniture, climate control and tiled floors, 3 with balcony. The big plus point is the terrace with a view over the whole bay; breakfast is served here. Double rooms from £29-35. (3638181, (3637955.

Ortakent and Yahşi

The villages of Ortakent and Yahşi lie inland. From here the road to the coast leads past citrus trees, whitewashed little houses and elegant mansions with manicured gardens. The two beaches, named after these two adjoining villages, are separated by a small port. Behind is an accumulation of hotels, guest houses, and holiday settlements which are predominantly occupied by Turks. During the Turkish school holidays, the scattered beach village is quite busy, before and after it's like a ghost town. The most popular places to stay are at the western end of Yahşi Beach.

Accommodation/camping: The accommodation is all well signposted.

Kaktüs Motel, at the eastern end of Yahşi Beach. A row of 10 recently refurbished rooms with green furniture, tiled floors, telephones, TV and climate control, all with balcony overlooking the shore promenade. Double rooms with H/B £46. Behind the motel is a garden-like area with cacti, palms, cosy nooks for relaxation and a bar — where you can also **camp** from Apr.-Oct. (2 people £9.50). (3483004, kaktüsmotel @ttnet.net.tr.

Aras Pansiyon, a family-run guest house behind the eponymous shop. Two minutes from Yahşi Beach. 40 very clean rooms with balconies and terrace, some with kitchen. Try to get a room at the back; rooms at the front get the noise from the garden of the hotel opposite. Double rooms £12.50, three-bedded £17, no breakfast. (3483140.

Kargıkoyu/Kargı Plajı ('Camel Beach')

For years tourists have been taking camel rides at sandy Kargı Beach, hence the nickname. It's also a popular destination for boat trips. The resorts here are well-camouflaged in the green woods along the undeveloped shoreline, whereas holiday settlements stud the surrounding slopes. **Bağla** and **Karaincir**, two bays further south, look similar. Between them is the '**Aspat Termera Resort**', which has a whole beach to itself and is much nicer than you might guess just passing the road entrance. For an entrance fee of £8.50 you can join the wealthy Turks and alternative-lifestylers who holiday here relaxing in hammocks and dining at the idyllic riverside restaurants. Entertainment includes a cinema and an open-air stage, as well as an open-air sculpture studio and various workshops. There are also nice bungalows to rent (doubles £46). Surrounded by the upper crust and intellectuals, you won't even notice the (fairly unattractive) beach. For details see www.aspat.com.tr.

Akyarlar

This one-time fishing and sponge-diving village is an enjoyable place for both day trips and for spending a few peaceful days; even in high season the tumult is kept within limits. The narrow beach is not intoxicating, but does have some flair, being lined by a few old Greek houses. The cosy fish restaurants are among the least expensive on the peninsula, with the menu including drink from about £8.50. Unfortunately, the skeleton of a gigantic resort in the west of the bay somewhat spoils the view. Further along the road towards Turgutreis, the beaches have completely lost their attraction now, due to the building of monotonous holiday settlements.

Accommodation: Motel Kılavuz, somewhat set back from the beach. 27 simple rooms in a garden full of mandarin trees, some with private terrace. Restaurant, own parking area. Double rooms £30. (3936006, www.kilavuzmotel.com.

Babadan Motel, right next door, but on the beach. 20 very plain rooms with private sanitary facilities, but with only 3 facing the sea. Double room £29.50. Adjacent restaurant with seaside terrace. Service isn't always very friendly. (3936002, (3937987.

Turgutreis

Not too long ago, this town, named after the famous 16th-century Ottoman sailor Turgut Reis, was still a sleepy fishing village. But now its population of 10,000 inhabitants swells to some 25,000 or so in summer, and it has become the second largest town on the peninsula after Bodrum, completely given over to tourism. Fishing boats are rarely seen in the port now; in their place are yachts of various sizes in the newly built marina. The people tanning themselves on the long sandy beach are predominantly holidaymakers

from Britain, and the local businesses appreciate their custom — virtually every restaurant offers 'bacon and eggs' for breakfast.

North of Turgutreis is the Bay of Kadıkalesi, popular with surfers. A few old Greek houses keep the resorts company here, while the few square metres of public beach in between is hardly worth a mention. But it's worth coming here just to visit the **Pitos Café-bar** close to the Mark Warner Palm Beach holiday resort. Enjoy a relaxing (but not inexpensive) break in the beautifully land-scaped garden.

Getting there: Turgutreis has its own bus station on the road to Gümüşlük, with good connections during the summer to all the larger cities in western Anatolia. In addition there are regular connections by dolmuş *to Akyarlar and Gümüşlük.*

Accommodation: Hotel Water Ville, three-storey building north of the marina with seaside pool. Club atmosphere. 50 rooms with climate control, tidy and OK. Friendly service. Per person all inclusive £30. (3827332, www. hotelwaterville.com.

Plaj Pensiyon, nice inn on the promenade near the centre, also north of the marina. 7 plain but very clean rooms with photos of the area taken by the friendly owners. Unfortunately all rooms lead off the back courtyard and are quite dark. Double rooms £19. Kumsal Sok. 32, (3822230, (3943087.

Food and drink/nightlife: Full English breakfasts to steak. But also Turkish cooking at **Anadolu Çorba Salonu** near the promenade and the popular **Tash's Bar**

(see below): kebabs, various soups (including sheep's-head, sheep's-foot and entrail) and *mantı*. Fair prices, nice service. Nights are quieter than in Bodrum. Among the most popular places for a beer is **Tash's Bar**, the nearby **Radio Bar** and **Shaina Bar** near the Aegean Dream Resort Hotel. *Tip:* Just because it says 'Guinness' outside doesn't mean you'll find it inside — you may have to settle for Efes Dark.

Practicalities A-Z

Boat trips: Boat trips to Kos start at 10am each morning in the summer, returning in the late afternoon. Travel time is just one hour. Day return tickets cost £15, others double! No cars! Information in the brochures from the **Bodrum Ferryboat Association** close to the marina, (3827807. There are also daily tours to bays south and north of the town, £13 per person including lunch.

Shopping: There is a large weekly market in the centre on Saturdays.

Gümüşlük

Gümüşlük is by far the most tranquil place on the Bodrum Peninsula. There are plenty of restaurants lined up alongside the quay in an idyllic setting. Anyone who knows Bodrum well will tell you that an extravagant meal in one of the Gümüşlük fish restaurants is a must.

Gümüşlük consists of little more than the restaurants and a few guest houses. A stop on all building has so far ensured that this remains so. And as a result, the narrow, predominantly shingle beach never overflows in the summer. On the small offshore island (to which you can wade through the shallow water), rabbits jump around between the meagre remnants of ancient **Myndos**, which in earlier times gave its name to what is now the Bodrum Peninsula. Most of Myndos lies under water today, the 'Sunken City'.

Every evening in spring and late summer, the Bay of Gümüşlük offers one of the most beautiful sunsets on the entire west coast — a tip for the romantics among you.

From Gümüşlük there's a lovely walk to Karakaya, a picturesque village (see Walk 2).

Accommodation/camping: Mostly simple guest houses or apart-hotels. In summer best to reserve in advance.

Sysyphos Pansiyon, long-established pension at the south end of the bay. Lovely old stone building, restaurant with seaside terrace, idyllic little courtyard garden. Very cosy. 20 simple clean rooms with bath, most with balcony, double rooms £30 with breakfast. Also 2 apartments for 4 people maximum, without breakfast £35 per night. (3943016, (' 3943656.

Özak Pansiyon, near Sysyphos. 14 tidy, simple rooms around a well-kept green area with hammocks, beach volley ball field and 'campfire bar'. Restaurant. Double rooms £19. (3943388, (' 3943037.

Arriba Apart Otel, on the beach. 4 large, simple, clean apartments (for up to 4 people), with balconies overlooking the sea or terrace; £32 per day. Also 5 cosy wooden cabins in the garden behind, with fridges and terraces, rented as double rooms with breakfast for £25. Friendly service. Restaurant. **Camping** possible in the garden. ☏ 3943654, arribaapart@yahoo. com.

Gümüşlük Hotel, in the centre by the fish restaurants. 5 small double rooms (£22) — extremely spartan, but with lovely views over the bay and port. If you stay here, you get a discount in the hotel's own restaurant. Note that they plan a change of name. ☏ 3943045.

Food and drink: All the restaurants are pleasant and serve good fresh fish — the *meze* displays provide the competition. For a complete meal with wine reckon on about £17 per person. Despite the boards with fixed menu prices, it's usual to bargain. There is a particularly beautiful view (fantastic at sunset) from the **Café-Restaurant Limon** near the road to Yalıkavak, about 20 minutes on foot from the centre. If you take a good book, you could spend all afternoon here lounging around on the ultra-comfy cushions.

Practicalities A-Z

Information: The Tourist Office is in the centre near the fish restaurants. Very friendly and helpful staff. In the high season open daily from 08.00-13.00, reduced opening times in winter ☏ 3944487.

Diving/snorkelling: Officially, this is banned around the Sunken City. But since the most important finds have already been saved, a blind eye is *usually* turned to snorkelling. But whatever the Tourist Office says, the *jandarma* may think otherwise, so do enquire again!

Yalıkavak

This former sponge-diving centre is a dignified resort today. The village centre, where the old men meet to socialise, still looks pretty much as it must have done originally. The small stretch of bazaar is straw-covered, no one pesters you, and there are no crowds. You can dine royally in the fish tavernas a few steps further along (the new marina, with space for 450 yachts, provides them with plenty of up-market clientele). The narrow beach is admittedly not the most spectacular, but it's OK and not ruined by any large hotel blocks. Similarly, at the only two attractions, there are none of the usual hassles: in the centre, changing art exhibitions are shown in a late 19th-century *sarnıç* (open sporadically, no entrance fee); at the port there's an old restored windmill with covered sails.

Accommodation: Lavanta Hotel, Luxury inn with breathtaking view over Yalıkavak. Extremely comfortable, individually decorated rooms (antiques, expensive carpets, wood floors, etc.). Beautiful pool area. Good wine cellar and good cooking. Double rooms from £98, self-catering apartments for £420 per week. Signposted off the road to Gündoğan and Türkbükü. ☏ 3852167, www.lavanta.com.

Adahan Hotel, about 100m from the new marina, in a caravanserai-like building. 22 very tastefully decorated rooms. Antiques scattered throughout. Pool with classical music, library. A1 cooking; family-run. Open all year. Double rooms from £65. ☏ 3854759, www.adahanotel.com.

Taşkule Hotel, chic hotel on the promenade, refurbished in 2005. 15 quiet rooms. Small pool. Double rooms with climate control £65, singles £57. ℂ/℡ 3854935, www.taskulehotel. com.

Cüneydi Pansiyon, clean, well-kept family guest house with 15 rooms on the promenade. All rooms with stone floors and bath, nice little garden. Double rooms £32. Plaj Cad. 14, ℂ 3854077, ℡ 3854824.

Dost Pansiyon, very simple, but with the advantage of being right on the sea. 10 plain little rooms with private bath, 2 of them with a fantastic view of the beach. Another plus: airy, cheerful bar with a delightful balcony and roof terrace. A good place for young people. Double rooms £22, singles £11, three-bedded £25. ℂ 3854080, dostpansiyon@ yahoo.com.

Food and drink: Of those on the promenade, the chic, high-priced **Cumbalı** stands out. It's in an old stone house, with a welcoming terrace in front. Fish with salad and beer will set you back about £10. ℂ 3854995. In the little centre, opposite the mosque by the cistern, **Gülten Abla** offers honest Turkish home-cooking (stuffed vegetables, *köfte*, soups). Main course about £3. Seating is on benches under shady trees.

Practicalities A-Z

Boat trips: Swimming trips are on offer at the port for about £13 per person including lunch.

Shopping: There is a large weekly market on Thursdays near the Hotel Adahan.

Gündoğan

During the First World War the inhabitants of Gündoğan shifted their dwellings a few hundred metres inland from the coast, in order to avoid offering English warships a target to attack. Without realising it at the time, they lost their chance of ever becoming a major tourist destination. So today the inland village still has a small town, rural atmosphere. In contrast, the U-shaped bay in front of seaside Gündoğan is completely built up, and the noise level from local and foreign youngsters on the rough sand beach outdoes the noise of the sea. But the water is crystal-clear, and there is a huge choice of water sports on offer. There are also take boat trips to nearby Apostle Island with the ruins of a Byzantine church.

Accommodation: Expect exceedingly high prices, even in a guest house! One recommendation, right on the beach:

Begonvil Hotel, pleasant new building. 21 comfortable rooms with climate control, TV, telephone and mini-bar, some with balcony and beautiful sea view. Very good baths. Leisure dock at the water, peaceful back garden. Double room with breakfast £72, with H/B £85. ℂ 3879192, www.begonvilhotel.com.

Türkbükü

Türkbükü, in the north of the peninsula was still a fishing hideaway 20 year ago; today it's one of the most elite addresses in the country. On the other hand, the constant building and the bumpy, dusty roads between the villas and exclusive mini resorts detract from the charm. The small esplanade with its chic restaurants is where the rich and famous stroll. Rumour has it that you'll always meet some celebrity or other in Türkbükü. Since the narrow sand beach is unsuitable for sun-bathing, you get your tan lounging on wooden jetties over the sea, with rottweilers and golden retrievers for company. When you're busy seeing and being seen, don't worry if your money runs out quickly — there are ATMs right on the beach…

Accommodation: While we await all the new building works to finish, the three best addresses at time of writing were (all signposted):

Ada Hotel, the most expensive hotel in this book, but worth it. The building, in a small fort, is one of the best hotels in Europe. Top-class luxury and service. Only 8 rooms and 6 suites with small private terraces, own *hamam*, 2 pools, relaxing garden, theatre, private yachts, etc. Double rooms, depending on size, etc. from £215-440. High above the bay. (3775915, www.adahotel.com.

Maki Hotel also merits stars. At the north end of the bay, without direct access to the beach. Minimalist-functional décor. All rooms with balcony. Pool above the sea. Private yacht to take guests to various beaches. Double rooms from £165, in the shoulder season discounts of 50% or more. (3776105, www. makihotel.com.

Kaktüs Çiçeği Hotel, right on the beach. Old-established, romantic 16 room hotel, run by a warm-hearted lady from Istanbul. Welcoming rooms decorated in warm colours. Excellent restaurant. Double rooms with H/B £125. (3775254, (3775248.

Getting there: Türkbükü and adjacent Gölköy are somewhat confusingly signposted as 'Göltürkbükü' from the Gündoğan/Torba road.

Gölköy

Gölköy, which you pass on the way to Türkbükü, is a simpler variation of the latter. Gölköy's beach is no better than Türkbükü's, and you have to make do with bars instead of posh restaurants … because here in Gölköy you'll also find ordinary holidaymakers like Fred and Gladys sunning themselves. With all the holiday developments, the beauty of this bay has been totally lost.

Getting there: see Türkbükü above.

Accommodation: Gölköy isn't cheap either. You'll only find a double room in a simple family-run pension well back from the beach for £20-26 with luck. One beach-side suggestion:

Şeker Otel, simple hotel with a beach-side restaurant. 11 plain rooms, all with balcony, many with sea view. Double room £42 (with climate control) or £35 (without). (3577129.

Torba

This last port of call on the Bodrum Peninsula is of very little interest for individual travellers. There are chic club resorts all along the bay, and between them not a single square metre of beach for the day visitor.

Walk 1: From Akçaalan to Akyarlar

Distance/time: 3h
Grade: easy-moderate, mainly over footpaths and tracks (often stony underfoot); initial ascent of about 275m
Equipment: see pages 21-22.
Travel: 🚐 dolmuş from Bodrum to Akçaalan mosque (Bodrum/Turgutreis service, frequent departures, journey time 20min); return by 🚐 dolmuş from Akyarlar to Turgutreis, then 🚐 dolmuş back to Bodrum
Shorter walks
1 Akçaalan — Karabağ — Turgutreis (under 2h; easy; good shoes and sun protection are all you need). Follow the main walk as far as Karabağ. Return along the road by which you entered the village, following it down to the main road. Turn left, down to the seafront at Turgutreis.
2 Akçaalan — windmills — Turgutreis (under 3h; grade as main walk). Follow the main walk to the windmills, walk back to Karabağ and on to Turgutreis, as in Shorter walk 1.

The dolmuş journey out to Akçaalan takes you westwards from Bodrum through the village of Ortakent, or 'middle town', to give it its English name. Once beyond Ortakent, notice how the scenery changes. The greenery-cloaked, rounded limestone hills, so familiar around Bodrum, are replaced by the open volcanic landscape that covers the whole of the western half of the peninsula. As if to emphasise the starkness of the landscape, a lone tree might find a foothold. The hollows at a lower level collect and hold the soils washed down from the mountainsides, sometimes forming areas large enough for cultivation. Imagine such a pocket of cultivation — an emerald green meadow, walled in brown stone;

imagine it with a solitary white farmhouse built on the very edge, so that it takes up little or none of the valuable land for cultivation; picture the white farm with the luxury of a little shade from the single tall leafy green tree. See all this in your mind's eye against the brown barren hills rising steeply behind, and you have an image of the dramatic contrasts which are so typical of this intriguing landscape. This walk follows an old route between two lovely villages, passing some delightful old windmills which grace the skyline almost from the start. At the end of the walk lies Akyarlar (see page 76).

Start out in **Akçaalan** with the mosque on the right, by heading momentarily uphill. Turn right by a shop into Okul Sokak (School Street). After a short way the street ends. Continue more or less ahead (there is a small **tower house** on the right) and take the surfaced road to the right of the **Amiral Turgutreis Ilk Okul** (Infant School) and fountain. Once past the school, you pass a *sarnıç* (water cistern, see page 87) on the left and a **mosque** to the right. Looking ahead, you can see three windmills on the skyline. Keep along the road as it swings right and shortly becomes walled-in. There is a lovely pastoral feel to the walk, as you head past well-tended farmlands on your left. Viewpoints open up as you climb.

Shortly the road you are on joins a narrower road on a U-bend: turn left here. A minute up this road gives you your first view of Karabağ above; it is perched on a platform nestling into the hillside. Higher, to the right, are the windmills. Continue up into the village of **Karabağ** (**45min**), to pass first a water fountain with a tap and then a mosque on the left. Walk past the mosque and turn right along Yaka Sok. Then take the first left uphill, then the first right. The road now becomes a track as you leave the village, swinging round the back of new holiday homes. Turn right at the next junction and keep on the track to the crest of the hill. To inspect the **windmills** and enjoy some spectacular views, take the path uphill to the right. Looking at the craggy hilltop surrounded by pink-hued rocky terrain over to the east, the eye can just make out the remains of farm buildings

which blend so well into this hostile environment. This may also have been the site of ancient Termera which is known to be in this region.

Head back from the windmills and turn right when you rejoin the track. Follow the track as it continues over the crest of the hill. As the track reaches its highest point, eye-catching splashes of yellow and green lichen decorate the rosy-hued rocks where, in autumn, *Cyclamen hederifolium* shyly hide and the white *Narcissus serotinus* waft around in the breeze. You pass through a **deserted hamlet**, then the track ends. The route

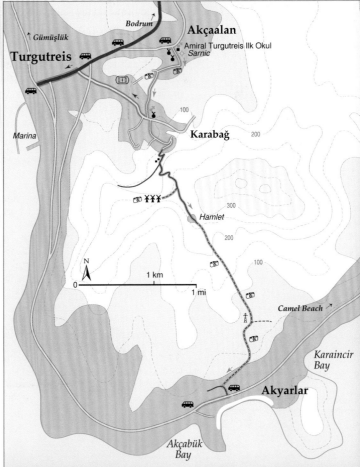

Unfortunately many of the peninsula's lovely old windmills have not only lost their sails — but their wooden frames as well (this photograph was taken on Walk 2 several years ago).

by a barbed-wire fence. Clamber (easily) round the right-hand side of the fence, but beware of the deep hole, covered by brushwood, as you do so. Dull red waymarks may offer some guidance. Keep downhill, in the middle of the two walls initially, moving more to the wall on the left as the right-hand wall sweeps away. As the wall on the left angles left, about three minutes later, take the less likely route to the left, heading down a shallow depression. The path is unclear at times but, keeping the wall on your left, head along the hillside towards a **solitary pylon** at the end of the ridge, which lies to the left of the Akyarlar peninsula (130° southeast).

Pass to the left of the pylon and, a minute later, reach a junction of trails. Turn right here to descend a rocky walled-in trail (if you encounter a brushwood gate, replace it behind you). The trail eventually widens out and heads more to the right of the Akyarlar peninsula. Edge over to the right, where you meet a strong path. But as the wall on the right swings away, keep ahead to continue alongside another wall joining from the right. Turn right through a gap at a junction of walls a couple of minutes later. Continue on the path contouring the hill, with a wall on your right. Make for the corner of a track that you can see ahead. When you meet the track, turn left to the **main road**. You can catch the *dolmuş* here. Or else turn right and then left, to reach the shore at **Akyarlar** (3h).

continues as a walled-in trail, with cactus lining the right side. The view opens out across to the Greek Island of Kos and the built-up coastline around Akyarlar.

Once into the descent towards Akyarlar, the trail becomes a path which is vague at times as it crosses the top of an open area of bedrock. Keep ahead, close to the wall on the right, to pass through a small rocky outcrop. In three minutes you reach a very wide walled-in trail, currently blocked

Walk 2: Karakaya circuit from Gümüşlük inland village

Time: 2h30min
Grade: easy, but the paths are very stony underfoot; ascent of about 150m
Equipment: see pages 21-22.
Travel: 🚐 *dolmuş* from Bodrum to Gümüşlük *inland main village*, frequent departures, journey time 25-30min; return by 🚐 *dolmuş* back to Bodrum, either from coastal Gümüşlük or from the main village. (Several villages on this peninsula are divided into two, with part of the village by the sea but the main village well inland. *Dolmuş* drivers expect to take tourists only to the coast, so may try to dissuade you: say 'tamam' ('OK'), to reassure them…)
Shorter walk: to the **windmill** and back (5.7km/3.5mi; 1h45min; grade as main walk). Follow the main walk to the windmill, retrace your steps, then continue down to the coast, as in the main walk.

Rickety wooden landing jetties in the unhurried sweep of the bay, waterside cafés and restaurants, a scattering of white buildings … and a peaceful unchanging life-style — this is Gümüşlük. This unspoilt fishing village (see page 78) has been denied growth because of the archaeological importance of nearby Myndos. And the local people prefer it that way. Traffic too is kept outside the village, but there is a car park. This short walk has been designed to leave you time to enjoy the peaceful ambience of Gümüşlük, perhaps to enjoy a meal at the water's edge and wander around the remains of Myndos (such as they are: most of the ruins are now under the sea). You might also visit 'rabbit island', which is joined to the mainland by a causeway. There is no problem if you want to go, but it does mean that you have to paddle across — and the water may be up to your knees in places. The walk itself takes you to one of the old windmills on the peninsula and, like Walk 1, explores the dramatic landscapes in this fascinating volcanic region. Gümüşlük takes its name from the Turkish word for silver, and there is evidence of old silver mines nearby.

Start the walk in Gümüşlük main village: with the **mosque/ PTT** on your left, head seawards, but in just *20 seconds* turn sharp right into an old trail, behind the buildings on the opposite side of the road from the mosque/PTT. Pass a *sarnıç* (water cistern; see page 87) on the left, then fork left and continue out of the village by taking the first right on a narrow surfaced road. The road passes behind a farmhouse and winds up the hillside to some **new housing**. Go to the right of the houses to pick up the path heading left up the hillside. This is a good place to catch your

Restaurants line the harbour at Gümüşlük

which was once used to grind corn.

Return to the Kayakaya road and follow it until it ends below the village. Continue along the path to the left which runs to a **junction of paths below Karakaya (1h05min)**. (If you explore Karakaya, return to this junction. Karakaya is a luxurious hide-away for both upper-class Turks and tourists who rent some of the exquisitely refurbished villas.)

Continue on this path below the village. It leads into a steeply-descending trail, quickly taking you out of sight of Karakaya and into an open rocky area. Descend here, generally following the line of the wall on the left, and keep left where the path divides a few minutes later. Swing right with the wall at the bottom to continue on the trail. There are some captivating views of rocky formations over to the right, as you cross a stream bed, and a new softness comes into the landscape — especially in spring, when you glimpse fields white with Greek chamomile, *Anthemis chia*.

After passing a **fountain** in a large grassy area, continue ahead to cross a stream bed and descend to the main track. Turn right and follow the track back to the *sarnıç* and **inland Gümüşlük (2h10min)**. Continue back to the mosque/PTT, turn right on the main road and descend to **coastal Gümüşlük (2h30min)**.

breath and admire the views: a line of seven windmills on a hilltop to the east catches the eye, as do the offshore islands — of which Kos is the larger one. The three windmills silhouetted on the skyline to the south are visited in Walk 1.

Thorny burnett, *Sarcopoterium spinosum*, giving a realistic impression of wire-netting bushes, dot the way now along a stony, enclosed section of path. But the terrain opens up again as the path leads up left through a cutting, to give you a compelling view of Karakaya. The village clings to the hostile slopes of a rocky mountain, overlooking the green and fertile valley floor which this walk circumnavigates. Join the track which heads to Karakaya, but first divert left over some barbed wire by the **electricity substation** to visit the windmill. Pass beneath the furthest pylon on the left and follow the path around the contour to the right of the hill. Below the third pylon along, head up left to the top, then go right to the **windmill (45min)**. Flower-filled meadows in spring provide a perfect setting for this old mill (shown on page 84),

Time: 4h15min
Grade: moderate; many of the paths and trails are stony underfoot; ascent of of 300m
Equipment: see pages 21-22.
Travel: 🚌 *dolmuş* from Bodrum to/from Yalıkavak *dolmuş* park, departures fairly frequent, journey time 25min.
Short walk: Sandıma (under 2h; easy-moderate). Follow the main walk to Sandıma and retrace your steps.

An adequate supply of water, for crops, for animals and for man, has been one of the major problems of survival in the arid volcanic western region of the Bodrum peninsula. There is no shortage of rain in winter but, with no great depth of soil to hold or store the water, there is need for some other system, hence the sarnıç. The sarnıç, or gumbet, is a lovely domed structure for storing water. It is often plastered and painted white. You will see many of these around the peninsula, but there is a particularly fine one along this walk (see below).

Apart from some glorious coastal views which stay with you for a good length of time as you climb above Yalıkavak, there are also two villages en route which are captivating for quite different reasons. Sandıma is situated in a bowl, at the base of a ring of barren hills. It is almost deserted; most of the population having moved down to the valley. The occasional splash of green from a cultivated meadow, or the glimpse of a woman bowed under the weight of sticks stealing silently down a far pathway, are reminders that this existence is still a way of life for a few of the older people. Friendly Geriş, in contrast, shines white and exudes vitality from its hilltop position — with the inevitable

building sites. Yalıkavak (see page 79) is a tourist resort with a large marina, but is still relatively unspoilt.

Start the walk from the *dolmuş* **park** in **Yalıkavak**: with your back to the mosque with the twin minarets, head almost due south along a concrete and cobbled road (Kayacik Cad.) — the road to Sandıma. (If you start at the **new bus station**, turn right, then left, and follow the same road.) Eventually a stream runs alongside on your left. Continue to the end of the cobbles and walk ahead on track. When the track starts to ascend, turn left towards a **bridge**, but turn right through a gate before the bridge. Then take the footpath that leads round to the picturesque *sarnıç*, the dome- covered cistern shown below. It is worth a stop to enjoy both the panorama and the setting. Flowers decorate the way — from wild orchids like the

Rain falling on the outer dome of this sarnıç below Sandıma is channelled to the excavated interior, where it is protected from the evaporating rays of the sun. A door and steps inside the dome give access to the water. Most sarnıçlar are unused today; the one in Yalıkavak is used for art exhibitions.

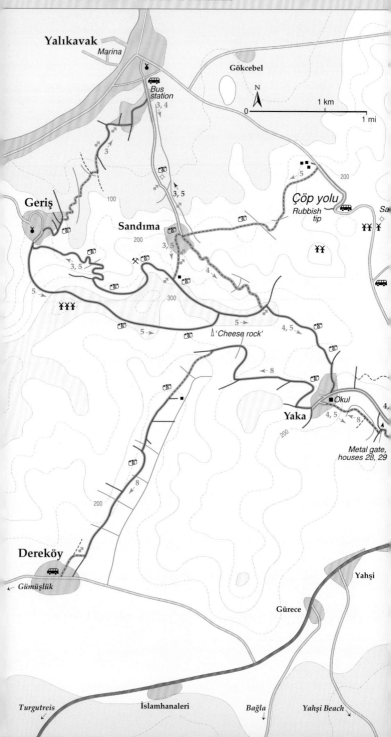

Yalıkavak

Marina

Bus station

3, 4

Gökcebel

N

0   1 km

1 mi

3

3

3, 5

Çöp yolu

Rubbish tip

5

200

Sa

Geriş

100

Sandıma

200

3, 5

3, 5

4

5

3, 5

300

5

5

4, 5

△ *'Cheese rock'*

8

Okul

Yaka

4, 5

4,

8

Metal gate, houses 28, 29

200

8

200

Dereköy

← *Gümüşlük*

Yahşi

Gürece

Turgutreis   *İslamhaneleri*   *Bağla*   *Yahşi Beach*

holy orchid (*Orchis sancta*) to the more shrubby fringed rue, *Ruta chalapensis*, which grows around the fountain reached four minutes later. The stream bed on the left which you have been following changes course: cross it and continue the ascent.

Alpine gardeners may well eat their hearts out at the sight of some delightfully-shaped stone troughs scattered around the well on the approach to **Sandıma (50min)**. Silence hangs heavily around this nearly-deserted village, creating an atmosphere of the unreal, as though you have just walked onto a huge film set. Photographic opportunities abound. As you first enter the village there is a **large grassy area** (Walk 5 comes in here from the left) and some tall eucalyptus trees over to the right — a delightful spot with fine views.

To continue from here, head right, aiming for the **eucalyptus trees**. But turn sharp left into a walled-in trail just before reaching them. Head uphill, almost due south, through

the right-hand side of the village. You will come to a **double ornamental fountain**: the small-bore **metal pipe** which supplies the fountain with water acts as a guide for a time. Continue in a fairly steep ascent following the line of the pipe, in two minutes passing a running water source and a trough on the left. The path is somewhat indistinct over the hard rock, but keep the pipe and a wall on your left until you **cross the pipe** before it passes through the wall ahead. This a good place to catch your breath and take in the captivating views back over Sandıma. The climb becomes more gradual as you press on, keeping a wall on the right, and you find that you are being channelled into a walled-in trail.

After passing a **farmstead** on your left you reach a track (**1h20min**); turn right. *Cyclamen hederifolium* shelter beneath the spreading plane tree here in autumn. Follow the track, passing a water trough on the left, enjoying the superb coastal views as you go. Turn sharp left uphill before a small **quarry**. There is another fine view of Sandıma from this point and, above the village, you can see the rich meadow (*yayla*) which once sustained it. See also how the flat-topped houses are built on the naked rock to preserve the productive land. Continue to the **highest point of the walk** (**1h40min**).

Ahead now is a beautiful fertile valley, where walled terraces weave their own patterns into the landscape. Geriş comes into view only moments later, glistening white in the sun from its hilltop position. About 10 minutes from the views of Geriş, at a junction of tracks, be sure to turn sharp right. Descend to the valley floor and cross a dry stream bed. Swing right here and head up towards Geriş. At a junction of tracks about 10 minutes later, turn right and keep ahead into Geriş on the cobbled road *(but turn left for Walk 5)*. You come into the **village square at Geriş (2h35min)**, with the mosque on your left.

Continue by skirting round the pylon ahead and taking the track immediately beyond it, heading downhill to the right from the corner of the square. Keep down right at the junction, then down right again. Just over a minute later, as the track starts to rise up round a development on the left, turn right down a rough track. Less than a minute later, as the track turns sharply left, keep

ahead, passing to the left of a rustic 'gate' (a few twigs nailed together!), to enter a narrow sunken path. Descend this stony path, enclosed by walls, to a stream in a small wooded valley splashed pink with oleander. Cross the stream bed and follow the path to the left. Shortly, pass through a shaded plant 'tunnel', as the path leads away from the stream past old, gnarled olive trees and back into a walled-in path.

Around eight minutes later, cross a stream bed; moments later, ignore a trail off left: keep ahead over bedrock. Almost immediately, meet a crossing of trails and go left (there may be waymarks). The countryside here announces its fertility with drifts of springtime colours.

Some 10-12 minutes beyond the stream bed, when you meet a track, keep round to the left. Pass a well on the left in a few minutes and then, as the track swings left, take the lesser track off to the right (by a fountain). Ignore the minor track off left in five minutes, but turn left two minutes later. The twin minarets of the mosque in Yalıkavak can be seen ahead.

You now enter new developments with a confusion of new roads and tracks. Just bear right and continue downhill, eventually arriving back in **Yalıkavak** on Kayacik Cad. (the road you started out on). Turn left and continue back to the **bus station (4h15min)**.

Yalıkavak

See map on pages 88-89.
Time: 4h
Grade: moderate; many of the paths and trails are stony; ascent of 300m
Equipment: see pages 21-22.
Travel: 🚐 dolmuş from Bodrum to Yalıkavak, departures fairly frequent, journey time 25min; return by 🚐 any dolmuş from Ortakent back to Bodrum.
Shorter walk: Yalıkavak to Yaka (just over 3h; grade as main walk). Follow the main walk until you reach the road at Yaka. Turn left here and walk on to the Yalıkavak road, where you can wait for a dolmuş back to Bodrum.

Apart from some dramatic scenery with weird rock formations, villages add considerable interest to this walk. The village of Yalıkavak (see page 79), where the walk starts, is famous for its sponges and still has a thriving fishing industry. Next along the route is the almost-deserted, but very photogenic village of Sandıma (described in Walk 3). Heading south from Sandıma, you cross over a hill to Yaka. If there is such a thing as a typical Turkish village hardly touched by tourism on this western part of the Bodrum peninsula, then it must be Yaka, which sits near the top of a hillside, looking down over the pastures which sustain it. If you are looking for shops or any other facilities, then wait until you reach Ortakent. Ortakent is another of those villages which exist in two parts, one inland and one by the sea. This walk ends at inland Ortakent. If you have time in hand, then it is worth having a look around to see some fine examples of old Turkish architecture, including the Mustafa Paşa tower house which dates from 1601. To reach the

Ortakent beach from here requires a further journey by dolmuş.

Start the walk at **Yalıkavak** by following Walk 3 (page 87) to **Sandıma (50min).** Walk 5 comes in here from the left, but keep ahead and enter the confines of a walled-in path for a short while. Although the path may be obscure at times, it basically follows the line of the gully over to the left, heading straight up the valley. The steep gully is brightened by pockets of pink oleander, prickly pear cactus (*Opuntia ficus-indica*) and the century plant (*Agave americana*). The latter's flower-spikes take several years to form and resemble a telegraph pole in height and thickness.

After you pass to the right of a ruined building above the gully, the route ahead can be seen more clearly. Cross the middle of bedrock about six minutes later, to be channelled back into a walled-in trail. On reaching a further area of bedrock a few minutes later, keep by the wall on the left initially, then head up more towards the wall on the right — to pass through a rocky outcrop.

Around eight minutes later, meet a dry stream bed and keep round to the left. Still ascending steadily, stay more or less beside the wall on the left as the path crosses an area of *Phrygana* and enters another walled-in section. Some four minutes later, at a junction of paths, go left along the stream bed, before rising up right onto the path alongside it. Shortly, before the path dips down to meet a confluence of streams, take the path uphill to the right; it becomes walled-in.

Yalıkavak's old harbour

You rise up onto a **track, by a well** (**1h45min**), where Walk 5 joins from the right. Turn left here and, almost immediately, go right, to continue up onto a saddle, from where there are new vistas down to the southern coastline.

Now the track snakes downhill, with the '**cheese rock**' and valley encountered in Walk 8 over to your right. Eventually the track passes into the Yaka valley. Five minutes later, join a track coming in from the left and keep ahead. As the track swings right three minutes later, the village comes into sight. On meeting the surfaced road, turn right and walk into **Yaka** (**2h30min**). *(But turn left here for the Shorter walk.)*

Keep left at the fork two minutes later, just after passing the **school** (*okul;* down on your left, hidden by tall cypress trees). Less than a minute from this junction, head sharp left down a road signed 'Karaban Mah'. Then fork left on a track and, on a bend, fork left again, to pick up a footpath running down by a stone wall and barbed wire (there is a **farm** to the left).

Continue along the left bank of the stream and go straight on when you meet a track. Take the next left fork, ascending, then turn right by some new **houses numbered 28 and 29**. Walk on to the end of the track, by a **metal gate**, then carry on along a footpath. The path crosses to the right side of the stream, then back to the left, before widening to a track with the stream running down it (in spring). The path continues on the right side of the stream through lush greenery. In a few minutes the path emerges on a track: fork left here, following the course of the stream on your right.

The track then swings away from the stream, to the left, and gently descends to the next junction, by a **pump house**. Turn right on the surfaced road here. The road swings right, running back alongside the stream, past some **ancient pillars** which once supported an aqueduct.

Continue to the main road and into the centre of **Ortakent** (**4h**), where you emerge opposite the *dolmuş* **stop** to Bodrum.

Walk 5: Çöp Yolu • Sandıma • (Geriş) • Yaka • Ortakent

See map on pages 88-89.
Time: 6h30min
Grade: moderate-strenuous; the footpaths are often stony; there are two ascents to contend with, the harder one taking you up to about 350m.
Equipment: see pages 21-22.
Travel: 🚐 *dolmuş* from Bodrum (Bodrum/Yalıkavak service, departures fairly frequent, journey time 20min. Ask the *dolmuş* to stop at the *'çöp yolu'* (pronounced churp yoloo; *çöp* means rubbish), an obvious track to a rubbish tip seen about 1km downhill, off left on a bend, as the dolmuş starts to descend to Yalıkavak after the windmills. Return on any 🚐 *dolmuş* from Ortakent to Bodrum.
Short walk: Çöp yolu — Sandıma — Yalıkavak (2h; easy). Follow the main walk to Sandıma, then use the map to follow Walk 3 in reverse, down past the *sarnıç*, to Yalıkavak. Return to Bodrum by *dolmuş*.
Alternative walks
1 Çöp yolu — Sandıma — Yaka (3h30min; moderate). Follow the main walk to Sandıma. Join the route of Walk 3 (page 69), and climb away from Sandıma towards Geriş. But go only as far as the track reached at the 1h20min-point in Walk 3. Turn left here and continue climbing, to reach a track junction about 15 minutes later. Here you rejoin the route of Walk 5 on its return from Geriş. Turn left, using the notes on page 94 to walk on to Yaka. When you join the surfaced road in Yaka, turn left to the main road, where you can catch a *dolmuş* back to Bodrum.
2 Çöp yolu — Sandıma — Geriş — Yaka (5h45min; grade as main

walk). Follow the main walk as far as Yaka but, when you join the road leading into Yaka, turn left to the main road, where you can catch a *dolmuş* back to Bodrum.

*Windmills (*yel degirmenleri *in Turkish), have a charm of their own, evoking romantic images of a rustic age when sails turned lazily and life moved at a much slower pace. Life still does move at a slower pace at some places on the Bodrum Peninsula, especially in the hill villages and the high* yaylas *(meadows).*

Start out by leaving the *dolmuş* at the **çöp yolu downhill from the windmills**: walk down the road towards Yalıkavak, until the high banking on the left dips after about five minutes (50 metres before a track running up to some houses). Take the path sloping up into the field and follow a vague path diagonally uphill towards the wall over on your right. Continue uphill, close to the wall, to skirt a small rocky outcrop. Now head for the wall

View over Yalıkavak

at the left-hand side of the large rocky outcrop at the top of the rise, and find your crossing point — a gap in the wall. Pass through it and note the rising walled-in trail etched clearly along the hillside on the far side of the valley ahead. This is where you are going. To get there, first head left (southwest) — more or less along the contour of the hill, dipping round rocky outcrops. Head towards a large angular rock on the near horizon (the 'cheese rock' encountered on Walk 8). You meet a track and a wall rising up from the right and reach an area of bedrock at the end of the wall.

The start of the walled-in trail can now be seen below. Turn right and descend the steep field carefully, making for the confluence of streams below and staying fairly close to the wall on the right. The rubbish tip lies over to the left. At the bottom of the field, cross the stream bed about 10m to the left of the large olive tree. Head up diagonally right to the wall ahead (where it meets another wall). Pass through a gap and, 20 seconds later, cross over the low wall on the right. Join a path and turn right. The path dips to cross a stream bed and enters the walled-in trail.

Views open out as you climb to an area of bedrock. Continue along the path as it swings left through a narrow cutting only a minute later, to emerge over-looking Sandıma nestling in the huge valley below. On the left in this striking picture is a white *sarnıç* (water cistern; see page 87) and, over to the right, some fantastic rock formations. From the *sarnıç* a motorable track leads down towards the village, described in Walk 3.

As you enter **Sandıma (1h05min)**, keep down towards the bottom of the gully, watching for a sharp left turn where you cross the stream. As you climb into the main part of the village, meet a junction of paths (two minutes after crossing the stream). A left turn leads into Walk 4, but go *right* here, soon reaching a **large grassy area**. Swing left now towards the **eucalyptus trees** (*but keep straight down, past the* sarnıç, *for the Short walk to Yalıkavak*) and, almost immediately, turn left to enter a walled-in path.

Now use the notes for Walk 3 from just after the 50min-point (page 89), until you reach the **junction of tracks outside Geriş (2h40min)**. Turn left here, away from Geriş. The track affords good views over Yalıkavak and rounds the bowl of the valley, below some **ruined windmills**. Eventually a massive angular rock (the '**cheese rock**' from Walk 8) dominates the skyline ahead. You cross a shallow saddle and soon enjoy views of a fertile valley and the track from Yaka to Dereköy (Walk 8). Another saddle is crossed, to the left of the 'cheese rock', then you reach a track junction, where you turn right (*Alternative walk 1 rejoins here.*) Sandıma's valley now lies to the left. At another track junction, where Walk 4 joins from the left, pick up the notes on page 92 (from the 1h45min-point), to follow that walk up right over the saddle, just past the **well**, to **Yaka (5h)** and **Ortakent (6h30min)**.

Walk 6: From Dağbelen to the Bitez road

See map on page 97.
Time: 4h
Grade: moderate; some stony tracks and paths underfoot; ascent of just under 200m
Equipment: see pages 21-22.
Travel: 🚐 dolmuş to the Dağbelen turn-off (Bodrum/ Yalıkavak service, departures fairly frequent, journey time about 18min); return from the Bitez turn-off on 🚐 any passing dolmuş back to Bodrum.

This old route across the Bodrum Peninsula is still the only means of communication with the deserted village shown below — Kibrel, where old rose-coloured houses blend beautifully into the surrounding bare rock. The obscure Lelegian town of Side is also thought to be in this region, and the ruins of the tower that you pass on route might be connected with it. An interesting characteristic of Lelegian architecture is the use of roughly-squared blocks for building so, should you stop at the old tower to rest, then you can cast a critical eye and make your own judgement.

Kibrel

Many of the people in this area aim at nothing more than self-sufficiency in their farming and very often have just one or two cows, perhaps a bull or a few goats. In the morning 'rush hour' there is a constant stream of villagers taking their farm stock out to graze, and you may see this in the early part of the walk. Should you see any cows that look as though they may have strayed, then do take note of it — you may well be approached by a distraught villager asking if you have seen his lost cow (inek).

When you give Dağbelen as your destination on the dolmuş, you will be dropped off at the end of the road leading into the village. **Start out** by heading along the road to the village (on the same side as you leave the dolmuş). Eventually Dağbelen and its minaret come into view, perched on a hillside overlooking fertile land used for cultivation. You pass between an **Ottoman fountain** and huge plane tree as you enter **Dağbelen (30min)**. Stay on the road until it ends at a

T-junction two minutes later. Go up the track to the left, which is concreted initially (the fork to the right leads to the mosque). Rising steeply, you have lovely pastoral views as Dağbelen is left behind. Ignore the trail descending to the right 10-12 minutes outside the village, and pass a **fountain** on the left just over three minutes later.

Rise up to a high point and views of the northern shore, before starting into a gentle descent. Keep more or less ahead as the main track forks down to the left, ignoring a minor woodland track off right almost immediately. When the track sweeps right to a farm building, keep ahead along a sunken path. The pink and white of autumn-flowering *Cyclamen hederifolium* and *Narcissus serotinus* add splashes of colour along the route now.

You reach a **clearing with the ruins of an old tower**. Continue past the clearing along the path and spot the section of ancient wall to the left just before the **path from Gündoğan (Walk 7) joins from the left** (1h20min). The path keeps round to the right and soon starts to rise through a shaded stony section, heading towards the middle of the peninsula. Keep uphill, where a path joins from the right. Olive groves indicate the proximity of habitation, as you walk alongside a wall on the right three minutes later — and a white *sarnıç* (water cistern; see page 87) comes into view. On meeting a crossing path, keep right, towards the *sarnıç*. Two minutes later, follow the main path to the right again, passing a **graveyard** on the left. Just short of reaching the *sarnıç*

(a pleasant resting spot), your path goes left. Follow it downhill; it is a stony walled-in trail for a short while. Keep ahead on the path as it meanders between shrubs, ignoring a path off to the right. Two minutes later you enjoy a first sighting of Kibrel. When you reach a stone building and a wall on the right, ruined **Kibrel** comes into full view (2h). Walk ahead towards the village and, in a little over a minute, meet a path coming from Kibrel. Turn sharp right here. Follow this good path, which leads away from Kibrel, and comes up alongside a wall on the right with a stony field on the far side. Reach a vantage point three minutes later where, if you look back, you can see the village blending well into its rocky surroundings and notice that the path has described almost a semi-circle around the field.

Start heading down a valley on a steadily-descending track. At the bottom of the valley, turn left and continue along a dry, stony stream bed. The sides of the valley slowly close in around you, until you find yourself walking between the vertical walls of a very narrow and beautiful gorge. Out of the narrowest part of the gorge, you pass an old lime kiln on the right. The track then leads to a small **housing development** at the mouth of the gorge, from where you follow a road past a **cement works** and to the main road. Cross the road and head left to the junction with the **Bitez road** (*Bitez yolu;* 4h), for a *dolmuş* back to Bodrum.

Walk 7: From Gündoğan to Dağbelen

Time: 3h
Grade: moderate; some stony paths; ascent of 325m
Equipment: see pages 21-22.
Travel: 🚐 *dolmuş* from Bodrum to Gündoğan, fairly frequent departures, journey time about 20min; return on 🚐 *dolmuş* back to Bodrum (Yalıkavak service)

Alternative walk: Gündoğan to the Bitez road (4h; moderate-strenuous). Follow the main walk to the Dağbelen path. Instead of turning right, go straight on: follow Walk 6 (opposite) from the 1h20min-point to the end.

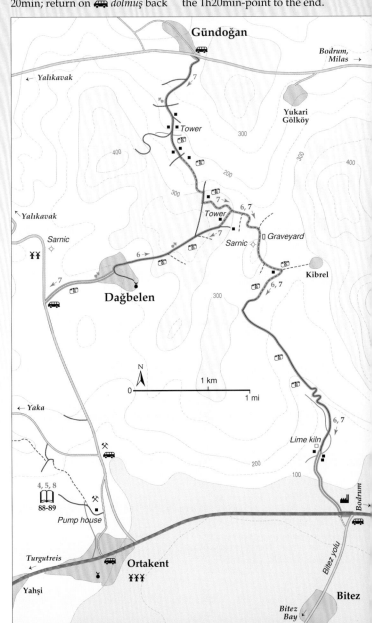

*Along any walk on the Bodrum
Peninsula there is a reasonable
chance of seeing a camel or a train of
them. Camels have been used as
beasts of burden here for many years.
A fully-grown camel is capable of
carrying a considerable load, which
is useful to both the remaining
farmers and the populace in general.
Camels move quietly and gracefully,
and the sight of one loaded with a
refrigerator, tables and chairs seems
incongruous in view of their aristo-
cratic demeanour. Camels are treated
much as other domesticated farm
animals: they are bred, reared and
turned out unattended to graze.
Tourism has brought change, and
the local people are now finding
these intriguing animals useful
revenue-earners, as at Camel Beach.*

Alight from the *dolmuş* just as it
turns right off the main road into
Gündoğan: watch for the village
of Yukari Gölköy on the left, 20
minutes from Bodrum, and ask
to leave the *dolmuş* just over the
next rise). **Start out** by crossing
the main road opposite the
junction, to find a track which
dips down from the road. The
track briefly heads left, parallel
with the road, then swings right
into the countryside. Where a
track forks down right, keep
ahead uphill, to pass a large
water tank on the right at the top
of the rise. Ignore a left fork just
past a renovated farm building
(also on the left). Continue uphill,
to pass a house on the right and a
stone tower on the left. A little
under two minutes later, the
main track swings right and it
can be seen carving its way up
the hillside; take the lesser track
to the left.
The ascent steepens for a while,

then a small **hamlet** is reached
(**40min**). At the junction of tracks,
continue ahead into the woods,
along what appears to be a small
stream bed at first. Initially
leading round to the left, it soon
meets an old trail, where you
turn right. This lovely shaded
section of the route meanders
upwards and widens into a
woodland track. It rises to a track
less than a minute later: turn
right here.
Now heading towards Dağbelen,
the track passes above a farmed
yayla (meadow) down to the left.
Almost past the *yayla*, turn left
down a woodland track. Keep
right where the descending track
forks almost immediately and
soon narrows into a path. The
path skirts to the right of the
yayla and a farm building on
the edge of pine woods. Soon the
path rises again and, although it
leads briefly to the right in three
minutes, it remains on the edge
of the pine woods. When you
meet the **junction with the
Dağbelen path** (the 1h20min-
point in Walk 6), turn right. *(But
keep straight on for the Alternative
walk.)*
From here continue to Dağbelen
by following Walk 6 in reverse:
stay on the path; it leads into a
track. Keep straight ahead where
a track runs back to the right. The
track keeps to a high level before
descending into Dağbelen, which
can be seen for some time on the
approach. Once in **Dağbelen**,
take the surfaced road off to the
right, and follow it to the **main
road** (**3h**), where you can catch
the Yalikavak/Bodrum *dolmuş*. A
couple of restaurants on the
right, just before the main road,
are a welcome oasis.

See map on pages 88-89.
Time: 3h50min
Grade: moderate; the paths and tracks are usually good underfoot, but there are some stony sections; ascent of about 275m
Equipment: see pages 21-22.
Travel: 🚐 *dolmuş* to Ortakent (using the service from Bodrum to Ortakent, Turgutreis or Gümüşlük), frequent departures, journey time about 10min; return by 🚐 *dolmuş* back to Bodrum (Gümüşlük service).
Shorter walk: Ortakent to Yaka (2h15min; easy). Follow the main walk to Yaka. Turn right on the main village road and follow it out to the main Ortakent/ Yalikavak road, to catch a *dolmuş* back to Bodrum.

As you travel from Bodrum to the start of this walk, you may notice a partly-constructed wooden boat by the roadside (although most are built in shipyards now). Boat-building is an old industry in these parts, given a new lease of life by popularity of the gulet — taken from the Italian gouletta (a kind of schooner incorporating features from the Arab baggala). Usually built from local Aegean pine, the hull has evolved considerably, as has the rigging — but the latter is now for show, since the gulet is powered by a large diesel engine. You might wonder how the boats are transported down to the sea. If you are unlucky, you might just find out first hand! It is a slow process: greased blocks, which are moved constantly from back to front, are used as a sledge. Given the roads in Bodrum, it virtually stops the local traffic.
The walk starts off in a region green with cultivation, where trees sometimes arch over the route. You then

head into a stark and barren landscape, before returning once again to cultivation. There is a variety of interesting wild flowers and shrubs along the way, including autumn-flowering cyclamen, two different kinds of wild lupins, and mandrakes, Mandragora officinarum, *about which so many interesting tales are told (see Walk 9). Particularly eye-catching, especially in the spring, is the giant fennel,* Ferula communis, *with its spread of light green ferny foliage. It provides a delightful complement to other wild flowers. Ortakent, where you leave the dolmuş, is an old village with interesting tower houses and a row of ruined windmills on the barren hillside. If you have time, it is worth a few minutes looking around. The dolmuş leaves you in the centre of Ortakent, by a plaza with a taxi rank and PTT.*

Start the walk in **Ortakent**: take the road opposite the plaza, heading inland and then following a stream past some **ruined pillars** that once supported an aqueduct. The road swings right, away from the stream, then left. Continue to a water **pump house** (beyond which lies a disused **quarry**). Turn left along the track just *before* the pump house and follow it round to where it dips to ford the stream. Leave the track here and turn right on the path running alongside the stream. The path crosses over to the left-hand side and continues following the stream through lush greenery. When the stream divides, continue straight ahead on the left bank, then cross over to the right. You emerge on a dirt track by a **metal gate** on your right.

Continue up the lane, rising to the main track junction. Turn left by **house number 28** and continue into a dip; then fork right, cross the stream and continue on the footpath along the left-hand side. At a bend in the stream, go straight on; the path then crosses the stream and rises to a stone wall. Cactus and asphodel line the route as the path swings left to a **well** and a **huge plane tree** that is split into three. Cross the stream and start ascending, taking the right fork through lush vegetation (an old olive grove is below on your right). The walled-in path follows the course of the stream, climbing towards the village of Yaka. It rises to a track, where you continue up to the village houses, forking left uphill to the main road in **Yaka (1h30min)**.

Turn left and continue past the **cemetery**, from where you take a track uphill. *(But turn right along the road for the Shorter walk.)* Still climbing, swing right when you meet another track six-seven minutes from the main road, to continue across the top of Yaka, with good views down over the village and beyond it. Some five minutes later, the track goes sharply round to the left, and the village is left behind. Soon you reach the **highest part of the walk (2h)**, at the top of the hill between the valleys. From here you can see a hilltop with a mast over to the left. Follow the track into a descent through patches of *Phrygana*, where lavender, *Lavandula stoechas*, can be detected by its aromatic perfume, if not by its dark blue flowers. When the track forks four minutes later, keep down to the right.

Dominating the view now is a large, pitted, **angular rock which resembles a wedge of cheese** — it is a useful waymark for other walks in this area. Your way leads down into the valley, to an area of bedrock at the base of this 'cheese rock'. Below the rock, where there is a dip in the track and a wall to the right, take a path forking off left. It curls left towards a white house with a red roof, almost hidden in the trees. Some two minutes later, you pass to the right of the house and head left into a walled-in path, via a rustic gate. Enjoy the flavour of this lovely section of walled-in path, where oleander provides the colour and myrtle the scent, with an accompanying stream to the left — all the time under the watchful gaze of the receding 'cheese rock'.

Cross a dry stream bed and, five minutes later, meet a track by a house on the left. Continue along the track to the right. At a junction of tracks under 10 minutes past the house, keep ahead. Dip down to cross a stream 10-12 minutes later, ignoring tracks off to the left and then right. The track becomes walled-in, and a track joins from the right before a cobbled section comes underfoot. The track then dips down to cross another stream (some 10 minutes after the last stream crossing). Ten minutes later, fork right on an old trail. Then, almost immediately (by an old, colourful **fountain**), fork left. In two minutes you are in the **centre of Dereköy (3h50min)**. A minute along the road to the right is a pleasant, shaded *'cay bahcesi'* (tea garden) — a good place to sit and wait for a *dolmuş*.

Walk 9: Konacık • Pedesa • Bodrum

See map on page 103.
Time: 4h30min
Grade: moderate; mostly along a track; ascent of about 350m. The diversion to Pedesa requires a little scrambling and agility.
Equipment: see pages 21-22.
Travel: 🚐 *dolmuş* to Konacık using any westbound service (except Gümbet), frequent departures, journey time 5min. (Konacık is a fragmented series of habitations covering a large area, which can be confusing. If you take a dolmuş serving *only* Konacık, it will drop you off in the *new part* of the village — some 20min into the walk.) Return on foot to Bodrum centre.
Short walk: Konacık (under **2h**; easy). An opportunity to explore the interesting countryside around the old village of Konacık without too much exertion. Follow the main walk to the stony meadow, then return by the same route.

Old Konacık

This walk heads into the wild interior, following a valley towards ancient Pedesa, almost hidden in the foliage on its hilltop vantage point. The sense of history is never far away on the Bodrum Peninsula, with flowers as well as ruins around to remind you of past cultures and civilisations. One such plant that you can expect to see on this walk is the mandrake, Mandragora officinarum, *which was referred to back in Biblical times and is associated with many legends. It is recognised by its flat rosette of large, wrinkled, dark green leaves, often achieving a spread up to 50cm or more across, bearing a cluster of short-stalked, usually blue flowers, in the spring, followed by large round berries. Many of the legends*

arise from the shape of the tap root, which is often forked and strongly likened to the human figure. It was believed to have powers of curing infertility or to act as a love potion. It was also said to shriek when pulled from the ground, and that this cry brought death to those who heard it. The mandrake had a place in medicine, too; both the roots and the leaves have been used in various treatments.

Unless you are on a *dolmuş* serving *only* Konacık, ask the driver for Konacık *cami* (mosque). The blue-capped minaret of the mosque can be spotted to the right of the main road on the approach from Bodrum. Alight in front of a **café with a fountain** in front. **Start the walk** at the café in **Konacık** by heading inland along the road alongside the café. You soon pass the **mosque**, on the right. When the road forks after 10-12 minutes, keep right, to pass through the newer part of the village (the old village is to the left). The road then runs past a **newer mosque** (on the left) and down into a dip. Past the dip, turn left, following a road past olive groves on your right. If you are walking in spring, look for the mandrake down on the right, near another well, two minutes later.

Once beyond the newer part of the village, the road becomes a track and leads through the old, but still inhabited, **hamlet of Konacık (35min)**. Follow the track as it wends its way further into the countryside and up the hillside: the first indication of the ancient site are early **walls** over to your left as the track levels out. Continue along the track until the ruins on the hilltop come into view, then turn left on a path to **Pedesa (1h55min**; see history opposite). The tower at the far end affords the best views. From this vantage point you can appreciate the prominent situation of these fortifications — occupying a position on a hill in the centre of the Bodrum Peninsula, looking over the north shore just west of Torba and the south shore in the direction of Bitez.

Leave the ruins at the point where you entered them and return to the track, then turn left. Ignore a trail entering from the right as the route skirts to the right of the rocky outcrop and climbs away, giving good views of Pedesa. As the way levels out at the top of the rise, you can see your onward route ahead — a track which dips through an old hamlet (now used for cattle farming), before rising up past a lone building on the left. Descend through the old hamlet (**Gökçeler**). But before rising up past the lone building on the left, turn right and walk along the left-hand side of a stone wall. Head down the field, following the wall. Two minutes later, as the way becomes overgrown, cross the collapsed wall, into an olive grove. Continue down towards the left-hand corner of the field. Some old waymarks may be around to guide you for the next few minutes. Go back over the wall, then cross a dip, to rise up onto a rough path. Go right now, and keep right a minute later, just before reaching a crossing stream bed. With the stream bed on your left, dip down across an adjacent stream bed. Then bend left and pass through a gap in a wall, into a wooded valley. The path edges the stream bed, with short forays onto paths left, then right. The path then rises up to the right and becomes easier to follow. Here the path divides, but keep heading down the right-hand side of the valley, with the **stream bed** on your left (ignore the path entering from the right). You will pass **a number of ruins** — which may have been fortifications along the old route to Pedesa.

Bodrum comes into view as you emerge from the woodland. Four minutes later the path disappears in a **building site**. Drop down to a track/road and descend through woodland. Follow the road to the dual carriageway. Turn left past the Canerler **shopping centre** towards the BP petrol station, cross the road *carefully* and descend into a **concrete culvert**. Keep ahead on the road as you emerge from the culvert, and keep ahead again on meeting the next road. This leads round to the left, passing the **sports stadium** on the left. When you reach the dual carriageway in **Bodrum (4h30min)** turn right. The **bus station** is two minutes to the left.

Walk 10: Bodrum • Pedesa • Bodrum

Time: 4h50min
Grade: moderate; some stony paths/trails; short sections with no path; ascent of about 350m; agility needed to explore Pedesa. *Route-finding problems likely in bulldozed developments north of Bodrum; you need to have a good sense of direction and to persevere.*
Equipment: see pages 21-22.
Travel: on foot from/to Bodrum

Pedesa is situated in the region once known, and still referred to by the local people, as Gökçeler. It is one of the old Lelegian cities believed to date back to the sixth and fifth centuries BC, when it had greater power than neighbouring Halicarnassus. In the fourth century BC the people

were forcibly incorporated by Prince Mausolus into Halicarnassus, and the site was retained as an outpost. It is a fairly large site occupying a commanding position, but there have been no excavations, nor any reconstruction. There are no roads leading to it; the only way to get there is on foot. This walk explores some of the interesting and quiet countryside behind Bodrum and reaches Pedesa by what was possibly the old route to Halicarnassus. Sound carries in the peace of the countryside, and the tinkling of bells from the animals can often be heard from distant hillsides. Somewhere along the way in this walk we once heard the pure, sweet, clear voice of a girl break the calm morning air with

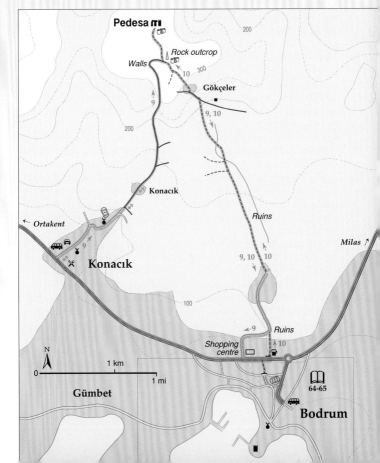

melodious song — followed in harmonious duet by a shepherd. It was unbearably beautiful and stopped us in our tracks.

Start the walk by leaving **Bodrum bus station** to the left of the WCs, near the ticket offices. Emerging on the dual carriageway, turn right towards the hills, keeping ahead at the traffic lights. Cross the road and in two minutes turn left (*not* the first minor left turn). You pass the **sports stadium** on the right. Follow the road as it leads round to the right, but then keep ahead on a minor road, when the major road sweeps left (three minutes later). Two minutes later, keep ahead into a culvert, rising up left to the busy **dual carriageway**. Cross *carefully*, heading slightly right, towards the culvert between the BP **petrol station** and the Canerler **shopping centre**. Then walk along the culvert/sunken path. A few minutes later you pass some old **ruins**, then the path disappears at the bank of a bulldozed road. Rise up to this road, turn right, and continue past new developments and up through pine woods. As you head away from the woods, the road veers right. Ahead you can see more **ruins** on the hillside.

Your ongoing path is hard to find because of all the new developments; watch out on the left of the road for a slight dip, where it should be possible to pick up the path heading inland through the woods (you will have a dry ravine below you on the right as you do so). Some 12 minutes along, notice more **ruins** down to the right. At a fork in the path 10

minutes past the view of the ruins, keep right. Two minutes later, the path begins to head along the stream bed, crossing and recrossing, before settling on the left bank and passing through a gap in a wall near the edge of the woods.

Continue alongside the stream, initially heading round to the right. But look for some old waymarks along a rough path up to the left. The route is not very clear at this point, due to invasive foliage, but the rough path heads uphill for a short distance and then over to the left. It dips down and crosses a collapsed wall, near a corner. Turn right and head uphill, with the wall on your right. But a minute later, cross back over the low wall, to continue uphill with the wall on your left. Rise up onto a stony track, with a **solitary building** up to the right and old **hamlet** to the left (**Gökçeler**; now used for cattle), and turn left to walk up through the hamlet.

At the top of the rise the main track forks left, but take the path forking right and keep near the wall on the right. From here the remains of a tower at Pedesa can be seen on the pine-covered hill to the right, as the path descends to become more obviously an old trail. The route becomes a sunken path as it skirts to the left of a **rocky outcrop**, and an overgrown trail enters from the left. As the path levels out beyond the outcrop, Pedesa sits atop the hill to the right, and **Walk 9 joins from a valley on your left (2h15min)**. Follow the notes for Walk 9 from the 1h55min-point (page 102) to visit **Pedesa** and return to **Bodrum** (**4h50min**).

3 GULF OF GÖKOVA

The bays of Çiftlikköy • The bays of Mazıköy • Çökertme • Ören •
Akyaka • Sedir Island • Karacasögüt Bay

Area code: (0252
Connections: *Dolmuş* connections are generally difficult; it's an advantage to have private transport when touring the gulf. *Tip:* Change money before you travel here; *no* banks or cash machines!

The Gulf of Gökova has so far hardly been touched by touristic developments and is still one of the most beautiful stretches of coast in all Turkey. The further you get from Bodrum, the more unspoilt the landscape: hills wooded with pine forests and olive groves alternate with green pastures full of cows in spring or golden stubble fields in high summer.

As you drive around, here and there you'll see signs advertising a 'Carpet Village' — one way the local agricultural community tries to profit from the tourist trade. Otherwise, signposting is a scarce commodity. You'll find yourself smiling wryly after going the wrong way for a few kilometres (all the maps are wrong), when a local farmer has to help you find the way. Relax — as compensation for the wasted petrol, there are breathtaking views all the way along over beautiful bays — which can only be reached by dirt tracks, on foot or by boat.

The bays of Çiftlikköy

The large farming village of Çiftlikköy is 20km southeast of Bodrum. Surrounded by wooded hills and fields, it's of little interest to tourists. But the stretch of coast a couple of kilometres *before* the village has several attractive bays. Those to the east have some all-inclusive club resorts, like Club Med and World of Wonders. Those to the west, on the other hand, are usually accessible and free. Coming from Bodrum, the first bit of beach you pass is near the Kempinski Hotel, and it's not always clean. **Yalı Beach**, which follows on, is much more inviting — a sand and pebble beach with several restaurants, surfboard rental and showers. But if you're watching the pennies, it's more economical to bring a picnic lunch.
Getting there: frequent dolmuş *connections to and from Bodrum.*

The bays of Mazıköy

If you keep driving east along the narrow country roads past Çiftlikköy, after about 35km of nerve-wracking curves you will come to Mazıköy. Below this sleepy village there are a couple of really fantastic turquoise bays, truly among the most beautiful in the whole country. Even the boat trips and jeep convoys cannot spoil this idyll. So far, these beaches are almost bare of buildings and not overcrowded, even in high season. Once in a while you'll even have a cow watching you swim. It doesn't matter which of the bays you choose — the narrow pebble

İnceyalı Bay, near Mazıköy

beach at **Hurma Bay** in the east or the two beaches at **İnceyalı Bay** to the west, separated by a small rise.

Getting there: It's best to have your own transport; dolmuş connections from Bodrum are few and sporadic.

Accommodation/Food and drink at Hurma Bay

There are three *pansiyonlar* right on the beach and more places to stay inland, including a very quiet campsite. In high season it is almost imperative to reserve ahead.

Sahil Pension is the top recommendation here — just a few metres from the sea. 13 clean rooms with pine furniture, per person with F/B £17. Meals are served on the lovely beach-side terrace or, in the evenings, in the garden full of mandarin trees. (3392131.

If Sahil is full up, try **Uğur Pansiyon** (3392043) or **Öztekin Pansiyon** (3392136), both of which are also near the beach. Both the **Mazıköy Restaurant** and the **Kayabaşı Restaurant** serve first-class fish dishes in lovely settings and at decent prices.

Accommodation/Food and drink at İnceyalı Bay

NRY Pension is the only guest house along the 300m long western beach. Just 5 very plain rooms, but with the sound of the sea to lull you to sleep. Nice terrace; some 'alternative life-stylers' among the clientele. Very inexpensive: from £6.50 per person. (3392039 or (0532-3124100 (mobile).

İnceyalı Dinlenme Tesisleri is on the eastern beach. 16 simple rooms with own bath and terrace (per person with F/B £19). Delightful restaurant right out over the beach, the only disadvantage being that it's a watering hole for the jeep safaris. If you like, you can pitch a tent in the garden under the lemon trees (sounds more idyllic than it is) for £4.50 per night. (3392125 or (0532-5687461 (mobile).

Çökertme

The coastal landscape east of Mazıköy is also an undisturbed paradise. Only bribery artists would get a building permit here. Çökertme is an inland farming village about 50km east of Bodrum, with a little port settlement at the sea. The latter consists of not much more than two rows of houses on a small beach more frequented by 'blue cruises' than sun-worshippers; the place has been completely ignored in most travel guides. So you may be able to spend the most memorable days of your holiday here — as long as your needs are simple. Spend a night for instance at the Çökertme Motel, and you're very likely to end up staying longer than you planned!

Getting there: There are dolmuş *connections to Milas and Bodrum, but very few daily departures. Be sure to tell the* dolmuş *driver that you want to alight at the port settlement. If you want to be collected by the* dolmuş, *telephone the Dolmuş Cooperative (℃5310334). To get there by private transport, Çökertme is most easily reached from Milas: shortly before Ören, turn right by an unmissable power station; from here it's another 12km or so. The route is extremely beautiful, and you'll pass lovely pebble beaches. Driving from Bodrum the route is more complicated: keep making for Ören and keep asking the way. Despite years of visiting, your authors have never made it on their own in one go!*

Accommodation/Food and drink
There are just a couple of simple guest houses. In July and August, if you haven't booked ahead, you will be very lucky to get a room. **Çökertme Motel**, while not right on the beach, is the best place to stay. The management is very friendly, the atmosphere very relaxed, and it's clean. 23 rooms, most with private bath and climate control, as well as (and this is a tip for those on a tight budget) 8 'bungalows': colourful little thatched huts in the garden (with stone floors, mosquito netting, showers and wash basins, but without loos). The best thing about the place is its beach-side restaurant with a delightful terrace, oriental nook for smoking a hookah, and wooden jetty for sunbathing. They also organise boat trips for guests. Motel rooms cost £11 per person with breakfast (£19 with F/B); bungalows £12.50 per person with F/B. ℃ 5310156, www.cokertme.com.

If the motel is full, try your luck at the **Akkaş Pansiyon** (℃ 5310125); prices are the same. The international yachting clientele patronise two restaurants in particular: **Captain İbrahim's** and **Rose Mary** — but that doesn't mean that the others don't serve good fish.

Ören

Ören, some 12km east of Çökertme, lies on a beautiful wide bay at the foot of Kocadağ. This 640m-high mountain is very popular with paragliders. So far there are no mega-hotels to spoil the long sand and pebble beach, behind which there are some discreet guest houses and holiday settlements. Unfortunately mayor Kazım Turan wants to make his town into one of the 'most important tourist centres in the world'. Let's hope he never gets his wish. At present Ören is still a good alternative to the hurly-burly of Bodrum — even though this little town of 4500 souls swells to 30,000 during the Turkish holiday season. In recent years foreign tourists have joined the mostly Turkish clientele. The actual village centre lies about 1.5km inland from the coast. Here you'll find the post office, a barber's, a couple of shops and, on Wednesdays, a colourful weekly market — but no bank. The nearest ATMs are 4km west near the unmissable power station. (The building of this power station in the 1990s was the reason why many international hotel chains which had already acquired building sites behind the beach left them undeveloped.) In summer the walkway between village and beach makes a nice stroll.

Ören was originally built on the site of ancient **Keramos**, first referred to in the 6th century BC and named for the son of Dionysus, God of Wine. Keramos is known as the founder of the potters' art (the word 'ceramic' is derived from Keramos). Only a few unspectacular remains of the ancient city are scattered in and around Ören.

Getting there: There are dolmuş *connections to and from Milas and Çökertme. In summer only, the* dolmuşes *run as far as the beach.*

Accommodation/camping
Since most of the visitors are Turks staying in their own holiday homes, the choice of accommodation is fairly limited. The places listed below are all on the beach-side promenade, but you can find more, simple apart-hotels, motels and guest houses inland. As a rule, you can always find a room, even in high season.

Hotel Alnata, at the far western side of the bay, is the most comfortable hotel in Ören. 50 bright, spacious rooms with marble floors, TV and climate control — ask for a room with pool and sea views! Tennis courts and a wide choice of sports. 7 rooms have wheelchair access. Friendly, young staff. Double room £42, with H/B £59, huge discounts in shoulder season. (5322813, www.alnatahotel.com.

Yıl-Tur Motel is on the east side of the bay near the fishing port. The simple but very clean rooms with private bath, fan and terrace are only separated from the sea by the beach promenade. Own restaurant with good home cooking. Double room £21.50. (5322114, www.yiltur.net (unfortunately not in English).

Camping: There's a simple and economical site near the Yıl-Tur Motel, also just separated from the sea by the promenade.

Food and drink: Fish restaurants and inexpensive bars cheek-by-jowl on the promenade. You get good value for money in Ören.

Practicalities A-Z
Boat trips: You can find various offers at the beach; typically the price is £6.50 per person with lunch.

Paragliding: Kocadağ, right on the doorstep, has become very popular due to its good thermals. You can get information about tandem flights in most of the hotels in the town (certainly at Alnata; see above). Reckon on about £57 for a flight, including transport and equipment.

Akyaka
This small holiday town, at the foot of the Kıran Mountains at the eastern end of the Gulf of

Gökova, owes its pleasant character to one man: Nail Çakırhan, a prize-winning architect from nearby Ula, who revived the traditional Aegean building methods with a lot of wood and oriels. Compared with nearby Marmaris, Akyaka is still a peaceful oasis, made even more pleasant by the constant light breeze. Since mostly Turks holiday in Akyaka (international tourism has been slow in coming), the peak season is only during Turkish holiday times. There are some tavernas just behind the narrow, palm-lined beach. A motorable track leads from Ören to Akyaka along the coast, past wonderful shingle bays and shady pine woods — as delightful as it is bumpy. Nearer Akyaka, the track is tarred. *Getting there: In the summer two* dolmuşes *a day to and from Marmaris; otherwise the only* dolmuş *connections are to Muğla, where you can transfer to a bus running along the coast. A taxi to Marmaris costs approximately £12.*

Accommodation: There's a good choice of mid-range pensions and hotels; most guests stay in apartments.

Club Çobantur Marina, at the western end of Akyaka, just past the campsite. Welcoming complex in a little bay (but with a couple of ugly concrete buildings at the back). Garden with duck pond, jetty giving access into the sea, nice terrace restaurant. Lovely mosaic floors in the hallways, spacious standard hotel rooms — be sure to ask for sea view. 24 rooms, 2 larger suites. Double room £57, larger suites £75. (2434550, www. turkuaz-guide.net/cobantur.

Hotel Erdem, one row of houses back from the beach. Small, well-kept two-storey building with pool, 22 rooms (double with breakfast £17), 4 apartments (for up to 4 people, £35) — all with terrace or balcony. (2435849, www.erdemhotel.com.

Yener Apart Pansiyon, near the Erdem, just 200m from the beach. Four well-equipped apartments with climate control, all with balcony. The landlady only speaks Turkish. For up to four people £26. Less expensive, but plainer, are the apartments at **Pension Fatih** just opposite. (2435858.

Camping: **Gökova Orman Camping**, outside Akyaka. Large, beautifully landscaped site in a shady pine wood with its own beach. Basic sanitation facilities. They also rent bungalows — not of the classic log cabin type, but real little houses with balconies and terraces. Idyllically sited restaurant. Not cheap. Two people with camper van £9.50, bungalows for up to 6 people £29-35. (2434398.

Food and drink: Good restaurants both at the beach and in the village, very reasonably priced in comparison with Marmaris.

Practicalities A-Z

Boat trips: At the port you'll find offers for trips in the Gulf of Gökova; prices starting from about £6 with lunch.

Car hire: There's little on offer, since most visitors have their own cars.

Sedir Adası

This island, in the south of the Gulf of Gökova, is also well known as **Cleopatra's Island**. An endearing legend has it that Mark Antony had the bay filled with white sand from Egypt for his beloved Cleopatra. Unfortunately no sultan ever did the same for his harem, because then the beach would have been larger… Today the island overflows with tourists.

The remains of the ancient city of **Cedreae** are here, including the ruins of a theatre, a temple dedicated to Apollo, an agora, a necropolis, etc. According to Xenophon, the inhabitants of Cedreae were semi-barbarians and were all enslaved in 405 BC by Sparta. Until fairly recently the island was private property; today it is in the hands of the Ministry for Tourism.

Getting there/prices: The easiest way to get to the island is with an organised tour from Marmaris, the most inexpensive way is by dolmuş *(4 times daily). The fare per person for the crossing is £3.75; there is then an additional 'island entrance' fee of £4.50. The turn-off to the ferry mooring is signposted 'Sedir Adası' at the village of Çamlı on the road to Muğla.*

Notes: It is illegal to take any sand from the beach. The restaurant on the island is very expensive, taking full advantage of its monopoly.

Accommodation/camping

Motel Sedir, in Taşbükü Bay opposite Sedir Adası (go past the ferry departure point and straight on for 5km). 16 simple rooms with furniture from here and there, balcony or terrace and private bath. Double room with climate control £19, without £15. Open all year. The nearest beach is about 1km away; it's 21km to Marmaris. (4958109.

Boncuk Camping, about 7km past the ferry departure point, the last 2km on unmade road; signposted. Located in a gorgeous setting — in a bay dotted with palms and with a narrow, sandy beach. Average sanitary facilities; also spartan rooms for rent. Mobile home or camper van £5.75. 24km from Marmaris. (4958116.

Food and drink: On the road to the ferry you pass the **Çınar Restaurant**, with a lovingly landscaped garden. You sit under shady trees, with a stream flowing behind you; ducks quack, and old cart wheels add to the atmosphere. Fairly pricey, but very popular — sometimes overflowing. They also rent nice rooms. (4958080.

Karacasöğüt Bay

This bay, with the small island of Karaca lying offshore, is south of Sedir Island. It's a meeting place for yachtsmen, who stop off at the 60-berth marina. If you are only heading here to swim, it's not worth the long trip; there are more beautiful bays closer to Marmaris. Some wealthy Turks have holiday homes here.

Getting there: From Marmaris take the road towards Muğla and after approximately 14km turn left. From there it's still about 12km to the bay. No dolmuş *connections.*

See map on page 113.
Time: under 4h
Grade: moderate-strenuous, with a tough ascent in the middle section of the walk, and some very stony terrain underfoot. Be prepared for encroaching foliage!
Equipment: see pages 21-22.
Travel: 🚌 *dolmuş* from Marmaris to Çetibeli (either the Muğla or Fethiye service, frequent departures from the *otogar*, journey time 22min); return by 🚌 any coach or *dolmuş* returning to Marmaris.
Short walks
1 Çetibeli circuit (1h35min; easy). Follow the main walk to the point where the track swings right (about 15min past the water deposit). Instead of forking left here, stay on the main track as it swings right. Keep right at the fork of tracks three minutes later, and keep down right again at the next junction. The next small track off left is where you rejoin the main walk: pick up those notes at the 3h-point, to get back to the main road.
2 Çetibeli to Çamlı (2h30min; easy-moderate). Follow the main walk until you emerge on the track above Çamlı. Then turn left, instead of right, and follow the track downhill, to join the road to Çamlı. Turn left here and walk back to the Marmaris road, to await the coach or *dolmuş*.

Natural woodlands, farmed areas, glimpses of old ruins, and wayside flora and fauna all contribute to the kaleidoscope of ever-changing land-scapes between Çetibeli and the Gulf of Gökova. Wherever you find water, particularly slow-moving or brackish water, keep an eye open for terrapins, which are commonly seen basking on stones or swimming

about lazily. It's likely that you'll pass beehives too. Usually arranged in neat rows, the square boxes are seen in great numbers — possibly in the fields or orange groves, or even lining the tracks, especially in the pine woods.

Alight opposite the Caglayan Pinarbasi restaurant as you enter **Çetibeli**, and **start the walk** by crossing the road. Take the track which leads uphill by the left-hand side of the restaurant. Almost from the start, the way climbs through a peaceful, pastoral setting. Keep up right when the track forks in one minute, and pause a minute later by a small **cemetery** on the right. Closer inspection of the neglected building with a verandah reveals it to be the old village mosque. The rich purple blossom of the Judas tree shines out from the hillsides in spring, while neighbouring shrubs like myrtle and storax quietly await their turn to bloom. You pass a **water storage deposit** on the left and continue uphill for another 15 minutes or so, until the track swings right. Fork *left* here, towards a gap opening into farmland. (*But keep right, staying on the track, for Short walk 1.*) Having forked left, take the footpath which leads up into the woods on your left, skirting the cultivated land.
The woodlands which flank the path to the left are brightened in early spring by a display of blue and white *Anemone blanda* and a lesser number of lovely yellow *Fritillaria bithynica*. Once beyond the *yayla* (meadow), the path heads more into the woodland and starts to descend a little, before a fork is reached some

111

seven-eight minutes along. Ignore the fork rising to the left, take the fork *descending* to the left — a **sunken path** through a tunnel of vegetation. A pine-covered valley falls away to the right, with the sea in view further to the right. *Take care* some 10 minutes from the fork: it looks as if the path continues ahead, but follow it round to the right, still skirting the valley on the right. When the charcoal burners are active in the nearby village of Çamlı, it is possible to catch the aroma even at this distance, as you start a steep descent (take care on the slippery pine needles). At a fork, continue ahead towards a ruined building, ignoring the path off to the right. Pass the building a minute later and emerge on a track above the plain. Turn right in the direction of the sea (*but turn left for Short walk 2*).

Continue along the track contouring around the base of the hillside above **Çamlı (1h40min)**. The track starts to rise; when it swings to the right, be sure to take the footpath leading up into the pine woods. The path joins a wide track under five minutes later. Turn right to continue uphill on a **bulldozed firebreak**. The firebreak rises up the centre of the ridge, descends a little, then continues to climb the hill ahead. Views open up: across the water, to the left, are the cliffs on the far side of the Gulf of Gökova. The firebreak narrows as it sweeps right, eastwards, and then rises to the **highest point of the walk (2h45min)**.

Continue along the track; some ten minutes later, looking ahead to the shrub-covered hillside, it is possible to make out some ruins — including part of a wall and a doorway. Several forts, both ancient and medieval, as well as some amphora factories, are recorded for this area; this may be one of the forts. (The amphora was a double-handled vessel used by the Greeks and Romans as liquid containers.)

Just over 10 minutes down from the high point, turn right at a junction. A minute later, take the minor woodland track off left. You meet a crossing track in two minutes. Turn left here, below the **hill with the ruins (3h)**. (*Short walk 1 rejoins here.*) The track descends towards a *yayla*, but take a path forking left *before* reaching this meadow. This skirts the edge of the woodland to the left of the *yayla*. As you descend into the pines, a path joins from the right. You pass a water trough on the left and reach a confluence of paths with a small stream bed over to the left. Keep ahead here, ignoring a path joining from the right and two paths on the left which merge to cross the stream (the route of Walk 12). You cross the same stream bed immediately afterwards. Follow the path to the right, along a small gully —the stream now on your right.

The path turns sharp left with the Marmaris road in view ahead. You have a very steep final descent down a firebreak, to a track junction. Take the track out to the **Marmaris road** (under **4h**), close to the **mosque**. A right turn here leads to some restaurants. Coaches and *dolmuşes* pass at some speed, so give an early and clear signal if you wish to stop one!

Time: 4h20min
Grade: moderate-strenuous; fairly good paths underfoot, but a steep descent of almost 300m down a stony trail, with a corresponding ascent to return. *Routefinding skills required from the 15min-point to the 45min-point, where the paths are confusing.*
Equipment: see pages 21-22.
Travel: 🚐 *dolmuş* to Çetibeli (Muğla service, frequent departures, journey time 23min; return on 🚐 any *dolmuş* or coach bound for Marmaris.

*The little-visited shores of the Gulf of Gökova provide a spectacular setting for this walk, which penetrates a fairly remote region. Images of an azure blue sea lapping a green shore-*line will provide you with a taster of solitude. Unfortunately, the farm-steads here have been abandoned, and it is no longer possible to continue along this superb coast on foot — the paths are hopelessly overgrown.*

Ask to leave the *dolmuş* at the mosque *(cami)*, which is located just beyond some restaurants on the left as you enter **Çetibeli**. **Start the walk** as you leave the *dolmuş* by crossing the road and taking the track at the right of the mosque; it heads directly for the hills. After six-seven minutes, at a junction of tracks, keep ahead on the path up the steep, wide **firebreak**. A minute later, stay on the path as it forks off left. You

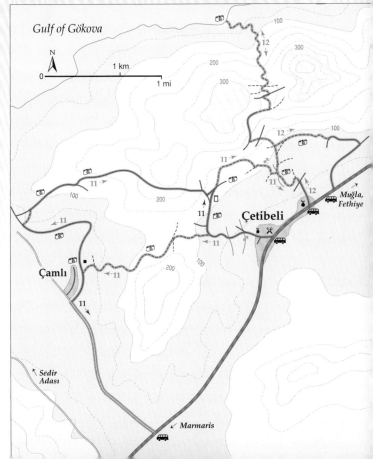

enjoy good views back over the fertile valley, to the pine-covered hills beyond, before turning sharply right into a narrow tree-lined **gully** (**15min**). Six-seven minutes along, cross the **stream bed** on the left and immediately take the path off right, to cross back over the stream bed a little higher up. Continue along the edge of the woods, keeping left at a fork a couple of minutes later. At the next fork, shortly afterwards, there is a stand of tall American aloes on the far side of the right-hand fork (easily recognised by their huge rosettes of thick, succulent, spear-shaped leaves). Keep left uphill again here, into the woods.

Brush aside encroaching *Pistachio* *lentiscus* shrubs and rise up to meet a strong crossing path in just a few minutes. *(NB: your return route will head downhill to the right at this point.)* Head straight across towards a *yayla* (meadow), to meet another path. Turn left to skirt the edge of the *yayla*, which is soon left behind as the path leads away from it and continues climbing. When you meet a track (five-six minutes from the *yayla*; **45min**), stay on the path which continues across the track in a steady ascent. (Watch out here for the purple limodore, *Limodorum abortivum*, the curious saprophytic orchid which finds a home in this woodland habitat.)

Turn right as you emerge onto a

Wherever the land is suitable, regardless of its isolation or difficulty of access, olives feature strongly as a crop. This walk is a classic example: having descended on a difficult, stony path for a considerable time, through heavily forested land, you arrive at the edge of the Gulf of Gökova to find … an olive grove.

woodland track five minutes later. *(Since you will be returning this way, take note at this point of the start of your (waymarked) path for the return — just before the track descends into a dip.)* Continue up through the woods to a large grassy *yayla*. Follow the track as it leads into this meadow, but keep right (now on a path) across the bottom end of the *yayla*. This path takes you back into woodland. The slender flower spikes of the man orchid, *Aceras anthropophorum*, are never easy to spot, but when it grows in the middle of the path, as here, then it is hard to miss! You descend to another meadow two minutes later and head slightly right, across the narrow part, to continue on a stony path.

This path leads to another *yayla* but, before it is reached — *or even seen* — you reach a fork and take the left-hand path. You emerge from the woods alongside a strong track and rise up onto it (by a waymarked white rock). This marks the **highest point of the walk (1h10min)**, and from here the way descends fairly steeply to the seashore. Turn right along the track for half a minute, then look for your waymarked path off left. Keep right at the first fork you come to (three minutes down); then keep ahead over a crossing path. You can already see the Gulf of Gökova through the trees, as the path crosses the head of the valley and leads down its right-hand side. The waymarked path descends the right-hand side of the valley and only edges more to the left as it nears the shore. *Care is required* in places, where the path drops more steeply and

takes on the appearance of an old trail at times, vague in places. Although footwork demands concentration in this steady descent, keep an eye out for bee orchids such as *Ophrys holoserica*. An **olive grove** announces your arrival at the bottom of the valley. The seashore is visible on the far side of the olive grove and is soon reached by bearing right across the grove, past a ruined farmstead. A small shingle beach at the **Gulf of Gükova**, shade from olive trees, a vista of dark green wooded slopes sliding into turquoise blue, the smell of pine, and the sound of the sea combine to provide an irresistibly relaxing setting … but if you swim, beware of sea urchins.

Return the same way until you come to the right turn at the bottom of the *yayla*. Here you meet the strong crossing path encountered earlier. Instead of turning right, however, continue along the path skirting the meadow; almost immediately you join the crossing path, slightly lower down. Follow it to the left downhill; a path joining sharply from the right in three minutes leads back to the fork with the American aloes — an alternative route back).

Skirt the edge of pine woods, with cultivated fields and scattered houses on the right, as the path zigzags down. Meet a track and turn left. Then, at a T of tracks, turn right and continue through a small farming community. You reach the main road just outside **Çetibeli (4h20min)**. Flag down any passing coach or *dolmuş*. (Or turn right, to some roadside restaurants.)

Time: just over 3h
Grade: easy, with good terrain underfoot; ascent of only 125m
Equipment: see pages 21-22.
Travel: 🚐 dolmuş from Marmaris to Akçapınar (Muğla service, frequent departures from the otogar, journey time about 30min); alight at the end of the road into Akçapınar (over the hill after passing through Gökçe). Return by 🚐 any dolmuş or coach bound for Marmaris.

Short walks

1 Akçapınar to Gökçe (2h35min; easy). Follow the main walk to the 30min-point, but take the track off to the right and start climbing. In about 25-30 minutes, just after a track has joined from the right (and where you can see a track junction ahead), take the path on the right — a short cut to a higher track. Turn right on this higher track to continue up through pine woods. When you meet cross-tracks, keep straight ahead, picking up the main walk again from the 1h50min-point.

2 Circular walk from Akçapınar (under 3h; easy). This is particularly suitable for those with their own transport. Follow the main walk to the cross-tracks on the saddle (the 1h50min-point). Turn right to continue downhill (the reverse of Short walk 1). As you approach a track junction five-six minutes later, take the path down to the left — a short cut to the lower track. Turn left and continue downhill, to meet the road used on the outward leg, where you turn left to head back to Akçapınar. (Under 10 minutes along the road, you could cross the bridge on the right and continue back along a track on the far side of the river.)

A great area of plain stretches eastward from the head of the Gulf of Gökova. Mountains rise all around it, but it is the foothills to the south which are the setting for this walk. The views over the green and cultivated plains make a pleasing contrast to the scenery on walks closer to Marmaris, and the bird life is different too. Particularly noticeable is the abundance of storks: they find plenty of food on the swampy fields of the plain. This migratory bird becomes evident in springtime, particularly April/May, when on the nest. Storks are regarded by the local people as harbingers of good fortune, so their presence is encouraged, and their huge nests are never disturbed, even when built on top of chimney stacks. No matter where the nests are built, their size always makes them look incongruous, but especially so when located on top of a telegraph pole... Starting at Akçapınar and running in a direct line across the plain, crossing the main Muğla/Fethiye road and continuing beyond it, is a magnificent 3km-long avenue of eucalyptus trees. If you want to have a closer look, make a short diversion from Akçapınar.

Leave the dolmuş at the end of the road into Akçapınar. **Start the walk** by heading into **Akçapınar**. Walk through the village and, where the road bends left across a bridge to the **avenue of eucalyptus trees**, turn right. Almost immediately there is a rural feel to the walk, with red-roofed houses dotting the hillside, citrus groves and views of the green plain. As the road leads in a gentle ascent above the plain, it provides the opportunity for watching for birds — the storks being easily spotted. Some 12

minutes or so along, the **bridge** over the river is an *alternative return for Short walk 2.*
Ignore a track rising to the right (**30min**). *(But take it if you are doing Short walk 1).* Continue into the village of **Sirinköy** and take the right-hand fork at the junction some three minutes later. Continue up the road, past a **house with lemon trees** in the garden, then turn left on a track. Rise to the next junction, turn left, and continue along the track. Just near a **cluster of eucalyptus trees**, on a bend, take the path up into the pines. This rises steeply and emerges on a firebreak. Continue uphill all the way to a crest, then descend to a track. Turn right on this high-level woodland track, enjoying panoramic views over the plain.
On reaching a **crossing of tracks on a saddle (1h50min)**, turn left into woodland. *(But head right downhill for Short walk 2.)* Grey-green leaves that rustle in the wind and sparkle silver in the sun announce yet more olive trees — this time buried deep in the pine woods. At the junction of tracks reached some 10 minutes from the saddle, turn right. From here you catch

glimpses of the red-roofed houses of Gökçe through the light pine woods. Nearer at hand are masses of the small, white *Gagea graeca* which grows so freely in the dry stony areas and is seen at its best in April. Down left, through the woodland, you can see a river in the valley bottom and, gradually, the views open to reveal more of Gökçe and the main road.
Eventually you reach an open area. Stay on the track as it swings right and then runs parallel with the main road below. Starting to descend, you enjoy good views over well-ordered citrus groves and towards the Gulf of Gökova. Once on the main road, turn left into **Gökçe** (just over **3h**). Any *dolmuş* or coach heading back to Marmaris can be stopped here — or walk into the centre, where there is a shop and restaurants.

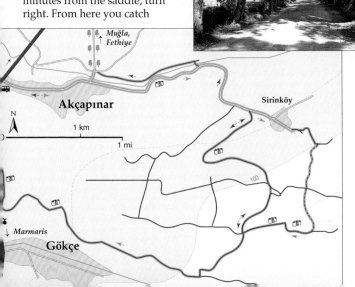

4 MARMARIS

Orientation • History • Accommodation/camping • Food and drink
• Nightlife • Beaches and diving • Sights • Practicalities A-Z

Area code: (0252
Information: The very
professionally run Tourist Office
is on the shore promenade near
the castle. In summer open daily
from 08.30-18.00, in winter
Mon.-Fri. from 08.00-17.00.
İskele Meydanı, (4121035,
(4127277, www.mugla-turizm.
gov.tr.
Connections: Buses operate
several times a day to Denizli/
Pamukkale (4 hours; £4.50),
Datça (1h30min; £2.50), Ephesus
(sometimes with transfer in
Aydın, 4 hours; £4.75), Fethiye
(3 hours; £3.50) and Antalya
(6h30min; £8.50). The bus station
is somewhat outside the centre,
on Mustafa Münir Elgin Bul.
Branches of the different bus
companies are located near the
Tansaş supermarket on Mustafa
Muğlalı Cad, from where nearly
all of them operate a shuttle
service to the bus station (otherwise you can catch a *dolmuş* with
the sign 'Otogar' opposite the
Tansaş supermarket.
Twice a day a **Havaş** bus runs to
Dalaman Airport: it leaves from
opposite the Turkish Airlines

(THY) building; officially it only
picks up passengers flying with
THY, but in practice they take all
comers (price £7).
Dolmuş: Constant departures to
İçmeler and Uzunyalı Beach
leave from the front of Tansaş
supermarket on Ulusal Egemenlik Cad.; they also stop at the
bend to the right by the Atatürk
statue at the port and along
Atatürk Cad. *Dolmuşes* to Muğla,
the bus station and Cennet
Adası leave from opposite the
Tansaş supermarket; the Turunç
dolmuş leaves from the *dolmuş*
station somewhat further north
on Ulusal Egemenlik Cad.; those
to Datça leave from the bus
station.
Water *dolmuşes* to the beaches
around Marmaris leave from
several places on the shore
promenade; they sail every 20
minutes to İçmeler and Turunç
(£3.75 return).
Taxis: Taxis are available at
almost every second corner. The
fare to Dalaman Airport or Datça
is about £40, to İçmeler £6.50 and
to Turunç £17.

I n Marmaris you can *really* 'take a holiday' and dispense
with all formalities — jacket, tie, shirt and trousers. In
Marmaris you can eat out in bathing shorts (which at least
has the advantage that you cannot be dragged by your
T-shirt into a shop). This informality appeals a great deal
to some people; others prefer a more refined atmosphere.
    Many other customs, none of them Turkish, prevail in
this small town of 30,000 inhabitants. With its sunshine
guarantee (300 days of sun annually) comes the 'anything
goes' of mass tourism. On the well-kept esplanade which
runs round the old quarter by the castle, painters, jugglers
and musicians are lined up cheek by jowl. Luxury yachts
and tour boats lie moored on the sea side; opposite,

waiters tout for business, inviting you to a candlelit dinner on their pretty restaurant terraces. Tourists stroll between the yachts and the restaurants, parading their sunburned bellies, which have shaded their still-white feet for most of the day. Marmaris the town is more chic than its tattooed, thirsty visitors. Every evening the masses flood into the centre from the hotel suburbs (especially when no Premier League games are on TV at the suburban bars). They roam through the modern bazaar, which is anything but oriental: everything on sale carries the trademark of well-known designers. The pushiness of the dealers can be so bad that sometimes the police have to intervene.

All the above aside, Marmaris is both an excellent walking base and a brilliant yachting centre — there are well over 1500 berths in the bay. The largest marina, and the most chic, is the Netsel, east of the castle. This is where Turkey's smart set meet. They virtually never go into the centre: The Turkish jet set wants nothing to do with the international proles.

Orientation

The old centre with its bazaar, restaurants and bars, lies around the castle. K. Seyfettin Elgin Bulvarıs runs west from here, towards İçmeler, before becoming Kenan Evren Bulvarı. To the right and left of K. Seyfettin Elgin Bulvarı is the hotel area called Siteler, from where you can catch a *dolmuş* to the centre day and night. If you get off by the Atatürk statue at the beginning of Kordon Caddesi, you can stroll around the castle to the marina.

History

Marmaris, founded as Physcus around 1000 BC by Dorian immigrants, was once a commercial port and Asia Minor's gateway to Rhodes and Egypt. In the 6th century BC the settlement came under Lydian rule. And by the 5th century BC Herodotus had already named it Marmarissos; it is assumed that this name was derived from the marble found in the area. From the 4th to the 2nd century BC Rhodes dominated the port. Marmaris was then constantly exposed to the changing balance of power, until finally in 1408 the Ottomans occupied the whole area. Since then Marmaris has been Turkish. The Bay of Marmaris has always played an important strategic role: where once Süleyman the Magnificent started his expedition to Rhodes and Lord Nelson prepared his fleet for the attack on the French at Abukir, there is now a NATO base (Aksaz Bay east of Marmaris is a restricted military area).

The largest changes in Marmaris's history were brought about however neither by the Romans nor by NATO military strategists, but by tourists. At the beginning of the 1980s only a few globetrotters stayed in the bay overnight; today some 100,000 holidaymakers sink into their beds every night during the

summer. The once-sleepy fishing town has become one of the largest international fairgrounds in Turkey. All the gaps between the buildings on the coast have disappeared, as have those in the second, third and even ninth or tenth streets in from the shore —

there is not a single strip of green left. New buildings and shells of buildings continue to spread ever further into the hinterland and testify to an optimistic view of the future.

Many foreigners move into the new apartments. The prices are

Marmaris

200 m

Food and drink

li Baba
zsüt
ofra Restaurant
aren Patisserie
armaris Lokantası
skos Bar
ellini

Nightlife

ack Street
reen House
alon Türkü Bar
li Baba Bar
each Club
aisy and High End
alk of the Town

Accommodation

1 Grand Azur
4 Öktem Motel
7 Interyouth Hostel
9 Candan Otel
10 Gülşah Pansiyon
11 Selenya Apart's Otel
12 Pekuz Camping
15 Club Bella Monte
18 Gözpınar Hotel &
    Apartments
19 Marina Hotel

Shopping

6 Solaris Shopping Centre
21 Point Centre

---

just too high for the bulk of the
Turks. Life has become too
expensive for even the average
wage earner in Marmaris. As a
result, a newly refurbished
branch of a bank simply couldn't
open, as no personnel could
afford to live and work in

Marmaris for the average
national salary.

Accommodation/camping

(see plan above)
The bulk of accommodation
developed over the past decades
was created for cheap mass

Marmaris — the yachting fraternity's Mecca

tourism. There are almost no more friendly guest houses or small hotels with any style left. Individual travellers take a big detour around Marmaris. Most hotels are located west of the old town behind Atatürk Cad. and further west, around K. Seyfettin Elgin Cad. in the hotel quarter of Siteler, where the highest density of accommodation can be found. The nearer the hotels lie to the centre, the older they usually are, with more antiquated equipment. Those looking for more modern rooms, of whatever category — without burns in the carpet — can find something more comfortable outside the centre for the same money. Recommended alternative places to stay are Akyaka, Turunç and the Bozburun Peninsula. There are some 800 different places to stay on offer; the following may help you choose.

Grand Azur (1), on the road to İçmeler, on the left. Extravagant five-star hotel. From the outside it looks almost futuristic. Beautiful entrance with marble pillars and minimalist décor. Tasteful, comfortable rooms, each with balcony. Large pool, indoor pool, private beach, tennis. Double room a horrifying £188! (4174050, www. hotelgrandazur.com.

Club Bella Monte (15), in the southeastern part of Marmaris Bay, about 6km from the centre. Well-kept hotel complex with 112 rooms divided amongst several buildings in a pine wood by the sea. One of the most peaceful and friendly places near Marmaris. All the rooms are comfortably equipped. Large pool, fitness centre. Entertainment. Only minus point is the narrow beach. Very good value for money. All-inclusive price per person £35. Access: leave the centre on Ulusal Egemenlik Cad., then head for the 'Otogar' and 'Günlüce'; from here the hotel is signposted. *Dolmuş* connections to the centre. (4133430, (4133434.

Candan Otel (9), on Atatürk Cad. 66. 39 classical-modern rooms decorated in bright colours. Well-kept and comfortable, attractive entrance area. Note that the rooms at the front, with views to the palms and sea, are noisy. In the back it's quiet, but you look out to an un-attractive neighbouring hotel. Double rooms £40, singles £26. (4129302, (4125359.

Marina Hotel (19), below the castle, on the promenade. Family-run old hotel with a personal touch. All rooms are different, not chic but nice all the same. Roof terrace with restau-rant. This alternative to the boring 'cloned' hotels is, unfor-tunately, as popular with party-goers as with those looking for peace and quiet. Double rooms £28, singles £18, three-bedded rooms £39. Barbaros Cad. 39, (/(4120010, www.marmaris marinahotel.com.

Gülşah Pansiyon (10), well-kept small family-run guest house in a central location. Somewhat set back from Atatürk Cad., so not nearly as noisy as the others. Rooms with laminate floor covering and balconies, very welcoming owners. Double rooms £15. In the winter they only take long-stay guests. Atatürk Cad. 52, (4126642, gulsahpansiyon@ hotmail.com.

Öktem Motel (4), 156 Sok. 1. Under 10 minutes from the beach and centre. Small, clean house with 14 simple, rustically decorated rooms. Obliging owner. Pool. Double rooms with climate control and breakfast £12.50. (4125383.

Interyouth Hostel (7), right in the bazaar, at 42. Sok. 45. Small

black- and white-painted rooms holding several beds (maximum 4 people, £4.75 per person) and double rooms at £10. Friendly staff. A good place to meet like-minded travellers. Laundry, Internetcafé. (4123687, inter-youth@turk.net.

Apartments: There are a lot of aparthotels, especially a few streets back from the coast, but they have little capacity for individual travellers as they are usually booked out by tour operators. In general, however, one rule holds true: you can't tell the book by its cover — what they promise on the outside is not usually delivered inside. Just two addresses:

Gözpınar Hotel & Apartments (18), a family-run hotel behind Uzunyalı Beach. Rooms and apartments, flower-patterned bedspreads and wallpaper give a little romantic touch. Mostly British guests. Closed in winter. Double room £24.50, apartment for 2 people £28. Seyfettin Kemal Elgin Bul. 230, (4122316, www.gozpinarhotel.com.

Selenya Apart's Otel (11), on 160. Sok. near Kemil Engin Bul. Clean building with 15 good apartments. Splash pool. Apartment for up to 4 people. £26. (4135306, (4139346.

Camping: The nearest campsite is **Pekuz Camping (12)**, 5km east of the town (leave the centre on Ulusal Egemenlik Cad. , then head for 'Otogar' and 'Günlüce'; from here the site is signposted. A very basic campsite on a singularly uninspiring bit of coast. The best thing about it is the seaside bar. Shade, but quite poor sanitary facilities. Convenient location, with *dolmuş*

Marmaris Bay

connections into the centre.
(0555-3438963 (mobile).
There are, however, far lovelier places on the way to Datça (see page 151) and near Sedir Island (see page 109).

Food and drink

(see plan on pages 120-121)
The selection is enormous: everything is available, Turkish, English, French, Italian, and Asian food, even international fast-food — something for every budget. The most expensive restaurants are those on the esplanade around the castle, where a Coke costs three times as much as anywhere else. But beer is always cheap.
Restaurants: There is a row of restaurants on the shore promenade between the Tourist Office and the marina. As a general rule, these are high-class tourist restaurants, pricey, serving fish and international

cuisine, often with lovely roof terraces and almost always with a very pushy tout out in front. This is why **Fellini (22)** is recommended: they don't hassle you, and the bill is always correct. You'll recognise it from its yellow chairs and nice roof terrace. In addition to high-quality home-made Turkish dishes, there's fish and various pot roasts served in earthenware casseroles. Main courses £3.75-6.50. (4130826.
The simplest place on the promenade is **Fiskos Bar (20)**, with a friendly owner, lots of Turkish clientele and simple dishes that are just right with a beer.
The top-class and most expensive restaurants are around the Netsel Marina; they are the best in Marmaris.
Lokantas: The *lokantas* in and around the bazaar look really reasonable from the outside, but

many are rip-offs: if there are no prices posted, you are advised to ask the price of every single thing you buy — even a Coke — before you order! It's better to go to the *lokantas* further away on 36. Sok. Good selections here are: **Sofra Restaurant (5)**, with every kind of kebab, *pide,* starters, and casseroles. It's very popular and open 24 hour a day. Right nearby is the **Marmaris Lokantası (13)**, the cheapest place in the old town, where you can get soup for £0.65 or a simple casserole with rice for £1.65. You can also eat well and inexpensively a bit further out, in one of the simple *lokantas* near the Tansaş supermarkt on Ulusal Egemenlik Cad. For instance, **Ali Baba (2)** is very nicely furnished and decorated for a *lokanta* and has kebabs, *döner* and casserole dishes. Friendly service. Per person with beer about £3.50. The only down-side is that it's on the noisy street.

Sweets: Karen Patisserie (9), on Atatürk Cad. near the Candan Hotel is a modern cake shop with delicious cakes, pastries and other sweets. They also serve breakfasts. What's really special here is the range of Anatolian specialities, which are usually hard to find on the coast. **Özsüt (3)** is another good address for those with a sweet tooth. Traditional Turkish sweet pastries, etc. On Atatürk Cad. (near Avis).

Nightlife

(see plan on pages 120-121)
There are two centres. One is **Uzunyalı Beach** (parallel with Seyfettin Elgin Cad.) — full of identical bars (with the same music and sometimes even the same seating plans). This is where many Brits settle in for the night.

At the **Beach Club (23)** crazy entertainers sometimes copy Tina Turner or Freddy Mercury; the **Talk of the Town (25)** attracts the transvestites. **Daisy (24)** is one of the biggest discos in town, and the nearby **High End (24)** stages a lot of foam parties.

The second night spot is **Bar Street**, which runs parallel with the shore promenade towards the Netsel Marina (signposted) and has countless bars and discos. Two popular places are the quite tastefully decorated **Club Green House (14)**, with aquariums, where they have laser shows once in a while, and **Back Street (8)**, only open in summer, an outdoor bar where you can dance under trees. Those with less energy head to the **Galon Türkü Bar (16)**, with Turkish music all night long, or the **Ali Baba (17)** hookah café, with its oriental atmosphere and backgammon players.

Beaches and diving

Marmaris Beach, jammed between the sea and the hotel blocks, is so full of beach chairs in summer that there isn't even room to build a sandcastle. So it's a much better idea to take a *dolmuş* or a boat trip to one of the lovely beaches in the area.

Çiftlik is one of the most beautiful beaches around Marmaris. It's best reached by boat, and you pass Kumlubükü Bay (see page 139) on the way. Driving there it's a long way (see 'Bozburun Peninsula' on page 136).

İçmeler Bay (see page 136) is a

beautiful beach, but it's plastered with sunbeds.

Sedir Adası (see page 109) in the Gulf of Gökova is most easily reached by organised tour.

Diving: Various companies offer dives to wrecks, caves and reefs. You pick these boats up at the port, and prices are much the same whoever you choose — about £24 for two dives with lunch. A four-day diploma course costs about £200. Always ask in advance how many participants there are — with some companies, you'll see about 50 people diving at the same time!

Aquapark: Atlantis Waterpark at Uzunyalı Beach near Point Centre (shopping centre). Large slides. Entry fee about £10.

Sights

Marmaris has very little to offer in terms of cultural or historical sites. On a hill in the north of the city are a few meagre remains of walls from ancient **Physcus** (see Short walk 14). A visit to **Marmaris Kalesi** is worthwhile — a medieval castle which was extended by Süleyman the Magnificent in 1522. There is little more to enjoy today, however, than a beautiful view over the old town and the port. Up until a few years ago the castle housed a museum with oil lamps, pots, vases, bowls and amphorae. But the city and region argued about who was responsible for the staffing and upkeep, so now it is closed. At the foot of the castle, by the Tourist Office, Süleyman built a **caravanserai** in 1545; today the arches shelter a few cafés.

Practicalities A-Z

Boat trips: At first sight, the hundreds of offers at the port look identical, but be sure to ask in advance whether you will have 30 minutes on the beach or three hours, and whether you have to sit on wooden planks or there are comfortable seats. Some boats have live music — you'll love it or hate it. Normally the boats leave at about 10.00 and return between 17.00-19.00. Moonlight cruises begin at 18.30 and end at about 22.30. Reckon on paying about £6 per person for a boat trip with lunch.

Marmaris has a **ferry connection to Rhodes:** A **catamaran** sails from the beginning of April to the end of October several times a day (journey time under 1 hour); no sailings in winter. There is also a **car ferry**: this sails once a week in summer and twice a week in winter. The embarkation formalities begin an hour before departure. A day return or one way ticket costs £24; open return ticket £44. The price for the car is £97. For information contact **Yeşil Marmaris**, Barbaros Cad. 11 (shore promenade), (4122290, yesilmarmaris@superonline.com.

Car hire: There are countless agencies; with the national firms you pay about £26 per day; with the internationals about £43.50 (including insurance). **Avis** is at Atatürk Cad. 10/D, (4122771, (4126413; **Thrifty** at Ulusal Egemenlik Cad. 13, (4134669, (4134670.

Doctors and dentists, English speaking: The private **Ahu Hetman** clinic has English-speaking staff. Otherwise, ask at the Tourist Office.

Events: There is a week-long international **Yacht Festival** at the beginning of May, with exhibitions and lectures, and the international **Marmaris Race Week** at the end of Oct./beginning Nov. In August there are frequent **concerts** and **theatrical performances**.

Launderettes: There are several, like **Çağdaş Laundry** on 33 Sok., near the marina; £2.50 per load.

Money: One exchange bureau is opposite the Tansaş supermarket.

Newspapers: English papers etc. are on sale along Atatürk Cad. and Seyfettin Elgin Cad.

Post: The post office is set back off Kordon Cad. in the bazaar.

Police: There are several police stations, for instance in the bazaar and set back off Atatürk Cad. (4121494.

Shopping and souvenirs: The lanes in the old town, roofed over with glass and steel, make a huge, if somewhat sterile **bazaar**, brightened by Turkish fast-food kiosks and some cafés.

The **Solaris Shopping Centre (6)** on Atatürk Cad. has various shops where they don't sell imitation goods. One of the shops is **Mudo City**, a large chic emporium with quality clothing and attractive accessories like vases, towels, candlesticks and the like. At **Paşabahçe** you can buy glassware made in the eponymous village near Istanbul. A further shopping centre with some good clothing stores and a supermarket is **Point Centre (21)** behind Uzunyalı Beach. Of course the really chic fashion shops are at the **Netsel Marina**. **Tansaş** supermarket on Ulusal Egemenlik Cad. has a huge choice of food. There is also a weekly **Thursday market** north of G. Mustafa Muğlalı Cad.

General note: Prices for souvenirs like carpets are about 70% higher in Marmaris than the national level. A good souvenir is the famous **pine tree honey** (*çam balı*) from the area.

Organised tours: There is a huge choice of both coach and boat tours. The going rate for a trip to Dalyan/Caunos is about £10, to Rhodes £22, Ephesus £30, Pamukkale £17, a two-day trip to Ephesus and Pamukkale £43.50, and a 'Turkey' trip (meaning to a rural village, which just happens to be a carpet-selling centre) £10.

Turkish Airlines: The THY office is at Atatürk Cad. 26B. (4123751, (4123753. See 'Connections' on page 118 for buses to Dalaman.

Turkish bath (Hamam): There is a nameless, historical bath in the old town close to the old caravanserai. Entry, with massage, £9.50.

Two-wheel hire: **Best Motorcycle Rental** on 158 Sok., (4129436, www.bestmotortr.com. has mountain bikes at £6.50 per day, scooters (100 cc) at £17, and motorcycles from a Suzuki TS125 at £24 to a Harley Davidson Sportster 1200 at £100. Usually prices are cheaper if you hire for a longer duration.

Yacht charter: In yachting circles it is almost a matter of course to hire a yacht with captain and crew for a week — the best way to see the Turkish coast. You can hire at one of the travel agencies or directly from the owners at the marinas. One well-known charter company is **Eser Yachting** at 35. Sokak 21. Reckon on £170 per person per week if you take one of the last-minute offers: this includes full board, but not drink. Otherwise allow £770 per day for an 8-cabin boat, £335 per day for a 4-cabin boat. (4123527, www.eser yachting.com.

Walking: Walks 11-20 are all well within reach. Another long stroll would take you to **Cennet Adası**,

the 'Paradise Island' in the south of Marmaris Bay. Take a *dolmuş* labelled 'Adaağzı' from opposite Tansaş supermarket and get off at the last stop, then walk.

Water sports: There's water-skiing, canoeing, banana-boating, etc. at all the larger beaches.

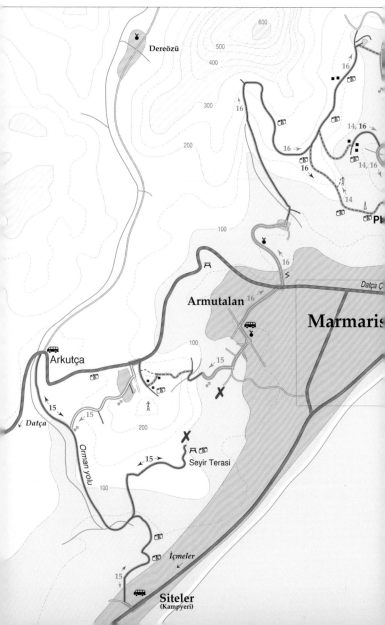

See also the town plan on pages 120-121.
Time: 2h40min
Grade: easy-moderate; reasonably good terrain underfoot; ascent of 200m
Equipment: see pages 21-22.
Travel: 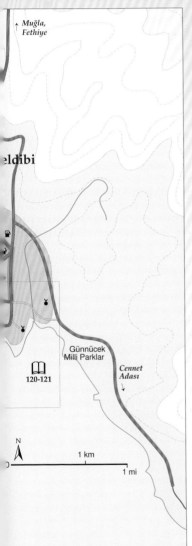 Catch the Beldibi *dolmuş* from Marmaris *dolmuş* station and note the start of the Beldibi road at traffic lights between the BP and Opet petrol stations (it is under 10 minutes on foot from this point to the start of the walk). Alight very shortly, about 300m past car workshops lining the road, near a cluster of short pylons on the right. Catch a return *dolmuş* or taxi at the same place.
Short walk: Physcus (1h; easy). Use this walk just to see something of Physcus and enjoy the fine views over Marmaris. Follow the main walk to the saddle (30min); return the same way.

Marmaris now occupies the site of ancient Physcus, a dependency of Rhodes, but little remains of that era — only some walls dating back to the Hellenistic period. These are set on a hillside overlooking Marmaris. They are overgrown with shrubs, and it's difficult to get close to them, but the compensation for the effort required is the splendid view over Marmaris. From here the route of the walk takes an interesting course, as it follows the line of a ridge of mountains separating Beldibi and Armutalan. The path switches from side to side along the ridge, with constantly changing views, before dropping down to Beldibi.

Start out where you leave the *dolmuş*: facing in the direction of Beldibi, turn left off the **Beldibi road** onto a narrow surfaced road (close to the **cluster of short pylons** on the right). Turn right, then veer right: ahead is the hill which hides ancient Physcus. The road crosses a **bridge** and then swings right, along the side of the valley. A few minutes later, just before the road dips and a track

The map includes the following labels:

Muğla, Fethiye

Beldibi

Günnücek Milli Parklar

Cennet Adası

120-121

N

1 km

1 mi

forks up left to a modern housing development, take a path forking up left along the rock-face, into woodland. The path follows a water pipe which you hurdle several times before it disappears into the shrubbery. As you wind up the hillside there is a small valley to the left, obscured for most of the time by foliage. Keep right at a couple of forks met a few minutes into the climb. If a brushwood gate is encountered, leave it as you found it.

Keep ahead as the path levels out, to reach a **saddle (30min)** with a terrific view of Marmaris, the sea and the islands. Looking left, you can see huge blocks of stone — remnants of the old Greek wall; sadly, these remains of **Physcus** are totally overgrown and unapproachable.

Leave the saddle by taking the uphill path to the right; it is not very clear at first, but it skirts to the left of the large rocky outcrop ahead. A couple of minutes later, the saddle comes into view just below. Keep heading up through a rocky area, with Marmaris Bay over to the left. The narrow path, edged with holly oak, leads towards another rocky outcrop on the left. The path passes to the right of the outcrop, from where there are good views to Physcus and the saddle. From here the path levels out a little, skirts a third rocky outcrop (on the right), and swings inland to a grassy meadow.

You now find yourself on a **ridge**, with Armutalan to the left and Beldibi on the right. From here, the onward route basically follows the line of the ridge. Head across the *yayla,* to follow the path along the left-hand

(Armutalan) side of the ridge, from where you can see the start of Walk 16. The path descends a little and continues towards a pylon ahead. Cross another saddle and pass close to the **pylon**, still traversing the left-hand side of the ridge. When the path forks just past the pylon, keep to the lower path, by the side of the ridge. The meadows are left behind now, as you enter light woodlands of pine, wild olive and holly oak. Keep uphill and reach another grassy saddle. Cross it diagonally and continue along the Beldibi side of the ridge. A minute later you emerge on a small *yayla* with a fine panorama over Beldibi, Physcus and Marmaris marina.

From here the path continues directly up the centre of the ridge, trailing fine views of Marmaris. As you reach the top of the ridge, bear slightly right and join a grassy track: it takes you down to a **main track (1h20min)**, where you turn right. *(Walk 16 joins here.)* From here on, the way back is all downhill. Just before a rocky outcrop on the right, take the faint **woodland track (1h25min)** which sweeps back down to the right. This shrinks to a path as it skirts to the right of a valley.

Head down into a cluster of farm buildings, turn left to join a track, and leave the farm through a gate. Initially, the track heads away from Marmaris, but it soon swings right and then down to the road. Turn right here. After 10 minutes you pass the path up to Physcus. When you reach the **Beldibi road (2h40min)**, wait for a *dolmuş* or passing taxi, or turn right and start walking back.

Walk 15: From Armutalan to Siteler

See map on pages 128-129.
Time: 3h
Grade: moderate; mainly on track; ascent of about 200m. The walk is in the Marmaris National Park, with information boards and maps (there is also a signposted trail to İçmeler).
Equipment: see pages 21-22.
Travel: 🚐 *dolmuş* from Marmaris to Armutalan, frequent departures, journey time about 10min; return from Siteler or İçmeler by any 🚐 *dolmuş* bound for Marmaris.
Short walks
1 Armutalan — Arkutca (2h15min; grade as main walk). Follow the main walk as far as the crossing track (1h45min), but turn right here to the Datça road at Arkutca (also called Arkutcha) and stop a passing *dolmuş* or coach returning to Marmaris. There is nothing at this point in the way of shade or refreshments.
2 Arkutca to Siteler (1h45min; easy). Catch a 🚐 *dolmuş* bound for Hisarönü, Orhaniye or Turgut or catch the Datça bus (all leave from the *otogar*). Ask to alight at

Arkutca (also called Arkutcha), in the bottom of the valley, after the descent over the hill from Marmaris. (This is where the road goes off right to Dereözü; see map pages 128-129). At the point where the road curves over the bottom of the valley, take the track forking down to the left. Follow it alongside the stream to the right. In under 30 minutes you pick up the main walk at the 1h45min-point (by a fountain on the corner, where the main walk track enters from the left). Follow the main walk to the end.
Alternative walk: Seyir Terasi (3h15min; moderate, with an overall ascent of 120m). Catch the 🚐 Siteler *dolmuş* and alight at the terminus. Continue along the main road towards İçmeler but, in a minute or less, look for a large wooden board on the right: *Yuruyus Yolu Sonu* ('end of the walking trail'). Head along the forestry track *(orman yolu)* to the right of the sign, *not* the tarmac road to the left. Follow the Kampyeri/ Seyir Terasi trail to a viewpoint and picnic spot, then return the same way.

Walks 15, 16: the liquidambar tree is endemic to Rhodes and southwest Anatolia. Its leaves are like those of the plane tree, and it occupies similar habitats.

Climbing the yayla *above the small stone building overlooking Armutalan*

This is a pleasing short walk which follows a forestry track (orman yolu) through quiet countryside and offers fantastic views of Marmaris along the way. One special feature of the walk is the liquidambar tree, Liquidambar orientalis, *which is endemic to Rhodes and southwest Anatolia. It is particularly common in the region around Marmaris and can be seen along many of the other walks in this area, as well as in Günnücek Milli Parklar just to the south of Marmaris. It is a member of the witch hazel family and is closely related to the American gum tree,* L styraciflua. *The name derives from 'liquid amber' and is a reference to the fragrant gum it produces, similar to the American gum tree, which is used in perfumery, as an expectorant, inhalant and in the treatment of skin diseases. Its leaves are rather like those of the plane tree, although generally smaller. It does tend to occupy similar habitats to the plane, by streams and rivers, in ravines and on flood plains, but they are not commonly seen growing together.*

Start the walk at the *dolmuş* station in **Armutalan** by heading south along the road, passing the *belediye* (council offices) and **mosque** on your left. You reach a large **roundabout** in a minute or so. Head right here, towards the road on the far side of the roundabout. A few minutes later, rise up and take the road off to the left, continuing to ascend. Just below the brow of the hill, turn sharp right into a narrow surfaced road ('Sinan Cad.'). Armutalan and the Datça road are now over to the right, as this road wends its way up the left-hand side of the valley. You reach a **fountain** on the left in 10 minutes or less; then the road reverts to track. A dry stream bed meets the track on a U bend five minutes later. Half a minute past here, head left up the hillside on a waymarked path/trail. This becomes very stony as it winds through the shrubbery, with the valley of the stream bed crossed earlier over on the left. Ever closer, on your right, is the

Datça road, but the traffic is mostly heard, rather than seen, and does little to disturb the tranquillity of your surroundings. Encroaching foliage may cause a moment's uncertainty some 10 minutes up, but press on uphill: the path/trail swings right and then left. Within five minutes, as the path/trail again swings to the right, go left and rise up onto a small *yayla* (meadow).

A stone building with sheet-metal roof perches at the bottom of the *yayla*, to your left, looking down over Armutalan. Turn right and head up the *yayla* towards a ruined hut; another ruined hut is now visible over to the left. Keeping to the left of the ruined hut ahead, cross a gully and ascend onto a woodland track. Turn right on the track and follow it to the **Datça road** (**55min**). (The path/trail joins here from the right.) Turn left, being wary of the traffic, as the road crests the brow of the hill. In half a minute, take the next track to the left. This track leads straight ahead to a small radio mast. Don't follow it up to the mast however; instead, soon take the motorable track forking down right towards a **small village**. Keep right as the track forks again on entering the village. The people here are friendly, and the village is an amazing microcosm of life before tourism … especially considering that it is so close to Marmaris. But it is not a museum, so please respect their privacy.

After you pass through the lower end of the village, the track sweeps right, alongside the valley on the right. A fountain is passed on the left. An open area, from where there are good views over the terrain ahead, is reached some five minutes later. Keep on the track as it bends round to the left. When the track forks (under 10 minutes beyond the open area), go down to the right, along the left-hand side of a wooded valley. The track turns sharp left about 10 minutes later and descends to a **crossing track** (**1h45min**), where you turn left. *(Short walk 1 goes right here; Short walk 2 joins here from the right.)* Liquidambar trees find a home in the stream bed along this track. Keep ahead along this pleasant woodland track *(orman yolu)* and ignore tracks off to the right, until you come to a fork of tracks in well under 20 minutes. (The left fork rises up 1.8km to the Seyir Terası viewpoint and picnic area which are visited in the Alternative walk, but a word of caution: the track beyond the viewpoint is *closed to the public*, although Armutalan and Marmaris appear close at hand.) The main walk forks *right* here, following the sign **'Kampyeri' (camp site)**. Rise up around the hillside, initially not far above the left-hand track. On reaching a high point, begin the descent towards Siteler. Good views to the Bay of Marmaris and Cennet Adası begin to appear through the trees, becoming more open as you descend, but disappear as the track snakes down through the wooded valley towards the sea. Emerging on the main Marmaris/İçmeler road at the bottom, turn left. In a minute you reach the *dolmuş* station at **Siteler** (**3h**), located on the same side of the road.

Walk 16: From Armutalan to Beldibi or Marmaris

See map on pages 128-129.
Time: 4h
Grade: moderate; almost entirely on forestry tracks which are good underfoot; ascent of just over 200m
Equipment: see pages 21-22.
Travel: 🚐 *dolmuş* from Marmaris to Armutalan, frequent departures; journey time around 10min; the walk ends in Marmaris, at the junction with the Datça road.
Alternative walks: This walk joins Walk 14 and, when you meet that route, two possibilities present themselves. Since they are of equal length, make your choice depending on your preference for walking on forestry tracks or on paths. The path walk demands some navigating skills.
1 Armutalan to Marmaris *mainly on forestry tracks* (3h40min; grade as main walk). Follow the main walk to the 2h05min-point, then pick up the notes for Walk 14 (from the 1h25min-point, see page 130) to walk down to Marmaris.
2 Armutalan to Marmaris *partly on paths* (3h45min; grade as main walk). Follow the main walk to the 2h-point, where Walk 14 comes in from the right. From here use the map to return to Marmaris following Walk 14 in reverse, referring to the notes for that walk if necessary.

*Rosy-hued, pine-clad hills form a green mantle around Marmaris. This walk explores with ease this seemingly impenetrable barrier. The number of rivers and streams in the whole of this region may come as a surprise to you — as well as the waterfalls along the walk, which passes through two distinct geolo-*gical areas. The landscape in the early part of the ramble shows barely a trace of the imprint of man; there are no signs of cultivation and no great profusion of wild flowers. Wild flowers give a clue — indeed many clues as you learn to read them — to the infertile nature of the soil generated by the underlying serpentine rock. Serpentines cover large tracts of this peninsula, from the area to the north of Marmaris and westward, sweeping down the Datça peninsula. Although the area is extensive, it is not always exclusively serpentine, and pockets of fertility (associated mainly with the limestone series of rocks) do occur. Villages and farming communities are few and far between in the serpentine region; usually regions of more fertile land of a different geology are cultivated. The high concentrations of metals like iron, magnesium, chromium and nickel from the serpentine render the soils infertile, and it is the high iron concentration that gives the rosy hue to the hills around Marmaris. Certain wild flowers are not only able to survive these soils, but actually flourish because of the lack of competition. The lovely cyclamen with the propeller-like flower, Cyclamen trochopteranthum, is one easily-recognised example of a flower which is only found on the serpentine soils in this region and, similarly, the liquidambar tree survives competition on this substrate. Should you find bee orchids or the evergreen Cupressus trees, then you have definitely wandered back into a limestone region ... and you could be near the end of the walk.*

Start the walk at the *dolmuş* station in **Armutalan**. Facing the Royal Plaza Hotel opposite, turn right and follow the road round to the right, to join the **Datça road** in a little over 10 minutes. Keep ahead, back in the direction of Marmaris, and take the first road on the left a few minutes later. Follow this road past an **electricity sub-station** on the right and go past a new **mosque** as the road contours round the hillside. When the road sweeps sharply back toward the sea, turn left past new developments, beyond which the road reverts to track. Just after passing a white house on the right, you cross a stream bed. Stay on the main track, heading up an isolated valley. Masses of oleander paint the banks of the stream a cheerful pink down on your left and, all around, the tall yellow spikes of the mullein vie for attention. The track starts to rise higher above the stream on the left, and in winter and spring there is the sound of water tripping over small waterfalls. There are larger **waterfalls** ahead along this delightful woodland track. Liquidambar trees add a splash of bright green by the water and confirm that this early part of the walk is taking you through a region of serpentine rock. Eventually your route swings right into an ascending loop (ignore the track off left). You head back in the direction of the coast, with your outward track down to the right.

A sharp left turn in the track leads you away from the waterfall valley, as you continue parallel with the coast, through beautiful woodland and past meadows. Reach the **high point of the walk** (**1h45min**) and start into a gradual descent. Walk 14 joins this walk briefly, at the

point where a grassy track comes in from a **knoll on the right** (**2h**; just before the track swings left). (*Alternative walk 2 descends to Marmaris here.*) Keep to the main track, to pass a **rocky outcrop** five minutes later (**2h05min**). (*Alternative walk 1 descends to Marmaris here.*) Fine views open out over Beldibi's valley below. The track heads north now, leading you away from Marmaris and keeping the Beldibi valley down on the right for quite some time. A small group of buildings is passed as the track weaves along the side of this lovely valley.

When you reach the **access drive to some apartments on the right** (**2h35min**), look for a waymarked path off right just 12 paces along the drive. (This is just 50m before a junction of tracks, where the left fork rises to meet a tarmac road and a right turn leads down and round back in the direction of Marmaris.) Follow this path down to meet the tarmac road and turn right.

Now heading towards Marmaris along the right-hand side of the **Beldibi valley**, you pass a **fountain** on the right. At a fork under 20 minutes past the fountain, keep right uphill. You pass the point where the track from Walk 14 joins on the right and, 10 minutes later, the **path up to Physcus** (Walk 14). Reach the junction with the **Beldibi road** (**3h35min**). You can wait here for a *dolmuş* or passing taxi. Or turn right, back to Marmaris (note that some shops among the car workshops sell drinks). In less than 10 minutes you reach the petrol stations on the main road. Go right here, into **Marmaris** (**4h**).

5 AROUND MARMARIS AND THE BOZBURUN PENINSULA

İçmeler • Turunç • Amos and Kumlubükü Bay • Bozburun Peninsula

Area code: (0252
Connections: Vary from very good (to İçmeler and Turunç) to fairly good (to Bozburun); other-

wise nil. See details with individual entries.
Walks: 17-19 (Walks 11-16 are nearby).

The landscape around Marmaris is just delightful — particularly the inviting Bozburun Peninsula (named after its largest village), with its isolated bays and villages, forests, and valleys where trout jump about in the streams. There are also some idyllic spots in the Gulf of Gökova, north of Marmaris (see page 105). As a rule of thumb, the further out you go from Marmaris, the more pleasant and tranquil the surroundings.

İçmeler

The Muğla Tourist Board tells visitors that 'In bygone days there was allegedly healing water in İçmeler, but don't try looking for it now, stick with bottled mineral water'. By the same token, İçmeler was once an unimportant village at the western edge of Marmaris Bay. But don't expect that today; with its 10,000 inhabitants, İçmeler is a busy holiday centre. Its beach used to be an unspoilt paradise, today it's a forest of sunshades with hardly anywhere to put down a towel. İçmeler is very popular with British package tourists, many of whom stay in the identikit (but very well-equipped) hotels and never make it further than the beach, where there is a large selection of water sports, or the beachside cafés. For those who want to see more, various tour operators and car and two-wheel hire firms from Marmaris have branches here.

Connections: A *dolmuş* runs to Marmaris every 10 minutes from 07.30-01.30; the last stop is in the south side of the bay. But the trip

by **water** *dolmuş* is much prettier (every 30 minutes, £3.75). There are also taxi boats to Amos, Kumlubükü and Çiftlik.

Accommodation: While there are a great many hotels, most cannot be recommended for individual travellers since they are pre-booked by (mostly British) tour operators.

Food and drink: There's a lot on offer in the centre. A top tip is the **Mona Titti** restaurant, sign-posted on the road to Turunç. This tranquil, jasmin-scented place has a pleasant terrace and tables around a little pool. They serve tempting dishes like 'spaghetitti', 'chicken titts' and 'Moby's Dick' — let them surprise you! Everything is simply beguiling (about 20 people a year come here to pro-pose marriage, and no one's been turned down yet). It's best to book ((4554046). Open from 19.00; they can collect you from your hotel. It's not cheap, but no more expensive than the restau-rants on the promenade in Marmaris. And while you're

View to İçmeler from Marmaris

having an apéritif, don't forget to read the 'History of Mona Titti'!
Nightlife: The 'in' place at time of writing was the open-air **Pleasure Disco**; they have a double-decker bus that brings people from the centre.
Market: On Wednesdays there is a big **market** on Çevre Yolu (the road to Turunç and Datça).

Turunç

Turunç is the Turkish name for a type of bitter orange. But compared with Marmaris or İçmeler, Turunç is quite sweet. This once-tiny fishing village, now with 2500 inhabitants, is still very laid back — despite the fact that over recent years it's been caught up in tourism more than any other place in the area. Located south of İçmeler on a long bay with some fine-sand sections, the village is no longer only a day trip destination, but increasingly a popular place to stay, especially among Dutch and British package holidaymakers. Very comfortable resorts have been built to the left, the right and above the bay. But there are also smaller, simpler and friendly places to stay. Cumhuriyet Caddesi, the main street behind the beach, becomes a pedestrian zone in the evening. Here's where you'll find jewellers and carpet dealers, bars and travel agencies.
Connections: A *dolmuş* runs to Marmaris every 30 minutes. In the summer there are **water dolmuşes** almost hourly to Marmaris and İçmeler, and once a day to Amos, Kumlubükü and Çiftlik.
Accommodation
The **International Academy Marmaris**, above Turunç, is a place for creative visitors near the Loryma Resort hotel complex (they fetch you with a tractor-shuttle). It's an art and culture centre where you can also stay overnight. The complex was set

up by Turkish artists and has workshops and an even an amphitheatre. You can breakfast by the pool listening to classical music. There are 23 very pleasant rooms with bath, most with balcony. Since IAM is a non-profit organisation, it's all very economical. Double rooms with H/B £39, singles £25. (4767081, www.akademionline.net.

İffet Hotel, a friendly hotel in a quiet spot on the north side of the bay and only separated from the bay by its own pool. 31 large bright rooms with tiled floors, half of which have a sea view. Per person £18 with breakfast. (4767040, www.iffethotel.com.

Hotel Han, right on the sea. 15 plain, but tidy and clean rooms with climate control — those in the front with fantastic sea views. Delightful terrace with restaurant. Friendly service. Double rooms with breakfast £19. (4767006, (4767021.

Şule Pansiyon, on the shoreside road. It's a wonder that this guest house hasn't been made into an expensive hotel. The rooms (with bath) are spartan, so the place would be nothing special were it not for the beautiful terrace overlooking the sea. One can only hope that this 'fossilised guest house' will stay in business for some time yet! Double rooms £11; no breakfasts available, but there are shared kitchen facilities. (4767314. If no one is there, ask at the Burak Supermarket 100m inland.

Food and drink

Dionysos Sea Club, near the İffet Hotel on the north side of the bay. Really lovely garden restaurant under old trees by the water's edge. Small, well-chosen menu with high prices (fish carpaccio £6.25, giant prawns with garlic £9.50). (4767832. The **Aydede Beach Café** next door is simpler, cheaper and has very good grilled fish.

Arcade, on the main through road. Very popular and with good reason. Well-kept, high-quality local with terrace, decent music and very pleasant service.

Sometimes you have to work quite hard for the best views, as here on Walk 19 between İçmeler and Turunç.

A huge choice: apart from simple casseroles, *pide* and pizza, there are tasty starters and fantastic *güveç* variations. Wait for a surprise at the end of your meal! Main courses £2.75-7. ✆ 4767372. **Sürmen**, on Cumhuriyet Cad., is another well-kept place where you eat on a lovely terrace by the sea. The speciality is oven-roasted lamb. Otherwise there are Turkish dishes and the standard international fare at tourist prices.

Nightlife: Nightlife is focused on several music bars — especially **Fidan** on the main road behind the beach. It has a restaurant facing the sea and terrace facing the road (sometimes with foot-ball on TV). Readers call it a really nice disco, open till 4am in season.

Practicalities A-Z

Car and two-wheel hire: **Star Moto** on Cumhuriyet Cad, the main street, has scooters from £17.50 per day and cars from £25. ✆ 4767286, ✆ 4767286.

Organised tours: Various companies offer the same coach and bus tours as in Marmaris.

Water sports: Everything is on offer, from jet skis to parasailing.

Amos and Kumlubükü Bay

From Turunç a side road heads south, high above the coast. After a few kilometres a narrow little road branches off to the left, and goes steeply downhill to small, beautiful **Amos Bay**. First you pass the little holiday homes belonging to the staff from the universities of Marmara and Anadolu, then you come to the sand and shingle beach, just 100m long, where you can hire sunshades and sunbeds, and enjoy a meal at the good restaurant.

If you ignore this turn-off to Amos, you soon pass **Asarcık Hill**, which separates Amos Bay from Kumlubükü Bay. On top of the hill lie the stony remnants of **ancient Amos**. Surrounded by the impressive remains of the **town wall**, are a **temple** in quite poor condition and a fairly well-preserved **theatre**. Apollo, who was called Samnaios in this area, was the city's god.

In **Kumlubükü Bay** an enormous, unwalled villa immediately comes into view — it belongs to the chairman of the Garanti Bankası. Otherwise the bay hasn't much to offer, as its shingle beach isn't among the most beautiful in the area. There are some restaurants and accom-modation.

Approximately two kilometres south of the bay, you can visit a cave — ask someone to point the way out to you.

Connections: Between 10.30 and 13.00 **taxi boats** make the trip from Turunç and İçmeler to Amos, heading back at 17.00.

Bozburun Peninsula

By *dolmuş* the bays and villages on the Bozburun Peninsula are either inaccessible or hard to reach; Bozburun is an exception.

Bozburun

The sleepy little town of Bozburun is about 54km from Marmaris and has long been a centre for boat-building. In recent years the place has had a bit of a face-lift, in order to catch the attention of the lucrative tourist trade. In the hopes of attracting the yachting fraternity, they have built a new marina and eschewed hotel blocks. So the place has retained some charm and authenticity; it's a peaceful spot with a relaxed little esplanade. At time of writing only one carpet place had set up shop.

Connections: There are buses from Marmaris up to six times a day.

Accommodation: There is a good choice of simple, friendly guest houses and hotels along the shore promenade. But most visitors to Bozburun spend the night on their yachts. One good place to stay is the **Hotel Möwe** at the port: just six rooms with bath in 'South American style' — colourful walls, rag rugs, and sea-shell decorations. Simple but quite adorable. The three upstairs rooms have balconies with wonderful sea views. A good local restaurant is next door. Double rooms with breakfast £20. (4562661, www.moewe-tr.com.

Sabrinas Haus, is an exceptional place in an isolated position near Bozburun. A 20-room complex under Turkish/German management, far from the madding crowd. Pleasant, large rooms, wonderful garden. Classical music with breakfast, well-stocked library, fireplace nook, restaurant with both international and Turkish cuisine, kitchen priviliges and some other amenities. It's important to book ahead — best done before you leave home.

They will send you brochures. Double rooms with breakfast (in high season) £26-40 per person. (4562045, (4562470, www.sabrinas-haus.com (the site is also in English). Access: It's signposted at the entrance to Bozburun, but you cannot reach it by car. You can only drive as far as the Hotel Mete, from where it's another 15 minutes on foot — or telephone them, and they will send a boat to collect you.

Food and drink: The quality of the **restaurants** is good everywhere; to single out any in particular would not be fair. In the evening a good spot is the **Bar Arşipel** 200m south of the port, a nice 'world music bar' (as they style themselves) in a stone-walled building with a roof terrace. Usually live music, some places to go for a swim.

Söğütköy

Apart from Bozburun, the villages on the Bozburun Peninsula are predominantly farming or fishing communities — or both. For example, one half of Söğütköy is located high up on a hillside with fabulous views over the coast as far as Symi, while the other half lies on quiet **Saranda Bay**.

Accommodation, food and drink: Just at the Kızılyer boat dock in Söğütköy is the **Aşkın Pension** (signposted). You could hardly find anywhere more quiet and peaceful. Aside from a couple of yachts which come in by mistake, there is simply no traffic. 12 very well kept rooms with bath, some with a little garden in front. The place is only 20m from the sea but, unfortunately, there's no sandy beach. Double rooms with breakfast and climate control £46.50. The adjacent **Octopus Restaurant**, idyllically located at the water's edge, is an excellent place for fish. (4965047, askinpension@hotmail.com.

If Aşkin is full, another good guest house is the **Saranda Pansiyon** right at the southern end of the bay (also signposted). Under Dutch/Turkish management, nice garden, also right on the sea. (4965057, (4965088.

From Söğütköy to Selimiye Bay

In the south of the peninsula, where the pine forests are replaced by barren landscape, you can walk from the forgotten village of **Taşlıca** with its space-age mosque to the ancient ruins of **Loryma** (ask someone to show you where the path begins; it's quite a long walk). Surviving remains include, among other things, the walls of a fortress built to protect **Bozukkale Bay**, a popular stopping point on 'blue cruises'.

Heading north, there is the sleepy town of **Bayırköy**, where the men gather in the teahouses around an (allegedly) 2000-year-old plane tree. To amuse themselves — since nothing much ever happens here — they fixed a sign to the tree to the effect that anyone who walks around it will have a lucky life. At first they used to have a good laugh watching tourists circle the tree, but now they no longer pay much attention.

Past Bayırköy you come to delightful **Çiftlik Bay**, which has one of the best beaches around Marmaris. Sadly it is no longer the idyll it once was; today there are just too many visitors — an armada of boats sails in from Marmaris, disgorging several thousands of tourists every day … frightening the Russians and Germans who stay at what is so far the only hotel. To beef up this small outpost of tourism, new resorts will be built.

Turgutköy is a popular stopping point for jeep safaris and the coach excursions usually called the 'Visit Turkey Tour'. These tours promise a visit to a typically Turkish village; it doesn't take much imagination to realise this means one where carpets are sold… But the tour usually includes a stop at the nearby waterfalls (signposted as 'Şelale'). Don't expect too much here either: in summer the roar of the falls is little more than the flush of a domestic toilet. The water collects in several small pools, where you can swim. There are several trout restaurants along the stream.

Selimiye Bay

The landscape around **Selimiye Bay** is beautiful, with the ruins of an old castle towering above. This bay lovely to look at, but beaches are in short supply. Instead there are seaside restaurants. In recent years a few hotels have been built here, in the form of small, charming houses rather than blocks.

Accommodation, food and drink: The **Beyaz Güvercin Hotel**, in the western part of the bay stands out for its lovely garden with hammocks, palms and a play area for children. The 20 rooms, on the other hand, are nothing special — but OK. There's a small beach and little jetties out over the sea for sunbathing. Double rooms with breakfast £49.50. (4464274, www. beyazguvercin.com.

Sardunya is a first-class fish restaurant with a romantic terrace right on the sea. Fantastic Aegean cooking with the best olive oil. Good service; high prices. The restaurant also rents out rooms and bungalows (double room with breakfast £26). (4464003, (4464286.

Beside these, there is also a **row of simple, cheap guest houses** in the village.

Orhaniye Bay

There's a marina at the entrance to this fjord-like bay, but yachts trying to get further in have to take great care, as there is a sand bank just below the surface of the water.

Accommodation, food and drink:
There are a few simple places to stay. **Zuhal Restaurant**, near the marina, is a favourite with yachtsmen. Tasty salads, top-quality fish, quite pricey.

Hisarönü Bay

This bay has a long, narrow and somewhat untidy beach backed by a few scattered guest houses, hotels and campsites.

Accommodation/camping:
Club Rena is a lovely place in an idyllic setting, opened in 2003. It's a mini-resort — just 5 very pleasant bungalows (with bath, tiled floors and large windows and glass sliding doors); another 5 bungalows will be added. In front of the complex is a pool, restaurant (excellent food at good prices), palm trees and the sea. Laid-back atmosphere, highly recommended. Double room with breakfast £28. (4666096 or (0536-6267806 (mobile). Can be seen at www.içmeleronline.com.
Hisar Camping, is a shaded site only separated from the sea by their beach bar. 2 people with camper van £3.75. May-Oct.

Seafront promenade at Marmaris, where Walk 17 begins

See plan of Marmaris on pages 120-121 to begin the walk and the map on page 146 to end it.
Time: 3h (or as long as it takes)
Grade: easy. The main Marmaris/İçmeler road is never too far away, and a *dolmuş* or taxi is easily accessed at many points for a quick return.
Equipment: just comfortable footwear and sun protection. Food and drink are available all along the route.
Travel: ⚓ water taxis and 🚐 *dolmuşes* ply between Marmaris and İçmeler (and Turunç, but less frequently outside high season).

The promenade between Marmaris and İçmeler provides a traffic-free walking route with a diversity of scenery and interest along the way. At the Marmaris end, all is hustle and bustle with cafés/restaurants and souvenir shops cheek by jowl, but they dwindle out as you progress away from the centre. For much of the way, the promenade edges the shore, so there are plenty of opportunities to sit on the beach and absorb the activity in Marmaris Bay, stop for a swim or engage in an assortment of water activities. Pine woods invade the shoreline on the approach to İçmeler, giving a rural feel to the surroundings, while the setting of sandy İçmeler beach is incentive enough to linger awhile. This is a walk which can be savoured by all, with the chance to opt out at any point along the way. It can be joined at any point between Marmaris and İçmeler but, for the benefit of those travelling into Marmaris from other resorts, this brief description starts in Marmaris.

Start the walk from any point on the **promenade** at **Marmaris** by going right when facing the sea,
walking away from the marina. Initially, the promenade is accompanied by the main road but soon forks off left, away from the traffic (just before reaching the Hotel Selen). The first few kilometres, which skirt the deep straggle of tourist accommodation behind the shore, are lively and congested with plenty of interesting distractions. Towards the end of the Marmaris seafront, as the density of building declines, and pine trees edge the promontory separating İçmeler from Marmaris, a gentler ambience prevails. Those who wish to beat a retreat to the main road need to consider doing so before this point is reached, as the main road becomes less accessible for a while. This last section is the most delightful of all. The promenade meanders amongst shady pine trees where scattered café/bars offer a chance to sit and enjoy the view.
İçmeler comes into view once the headland is rounded, sitting at the back of a deep bay. It is hard to imagine being able to find a foothold along the steep green slopes of the hills across the bay here — but Walk 19 from Turunç finds a way!
On reaching **İçmeler**, the promenade continues left, to pass behind the beach with its facilities. The main road, from where it is possible to catch a *dolmuş* to Turunç or back to Marmaris, is close by to the right at this point. (You are also close to the starting point for Walk 18 here.) But the *dolmuş* for Marmaris actually *starts* from the far side of the beach, which is the best place to board at busy times, as they leave when they are full.

143

Walk 18: From İçmeler to Turunç

Time: under 4h
Grade: strenuous, with a fairly steep ascent of some 425m; mainly on paths which are often stony and overgrown in places. *Only recommended for keen hikers with route-finding experience (and perhaps secateurs!); Walk 19 is a far more straightforward option.*
Equipment: see pages 21-22.
Travel: 🚐 *dolmuş* from Marmaris to İçmeler, frequent departures, journey time about 20min. Another option is to catch the *dolmuş* to Turunç (less frequent out of season, so check at the *dolmuş* station), and start the walk at the 'Turkish House'. For the return from Turunç you can either catch a 🚐 *dolmuş* or 🛥 water taxi; access points for both (with timetables for the water taxis) are located by the mosque on the main street. Both offer a frequent service to İçmeler and Marmaris during the season. 🚖 Taxis are also found in the same location. Out of season, options are: 1) occasional *dolmuş* to İçmeler/Marmaris (check at the Marmaris *dolmuş* station); 2) taxi to İçmeler, then *dolmuş* to Marmaris.

This walk between İçmeler and Turunç is probably a very old route dating from long before the road was built. It is still partly used and kept open by the local womenfolk, who climb up almost daily to cut and gather branches from the strawberry trees. The cuttings are used as fodder for cows. The road follows an easier, but longer route to Turunç.
There is a straightforward division in this walk. The first part is constantly uphill, through delightful woodland that hides a host of interesting flowers, and the second part is steadily downhill with a

bird's-eye view over Turunç. Some of the flowers to be seen on the walk include three endemic species unknown outside southwest Anatolia: Cyclamen trochopteranthum grows in profusion in places, but you can only see its propeller-like pink flowers in early spring; Fritillaria sibthorpiana, which is a lovely spring-flowering fritillary with a pendulous bell-shaped flower in bright buttercup yellow, is best identified by its broad, grey-green lower leaf; Fritillaria forbesii is named after the British botanist Edward Forbes, who discovered this species in 1842 (it is also a spring-flowering yellow fritillary, but one with very narrow leaves). And there is yet a third yellow fritillary around, Fritillaria bithynica.

Alight from the *dolmuş* by the taxi rank on the right, as soon as it turns left into the wide road which runs behind **İçmeler**. (If you are travelling on Turunç *dolmuş*, it keeps ahead at this junction, so ask to alight at the 'Turkish House' restaurant and cafe/bar, located where the buildings are left behind and the road starts to wind up the wooded hillside over to Turunç. Then pick up the notes below at the 35min-point.) **Start the walk** by going along the road to the right of the **taxi rank**, with the **Atatürk memorial** on your right. In two-three minutes turn left opposite the **school** (*okul*). Keep left at the fork a few minutes later. Apartments now line the route which heads towards the old village of İçmeler. Follow the road through **old İçmeler** (**15min**), passing the mosque and then the bakery, both on the right. Towering rocks, decked in blue campanula, and a beautiful natural rock garden, on the left, brighten the way.

Keep ahead as the main road to Turunç joins from the right, following signs to the 'Turkish House' restaurant and cafe/bar. Soon a minor surfaced road goes off to the left, and on your right is the **'Turkish House'** (**35min**). *(Those travelling on the Turunç dolmuş join the walk here.)* Continue along the road towards Turunç, passing another minor surfaced road off left to a small factory. A few minutes later the road swings right to begin its ascent over the hill; turn half-left here on a path heading into the woods (about 50 paces past the 'Caution of fire' sign). This path runs up the edge of the escarpment and passes the **factory**. After about 100m you pass **three big stones**; after the last stone, fork slightly right, *downhill*. The initially faint path now moves off left, becoming stronger as you head up the valley. Woodlands soon close around the path where *Fritillaria sibthorpiana* graces the way with its dainty nodding bells, as it does at many stations along this climb. The path continues in a winding ascent, sometimes revealing views back down towards İçmeler. While the path is generally easy to follow, sometimes you may be uncertain about the direction. Watch for switchbacks — for instance, some 40 minutes uphill it heads sharply left (where the tendency is to continue straight on). After this sharp turn the ascent gets even steeper, and the path zigzags. Encroaching foliage from storax, strawberry trees and prickly holly oak sometimes

obscures the bends of the path but, once you brush (or cut!) it aside, the way is obvious. Eventually you approach **a high point in a scree-like area** (**1h35min** or so), where the path ascends in a zigzag. The scree is soon crossed and the way is easier going as you reach a more level, open area about eight minutes later. Continue as the path bears left and then right, heading to the right of a just-discernable **white rock** (about 2m high). Unusual amongst the flowers here is the white form of the orchid *Dactylorhiza romana*, normally found in shades of pink or yellow. Keep a tree-filled gully over to your right as the path rises more steeply again, until a **junction of paths** is encountered (**2h**).

Turn right here and continue on an almost-level path, towards a valley scattered with large white rocky outcrops. Wild iris catch the eye along this undulating section of woodland path, which ends about 12 minutes later at a cutting. Here you meet a track. Turn left to follow the track through the cutting, to an entirely different viewpoint over meadows. Continue to descend along the track, until you join the **Bozburun road** (**2h25min**), where you go left. Stay ahead through the cutting a minute later, when the road to Bozburun goes off right. Turunç is down below, but pine trees block the view.

From here the road winds down through a series of extended loops, but a path descends more directly, crossing the road several times on the way down. Once through the cutting, as the road

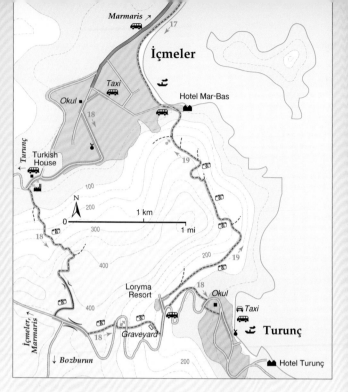

swings right, look on the left for the first part of the path. *Care is needed* negotiating this steep path which descends through the woods. On meeting the road again, turn left and, now with a clear view down over Turunç, look for the path which soon goes down sharp right (beneath power lines). It is a small shale path, which keeps above a concrete-roofed building and through olive groves. Emerging onto the road once more, by a fountain, cross straight over to continue along a stony track which later becomes a walled-in path. Skirt round the **graveyard** on the right and follow a line of pylons towards a building, then keep right to meet the road.

Follow the road to the left downhill, passing the entrance to the **Loryma Resort Apartments** (the start of Walk 19) on the left. When you reach a sharp right-hand bend, take the path off left, to again reach the road. Keeping left, barely touch the road before continuing into a fairly steep descent. This is a very rock-strewn section, and it is easier to walk down the olive grove on the right. Nearing the road again, move diagonally right, away from the rocky area (a high embankment limits access to the road at this point). Head along the road now, above a building with the sign 'Physkos', a bus shelter and a pylon, to locate the path which leads down left into the **school** yard.

Cross the school yard to the right and join the track which leads back onto the road. Turn right and keep ahead to the **mosque** in the centre of **Turunç (4h)**.

See map opposite
Time: 3h15min
Grade: moderate-strenuous, with an ascent of about 230m; way-marked throughout with orange flashes
Equipment: see pages 21-22
Travel: 🚐 hourly *dolmuş* to Turunç during the season (ask to be dropped off at Loryma Resort), or 🚤 water taxi from the waterfront at Marmaris (near the old town), then either take a taxi or walk to Loryma Resort (see map). Out of season options: limited *dolmuş* service between İçmeler and Turunç (check at the *dolmuş* station); alternatively, *dolmuş* to İçmeler and then taxi to Turunç (12km; alight by the taxi rank as you enter İçmeler; see the start of Walk 18). Return on 🚐 *dolmuş* from İçmeler, or 🚤 water taxi in season

Undreamed of views and solitude are the reward for the intrepid who defy the seemingly impregnable hill separating Turunç from İçmeler. Hidden amongst the foliage, which clings tenaciously to the craggy hillside, an old waymarked footpath forges an adventurous route along the contours. It has its gentler touches however, with grassy areas and, in autumn, splashes of colour from the Cyclamen hederifolium. *Surprisingly, there are no vertiginous sections, despite the steep slopes encountered at times along the way.*

Leave the *dolmuş* as it nears the end of its descent into **Turunç**, at the entrance to the road to the **Loryma Resort Apartments**. **Start the walk** by heading along the road towards the apartments. Then take the first concrete road off to the right (about six minutes along), to pass the tennis courts.

Keep ahead as the road reverts to track and then becomes a woodland path by a tree marked with a daub of **orange paint**. At the fork a minute or two later, take the *lower path to the right* (although it seems the less likely option). Continue through the woods — with some lovely views to enjoy down over Turunç. Orange waymarks guide you round the contour of the hillside. Then the path heads uphill, to rise to the top of a ridge. Go left here, and ignore another way-marked path which descends ahead. You are now on the İçmeler side of the ridge.

At a division in the path about six minutes later, keep left uphill, climbing steeply. In 15 minutes you will find yourself looking back down on Turunç. Notice how the route so far has almost completed a U around the contour and along the ridge, with Loryma Resort below. Soon after-wards you reach a **high point** and catch your breath with a wander through pine woods. There is time now to enjoy some fairly level walking through woodland, gaining a first view of İçmeler through the trees. You emerge from the woods into a more grassy and open area, with İçmeler still in sight. Five-six minutes later you find yourself looking down over the entrance to Marmaris Bay.

A little over 20 minutes from the Marmaris Bay view, the path appears to go straight ahead, but instead turns up to the left. The next 15 minutes or so comprise the **steepest part of the walk**, sometimes involving a little scrambling up the hillside. At the top of this ascent, begin to head

This walk affords some splendid views towards the bays and Marmaris.

downhill on a woodland path made slippery underfoot by leaves. There are some particularly magnificent panoramas towards Marmaris now, as the path climbs again, and İçmeler is

148

suddenly much closer. As the path decends again, you come to a fork: keep left uphill. The ridge ahead now blocks İçmeler from view. Some 15 minutes from the last fork, the path divides again: again keep left uphill, aiming for the dip in the ridge ahead. Crest the ridge and continue on the path ahead; İçmeler's beach is quite close below you. Soon after passing a **well** on the left, you reach a fork: descend the steep woodland path, to emerge on a saddle under 10 minutes later. The final descent is down a very stony path to the right. Not far down this path, the easier route is the path off to the right alongside a stream bed (keeping ahead here leads to a shale slope with access to the road). The path to the right emerges in a chicken run. Keep ahead, along the right-hand side of the run, to meet the road. A left turn here, opposite Hotel Mar-Bas, quickly leads to **İçmeler** beach and the *dolmuş* **terminus (3h15min).**

6 DATÇA AND THE REŞADIYE PENINSULA

Between Marmaris and Datça • Datça • Bays around Datça • Knidos

Area code: ℂ 0252
Information: Datça's Tourist Office operates in summer in a small wooden house on Cumhuriyet Meydanı (daily from 08.30-20.00); in winter it's in the Hükümet Konağı (government building) near Atatürk Cad. (Mon.-Fri. from 08.00-12.00 and from 13.00-17.00). ℂ/ℂ 7123546.
Connections: Regular **buses** to Marmaris from 07.00-21.00 (1h30min; about £2.50). For all further destinations on the south coast you must transfer in Marmaris or Muğla. Datça's bus station lies somewhat outside the centre, on the road into town, but most bus companies have branches in the centre. *Dolmuş:* Up to 6 *dolmuşes* run every day to Palamutbükü and Mesudiye (Hayıtbükü and Ovabükü), in winter once a day. One way £1.15. Note: On Sundays connections are very bad! The *dolmuş* station is on Atatürk Cad.
Taxis: There is a stand at Datça's *dolmuş* station (among others). A trip to Knidos, with a one-hour stop costs £37 — horrendous! Mesudiye one way £15, Palamutbükü £17.
Walks: Walk 20, circuit of Knidos

The sparsely populated Reşadiye Peninsula is a long and narrow strip of land stretching into the sea west of Marmaris. At the tip of the peninsula are the ruins of the ancient city of Knidos. Driving there you come upon many unspoilt bays — among the most beautiful in the area.

Not long ago the only way to Datça, the main town on the peninsula, was via a hilly road with endless hairpins, a test for both driver and car. Now the road has been improved, so all you need is some patience. On the way you have constantly changing views of wild ravines, turquoise-blue bays and steep, bare rock cliffs. Many of the villages en route are still caught in a time-warp, natural and unspoilt — especially when compared with Marmaris! Even Datça, with its 10,000 or so inhabitants, is still a quiet little town. The isolation of the peninsula has long been a deterrent to the development of touristic infrastructure. Whether the improved road will bring change remains to be seen. For those who enjoy camping, the Reşadiye is ideal: a whole collection of beautiful camp-sites lies between Marmaris and Emecik.

Between Marmaris and Datça

If you drive west from Marmaris, for quite a distance you pass little more than a couple of turnings to remote bays. Inviting campsites draw the eye (see below). You could say that the holiday centre of **Aktur** marks the end of the 50km-long 'camping stretch'; its beautiful beach is visible from the road. Some 8km further on, the small town of Emecik clings to a slope on the right. It's of no

149

particular interest for tourists. The **Bay of Karaincir**, 3km further along the coast, with its flat sandy beach, is equally uninteresting for foreigners, since it's usually populated with Turkish holidaymakers staying in their summer homes behind the eponymous village. About

1km beyond Karaincir Bay, however, is the kilometre-long, undeveloped sandy beach of **Gebekum**: the best-kept and most beautiful part of this beach is the eastern end (take the left turn to the classy Sunsail Perili Club). From here it's still approximately 14km to Datça.

Datça

Datça, the main settlement on the Reşadiye Peninsula, is a small, friendly coastal town, which still has little in common with the mass tourism of the large neighbouring towns of Bodrum to the north or Marmaris to the east.

Located 76km west of Marmaris, it is particularly popular with the yachting fraternity. The small marina is always busy, and a charming ensemble of bars, restaurants and souvenir shops has accumulated around it. The outlying areas look very different — hotels are springing up in an effort to emulate the holiday metropoli of Marmaris or Bodrum. If Datça is not careful, its frenetic building activity will scare off those who have been attracted to the place for its simplicity and friendliness. So far, however, it's just small beer relative to the large tourist centres. Symptomatic of this is the wholly undeveloped art of touting in front of restaurants — there are virtually no touts to be seen.

Datça, with its lack of culturally interesting historical sites, is trying to be proactive by building a museum which will accommo- date finds from Knidos. The plan is to build it on the end of the promontory near the amphi- theatre — but the plans have been on the drawing board for years…

So far only a few holidaymakers stray to **Eski Datça** (Old Datça), an idyllic village with narrow cobbled lanes, from which the coastal town got its name. Old Datça, approximately 2km inland from the coast, is worth a visit; there are even friendly places for an overnight stay.

Accommodation/camping
(see plan on page 152)
If money is no object, go to www. kocaev.com and read about the new boutique museum hotel, **Mehmet Ali Aga Mansion**, with double rooms from £115-310 per night (5km from Datça, not on the plan).

Villa Carla (16) is a delightful place to stay — a new building somewhat outside the centre, signposted off the road to Kargı Bay. 18 individual, lovingly decorated rooms, some with 200- year-old tiles. Book one of the rooms with balcony and sea view! Pool, super terrace, private pebble beach. Friendly, young staff. Advance booking recom- mended. Double rooms £35-37 with breakfast. ✆ 7122029, www. villacarladatca.com.

Datça Bay

Villa Tokur (16), near Villa Carla. Another little villa, also highly recommended and signposted off the road to Kargı Bay. German/Turkish management. 13 very pleasant rooms with cast-iron framed beds, plus 2 apartments for a maximum of 4 people. All with balconies, air-conditioning and central heating. Welcoming pool area. Open all year. Double rooms with breakfast £26, apartment £39.50. ℂ 7128728, www.hotel-tokur.com.

Hotel Luna (15), in the south-western part of Taşlık Bay. Nice building about 250m from the sea; 19 rooms with pale wooden furniture. Roof terrace, pool. Double rooms with breakfast £20 including breakfast. ℂ 7122001.

Huzur Pansiyon (10), guest house with a shady courtyard above the harbour. 19 simple and somewhat worn but clean rooms with en suite facilities, small balconies, climate control and fridge. Shared kitchen. Also 4 apartments for 2-5 people. Only 'down' side: some rooms are very near the minaret's loudspeaker. Double rooms with breakfast £19, apartments, depending on size, £19-29.50. Mevki Cami Arkası, ℂ 7123364, ℂ 7123052.

Yavuz Apart Otel (3), very friendly, well-run place between the *dolmuş* station and the sea. 8 apartments with large, very clean and well equipped rooms, all with climate control, good bathrooms and balconies. Half the apartments have sea views. Family atmosphere. Apartments for up to 4 people £35. Readers recommend it. ℂ 7123578, www.yavuzapart.com.

Tuna Pansiyon (4), simple, centrally located guest house with dripping taps. Rooms on the street are noisy, but those at the back from the second floor up have sea views and balconies. Clean. Double rooms without breakfast £12.50. Atatürk Cad., ℂ 7122014.

Camping: Ilıca Camping (17) is a lovely campsite at the south end of the bay, right on the pebble beach (some spots lack shade). The sanitary facilities are a bit of a disappointment. They rent large and small bungalows for the same price: £6.50 per person.

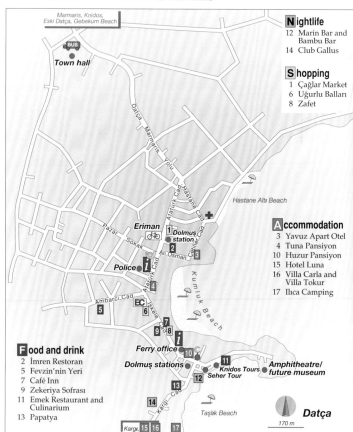

Nightlife
12   Marin Bar and Bambu Bar
14   Club Gallus

Shopping
1   Çağlar Market
6   Uğurlu Balları
8   Zafet

Accommodation
3   Yavuz Apart Otel
4   Tuna Pansiyon
10   Huzur Pansiyon
15   Hotel Luna
16   Villa Carla and Villa Tokur
17   Ilıca Camping

Food and drink
2   İmren Restoran
5   Fevzin'nin Yeri
7   Café Inn
9   Zekeriya Sofrası
11   Emek Restaurant and Culinarium
13   Papatya

Marmaris, Knidos, Eski Datça, Gebekum Beach

Town hall

Datça-Marmaris Yolu

Hastane Altı Beach

Eriman

Dolmuş station

Police

Kumluk Beach

Pazar Sokak

Ambarcı Cad.

Ferry office

Dolmuş stations

Knidos Tours Seher Tour

Amphitheatre/ future museum

Taşlık Beach

Kargı

Datça

170 m

2 people with camper van £10. Nice bar. ☎ 7123400.

At Eski Datça: Dede Pansiyon, signposted off the road to Datça. A real tip for a place to stay in an idyllic village. They rent six different, colourful suites, each individually and lovingly equipped, each with a different name. Little pool with palm trees, café/bar, everything very well kept. Double rooms with breakfast £40. ☎/☏ 7123951, www.dedepansiyon.com.

Faruk and Ursula Dinç, who own the Culinarium restaurant in Eski Datça (see under 'Food and drink'), also rent out two cosily outfitted apartments in stone houses for two people; one has a terrace and garden, the other a little balcony. Per apartment per day £20-24. Enquire at their restaurant, ☎ 7129770, www. peninsula-tr.de.

Food and drink/Nightlife
(see plan above)

The bulk of the restaurants in Datça, including many small, reasonably priced *lokantas*, can be recommended. The prices throughout are around 20 to 30% lower than in Marmaris, and the service is 100% better.

Emek Restaurant (11), at the port. Excellent grills and fresh-caught fish, plus such a huge selection of *meze* that it's hard to choose. Lovely terrace. Fairly pricey. (7123375.

Culinarium (11), near Emek; opened in 2004 under German/ Turkish management. The menu has a small but good choice of excellent Turkish/Mediterranean fusion cuisine. Every dish is freshly prepared and makes a great change from kebabs and grilled fish. Well-spaced tables, delightful roof terrace with a hint of 'ship's deck' atmosphere. Fair prices for what's on offer (meal with beer about £6.50-9.50. (7129770.

Papatya (13), in a detached old Greek house above the port. Pretty roof terrace with wicker and bright wooden chairs. Readers say they have seldom eaten as well as here. Pleasant view and quiet. A simple meal with beer costs about £4. (7122860.

Fevzi'nin Yeri (5), simple, very popular fish restaurant in the centre. Fresh fish prepared in an amazing variety of ways. Ambarcı Cad., (7129746.

Zekeriya Sofrası (9), a *lokanta* on İskele Cad. A couple of tables outside on the street and a couple more inside. You can check the casseroles and see what's cooking before you order. Tasty *köfte* too. Cheap and very popular.

İmren Restoran (2), somewhat off the beaten track on Şehit Ali Osman Çetiner Cad. Unprepossessing, simple *lokanta* with friendly service and good cooking. Daily menu changes, with more than enough casseroles to please everone. *Pide,* grills. Main course £1-1.25.

Café Inn (7), little café with European 'city-style' décor. Lavazza coffee — a welcome change from so much *neskafe!* İskele Cad., opposite Zekeriya Sofrası.

Nightlife is concentrated in a small area around the marina. Top meeting place is the **Marin Bar (12)**, with the brightest lights and blaring beats. Another popular place is the **Bambu Bar (12)** with bamboo chairs and décor, and stylishly presented drinks. If you want to dance, go to the **Gallus Club (14)** near the marina, on the road to Kargı Bay.

Beaches and diving

Datça has three public beaches: child-friendly **Kumluk Beach** north of the port, **Taşlık Beach** south of the port and **Hastane Altı** below the hospital. The last is the cleanest of the town beaches, with a blug-flag designation.

The most beautiful beach within walking distance of Datça is **Kargı Bay** to the south. Up to 10 *dolmuşes* a day go there as well. Further south is beautiful **Armutlu Bay**; Walk 20 (page 161) describes these bays in more detail.

But the most beautiful beaches around Datça are only accessible on boat trips (see 'Practicalities A-Z' below).

Diving: Datça Diving, at Taşlık Beach, runs daily trips with two dives and lunch for £35, including equipment hire. (7123759, www.datcadiving.com.

Practicalities A-Z

Boat trips: Captains at the port will offer you various tours, one of the most popular being to Knidos (see 'Getting there' on page 158). In high season there are also sailings to various beaches on the Reşadiye Peninsula (price about £9.50 per person, including lunch). In the shoulder season prices depend on how many people book. One of the most extensive programs is offered by **Seher Tour** (at the port), ✆/☏ 7123087, www.sehertour.com

Car ferries to Bodrum operate in the summer twice a day (usually around 09.00 and 17.00); they leave from Körmen Limanı (9km from Datça). The trip takes about 2 hours. Buses run from Datça to Körmen Limanı to coincide with departure times. In October and May the ferry runs 3 times a week; in winter there's no service. Tickets cost £6 per person one way, inclusive of the bus to Körmen Limanı, or £9.50 return. One car with driver costs £17 one way, each additional passenger £1.90. You can buy tickets in the **Datça Ferry Boat Office**, in an alley off İskele Cad., near the mosque. ✆ 7122143. In addition, some years a hydrofoil operates to Bodrum every day in summer (35 minutes); return fare about £13. Information about this is also available from the Ferry Boat Office.

Sailings to Symi and Rhodes: From May to mid-Oct. a hydrofoil runs to Symi on Thu. and Sat. It leaves from the port near the **Knidos Turizm** office (where you also buy tickets). The Saturday hydrofoil goes on to Rhodes. A return ticket to Rhodes costs £24, one way £20; prices for Symi are £6.50 lower. Note that the timetable can change! Smaller boats also sail to Symi once in a while (no fixed schedules).

Doctors: The local hospital is at the corner of Hastane Cad. and Çetiner Cad.

Car hire: Prices are much higher than in Marmaris, as there is no competition. Local firms like **Seher Tour** (see under 'Boat trips' above) charge from £37 per day.

Events: At the end of August the **Datça Knidos Kültür ve Sanat Festivalı** usually takes place in the local amphitheatre, with rock and folklore concerts, dance performances, sporting competitions and sometimes even bullfights.

Newspapers and magazines in English are available in **Çağlar Market (1)** on Atatürk Cad. near the *dolmuş* station.

Police: located in the centre on Atatürk Cad.; in emergencies call ✆ 155.

Post: also in the centre on Atatürk Cad.

Shopping: Compared with other holiday resorts, the choice is modest. Datça thyme honey and and some other kinds of honey are available at **Uğurlu Balları (6)** on İskele Cad. near the Ziraat Bankası. **Zafet (8)**, at İskele Cad. 59, is a beautiful shop with natural products from Datça (soaps, olive oil, honey or sage tea). On Friday evenings there is a **fruit and vegetable market**; on Saturdays a large general **market** (both near the post office).

Travel agency/Yacht charter: One of Datça's largest travel agencies is **Knidos Turizm** at the port (✆ 7129464, ☏ 7122464). Its main

business is yacht charter, but it also organises boat trips, etc.
Two-wheel hire: There are not many people renting, so prices are high. Both mountain bikes and scooters cost about £17 per day. One agency is **Eriman** on Atatürk Cad. opposite the *dolmuş* station. (7122915.

Bays around Datça

Körmen Limanı: This bay, 9km north of Datça, lies in a singularly unattractive stretch of the Gulf of Gökova and is nothing more than a quay for the Bodrum ferry, a bar and a campsite. There are a few scattered houses as well.
Getting there: Buses run from Datça to Körmen Limanı in conjunction with the ferries. The bus fare is included in the price of the ferry ticket. The port is signposted from the Mesudiye road as 'Feribot İskelesine gider'.

Hayıtbükü and Ovabükü: These two bays, which have only been accessible by road since 1996, lie 13km west of Datça, below the scattered settlement of Mesudiye. **Ovabükü Bay**, the further west of the two, has a wonderful beach, behind which are a few simple guest houses. **Hayıtbükü**, a quiet bay east of Mesudiye, is a little reminiscent of the idyllic bays in the Greek islands and is a well-kept secret among yachtsmen. It has a small beach which is never crowded. Many people only plan to spend the day here, then stay for a whole week.
Getting there: There is a dolmuş connection five times a day in summer to/from Datça (£1.15), but Sundays there are few, if any running.

Ovabükü Bay

Accommodation/camping/food and drink: There are a number of simple guest houses (double rooms starting from £11.50) in both bays. Some tips:
Gabaklar Pansiyon & Restaurant, for a long time the only guest house in Kızılbük, a small, palm-studded bay near Hayıtbükü Bay. 24 rooms, 12 of which were built in 2003. Lovely bungalows with modern plumbing, climate control and fridge. Unfortunately some of the rooms are separated from the sea by fenced-in scrubland. Double room in a bungalow £37, in the house (fewer facilities) £26.
(7280158, www.gabaklar. com. (The web site is only in Turkish, but very well done with many photos.)
Hoppala Pansiyon, in Ovabükü Bay. Old, established family business with some newer buildings (2004), about 100m

Sunday afternoon bullfight on the Reşadiye Peninsula

from the beach. Lovely rooms with top-quality baths and climate control, pleasant garden. Highly recommended by readers. Their restaurant features Turkish home cooking with vegetables from their own garden and home-made bread. Double rooms with breakfast £19. Open all year. ℂ 7280148, hoppalapansiyon @mynet.com.

Pansiyon & Restaurant Ortam, in Hayıtbükü Bay, one of the authors' favourite places to stay. Right on the beach, in a Greek house dating back more than 100 years. Four tiny, plain, clean rooms, two of them with private bath. Two gorgeous terraces. The restaurant has top-quality Turkish food and fish they've caught themselves. The owners, Süleyman and Mahmut, take wonderful care of their guests. Open all year. Double rooms with tasty breakfast from £11.50. ℂ 7280228.

Palamutbükü: This bay lies 24km west of Datça on the south shore

of the Reşadiye Peninsula. At the western end is a small fishing port with a handful of bars. There are usually a few yachts anchored here. The road to the eastern end of the bay has some restaurants and pensions. The beach is becoming finer all the time — changing from shingle into sand. The tourist infrastructure here is still in its infancy, so it's very pleasant. If you follow the bumpy little road east from Palamutbükü towards Mesudiye, you'll come to more small sand and shingle beaches.

Getting there: There is a dolmuş *connection six times a day in summer to/from Datça (£1.15), but Sundays there are few, if any running.*

Accommodation: You can stay right on the bay in various little guest houses. The loveliest place is **Kumburnu Pansiyon**, in the far eastern part of the bay — a white house with blue window frames and doors, lovely terrace.

20 simple but welcoming double rooms at £19 including breakfast. (7255503. Just before it is **Bük Pansiyon**, also with a terrace, where you could spend a whole week. The rooms here (a double costs £15.50) were once lovely but are now a bit tired, and the taps drip — but there are kitchen facilities. (7255136.

Food and drink: **Café Vino**, near the port, is the best place for a meal, with good fresh fish at fair prices. At time of writing they also had a couple of apartments to rent. Another good and economical place is the **Dostlar Restaurant** on the waterfront. The beach is the 'terrace' here, where you enjoy *meze* or grilled octopus under shady trees.

Knidos

Knidos, the ruined and only partly excavated site at the tip of the peninsula, attracts many visitors. While the ruins themselves are unspectacular, the combination of stony remains and wild landscape is really spellbinding. The ruined city is a beautiful destination for a trip and, after your visit, there is a small beach with crystal-clear water for a swim. The two ports at Knidos have been orphaned for two millennia. There's nothing stirring in the War Harbour these days (thankfully), but the commercial port is coming back to life, attracting boat trips and yachts.

An earlier place called Knidos, forerunner of today's Datça, was mentioned for the first time in the 7th century BC. Due to the increasing population, a new city of the same name was built in the 4th century BC on the western tip of the peninsula. This was laid out according to a Hippodamic grid (after the Greek architect Hippodamus), with right-angled roads. Inland, a 4km-long wall surrounded the city. For even greater protection from land-based aggressors, plans were made several times to close off the whole peninsula (it measures only 800m across at its narrowest point, some 30km west of Marmaris).

In its heyday the port city supported more than 70,000 inhabitants. Within its walls stood the Sanctuary of Apollo, the centre of the Dorian Hexapolis, where festivals were held every four years. Knidos was also known for its Asklepieion, one of the top four medical schools of the ancient world (the others were Pergamon, Kos and Epidauros). Knidos was a stronghold of science at the same time: the engineer Sostrates sketched out the Alexandria Lighthouse here, one of the Seven Wonders of the Ancient World. Art also blossomed in this wealthy city, although most of the works have been lost over the course of centuries (some treasures are in foreign museums — the famous statue of Demeter, for example, is in the Louvre). The stability of the Hellenistic era allowed Knidos to flourish. St. Paul the Apostle stopped here on his journey to Rome, creating an early Christian community. Knidos was first investigated by English archaeologists at the beginning of the 19th century, and excavations are still taking place today, most notably by the University of Konya Selçuk under the direction of

1 Port wall
2 Church E
3 Town wall
4 Athena Temple and altar
5 Apollo Sanctuary
6 Doric temple
7 Propylon
8 Bouleuterion
9 East-west road
10 Corinthian temple
11 Sund dial
12 Doric stoa
13 Church B
14 Church D
15 Stoa
16 Dionysus Temple
17 Roman theatre
18 Hellenistic house
19 Odeon
20 Large theatre

War harbour

Triopion Peninsula

Jandarma

Excavations depot

Restaurant

Excavations house

Commerc

Tic

Professor Ramazan Özgen.
*Getting there/opening times/prices:
Knidos is 35km west of Datça; the
road is asphalted throughout. Boat
trips sail from Datça daily in
summer at 10.00, stopping several
times at bathing beaches; £9 per
person including lunch (in the
shoulder season you can negotiate
the price). Boats also sail here from
Marmaris, but this is far more
expensive (up to £26). By taxi it
costs about £37 return from Datça
(including an hour for a visit).
There are* dolmuş *connections to
Yazıköy in summer (£1.50 one way),
but from there you have to walk or
hitch-hike the rest of the way (almost
8km). In summer Knidos is open
daily from 08.00-19.00; in winter it
is open from 08.00 until sunset;
entry fee £2.20. There is a restaurant
at the commercial port.*

Short walk round Knidos
(allow 1h30min)
From the car park, follow the
path down to the bay and the
one-time **commercial port**. When
there was a northery wind, ships
sailed in here from the Aegean; a
southerly wind brought in those
from the eastern Mediterranean.
From here you have a marvellous

once part of a **stoa**. Two officials in the *jandarma* station opposite make sure that no stones disappear!

On the way to the **war harbour** (which was once connected to the commercial port by a channel that could be closed with an iron chain if it came under threat), you come to **church D**; the floor of the middle apse was once covered with geometric two-tone mosaics. If you continue to follow the path along the bay, **church E** soon appears, which was also richly decorated with mosaics.

The path now heads uphill along the coast past the foundations of a **Doric temple**; its substructure was built using rose-coloured limestone. The **propylaeum**, which also forms the entrance hall to the **Apollo Sanctuary** on the hill, is a bit further east. To the north is an altar with a base of grey-blue marble. The steps where the spectators sat to watch the rituals are still visible.

If you go further uphill to the next terrace, you come to the impressive round base of the **Athena Temple**. It was long thought that this temple was dedicated to Aphrodite and housed the famous statue by Praxiteles (350 BC), one of the most famous sculptures of the ancient world. Praxiteles had the courage to model the Goddess of Love unclothed for the first time. Originally this monumental work was to be installed on Kos. But the conservative island did not want the statue, and so Aphrodite came to Knidos, where she was venerated as Goddess of the Sea and protectress of sailors. It is said that

view over the Triopion Peninsula (not to be confused with the Apollo Sanctuary called the Triopion, which was discovered during excavations near Emecik). The path goes past a **small theatre**, also known as the Roman theatre, which once offered seating for about 5000 people and is still in quite good condition. A short way west are the foundations of a **Dionysus Temple** which was later converted into a church — as were all the other temples in the city. Behind this, a few rebuilt columns catch the eye; they were

The two harbours and (below) view from the Athena Temple

Just before the main road, a sign points the way to the **Demeter Sanctuary** and the **acropolis**. If you make this tiring climb, you will be rewarded with spectacular panoramic views and will pass the fairly unspectacular **large theatre**.

If you instead follow the path further downhill, you come to a heap of rubble that was once a **Corinthian temple** from the 2nd century, behind which (on the sea side) is a Hellenistic **sundial**; if it still had its bronze gnomon, it would work. To the west of the temple was the **bouleuterion**. Continue further downhill and you reach the remains of the 114m-long **Doric stoa**, as well as **church B** with its three apses and figurative floor mosaics. Once past the small theatre, you arrive back at the commercial port. Before finishing your circuit of Knidos, don't miss the remains of the nearby **odeon** — below the access road, about 300m west of the town wall. It was built in the 3rd century BC and used for smaller events.

because of the naked Aphrodite, the Asklepieion of Knidos attracted more visitors during the following period than Kos.
Where the temple actually stood is still in dispute.
From here the path leads gently downhill away from the coast.

Time: 4h
Grade: easy-moderate; the roads and footpaths are generally good underfoot, except on the section just beyond Kargı Beach (where you must be sure-footed and have a head for heights).
Equipment: see pages 21-22.
Travel: coach from Marmaris to Datça, regular departures, journey time 1h30min. See plan on page 152: the coach stops at the bus station (*otogar*) on the outskirts of Datça, where a *dolmuş* connects with the centre. Return the same way.
Short walk: Kargı — Armutlu — Kargı (1h40min; easy, but you must be sure-footed and have a head for heights on one short stretch at the outset). Access by *dolmuş:* up to 10 times daily from Datça. Follow the main walk from Kargı Beach to Armutlu and return the same way.

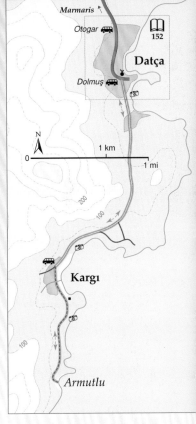

Datça is a delightful coastal village west of Marmaris, about halfway along the Reşadiye Peninsula. It's very picturesque, so you are sure to leave with some treasured photographs. But it is quite small — too small to keep you occupied for a full day. This walk has been designed to fill the time, to make the whole day a more enjoyable experience. It explores the region to the south of Datça, largely following the coastline, and it visits two lovely bays. Kargı is the first and the larger, where some of you might be content to spend the whole day. However, the second bay, Armutlu, has the intimate charm of seclusion and is well worth the extra effort to get there — even if you just do the Short walk.

Start the walk at the *dolmuş* station in **Datça**, near the harbour. Turn up the road on the right, opposite the mosque (Kargı Cad.). It quickly leads away from the village into countryside and gives some of the best photographic viewpoints back towards Datça. In about 20 minutes the road leads away from the shore and cuts across the headland towards Kargı.

It is hard to believe that the surrounding countryside, seemingly arid and shrubby, could hide a wealth of interesting spring flowers but, if you keep your eyes to the right, you could expect to see a number of bee orchids — including the yellow

On the way to Armutlu Bay

bee orchid, *Ophrys lutea ssp galilaea* and the sombre bee orchid, *O. fusca*. The small yellow *Gagea* species are everywhere and add plenty of ground colour, but look twice if you see a red anemone, for it may really be the red turban buttercup. They are similar in size and colour, so the only way to be certain is to inspect beneath the flower, to see if there are green sepals immediately below the petals; if so it is the buttercup, *Ranunculus asiaticus*. It has limited distribution, with the yellow and white forms only growing on Crete and the red form on Rhodes — and now near Datça.

The road crests the hill and, as you begin your descent to Kargı, the bay spreads out before you like a map. Follow the road beside the shingle beach and the sparkling sea. Kargı is still little more than a farming community enjoying a very fine location

beside this enchanting bay, but it is surely destined for a greater role in tourism. Leave the road/track when it swings away from the shore and continue along the shingle beach, crossing a small stream on a **plank bridge** Pass **Kargı Restaurant (1h10min)** and continue to the end of the beach. Then follow the path around to the right, by the wall, and head inland. As you pass a small building on the left in about a minute, turn left, and then diagonally right, to climb a small hill, heading for the centre of the saddle.

Crossing the **saddle**, you descend a well-defined path leading through a boulder-strewn area, just above the sea. The path becomes a little obscure as you cross an area of bedrock, but head upwards to find a clear path. Again, a minute or two later, you must climb a little to continue along the path. *Care is needed* where the path narrows on the steep-sided bank, and some walkers may find this section unnerving.

The path meanders around the coastline, giving fine views — especially as you approach a cove. The next cove looks particulary inviting, with the ultramarine sea lapping the shingle beach, and the path leads down to it. This is **Armutlu (2h)**, a delightful place to relax — either in the sun or under the shade of the nearby trees.

From here return the same way to **Datça (4h)**.

*History • Accommodation/camping, food and drink, nightlife •
Sights * Hierapolis*

Area code: ☏ 0258
Information: The Tourist Office is just opposite the travertines, right by the main car park (northern access). Information in English. Open daily from 08.30-12.00 and from 13.30-18.30. ☏ 2722077, www. pamukkale.gov.tr.
Connections: Travelling by **private transport** there are two approaches. The loveliest route leaves Pamukkale Köy towards Karahayıt and then turns right through the necropolis to the main car park above the travertines. The shorter access road is from Pamukkale Köy direct to the southern entrance of Hierapolis, from where you continue on foot through the 5th-century Byzantine gate. **On foot**: At time of writing it was permissible to climb *shoeless* from the Tourist Police office at the bus stop in Pamukkale Köy up to the tourist path in the travertines, but things may have changed by the time you use this book (at least this way you pay no entry fee). *Dolmuş:* There are connections between the travertines, Denizli and Pamukkale Köy at least half-

hourly. **Bus:** There are buses from Pamukkale Köy and Denizli to all the main tourist resorts on the south coast (for instance, Marmaris: 4 hours, £4.50). The buses from Denizli are hardly less expensive than those direct from Pamukkale.
Organised tours: In Pamukkale Köy you can book a day trip to Aphrodisias or other attractions in the area for about £6.50 (excluding entry fee); there are several operators.
Opening times: The travertines are open round the clock, but the archaeological site near the theatre is closed at night. The museum is open daily (except Mon.) from 09.00-12.30 and from 13.30-17.00.
Entry fees: For both the travertines and Hierapolis £2.20. You can come and go using the same ticket on the day of issue. Sometimes, with luck, you can get a cheaper ticket late in the afternoon which can also be used the next day. Entry to the museum costs £0.90 extra.
First aid: There's a little first aid station above the travertines (open in high season).

Be aware before you go: if you expect to be able to bathe in the beautiful turquoise waters of the travertine terraces you are going to be disappointed. Bathing has long been forbidden, and today you have to enjoy this tourist magnet by walking single file behind coachloads of other visitors. A visit to the ancient site of Hierapolis above the terraces is some compensation…

The emergence of these unusual white lime travertines is based on a simple chemical reaction. A hot spring (53°C) contains large quantities of dissolved calcium bicarbonate. When it cools on the surface, it is converted into water, carbon dioxide and calcium carbonate (lime). The carbon dioxide escapes, while the travertine lime is deposited and clogs the drainage canals for the water. The water then overflows and spreads fan-like over the slopes, thus forming the white travertine terraces — enormous, graduated basins like oversized bath tubs, one above the other. From below, with a little imagination, the 120m-high incline resembles a large frozen waterfall.

Directly below the travertine terraces is Pamukkale Köy, a settlement consisting of guest houses, hotels, restaurants and bars. Karahayıt, a few kilometres north of the terraces, is its better-kept (if not necessarily more attractive) counterpart. The next nearest city is Denizli with some 300,000 inhabitants — a lively, provincial centre 18km south of Pamukkale, usually covered in smog. It's of no real interest for tourists, since all its historical buildings have been destroyed by earthquakes.

History

For thousands of years, the inhabitants from the surrounding area knew about and appreciated the healing properties of the Pamukkale spring.

The Hittites and Phrygians established altars here, while the Pergamon King Eumenes II founded the city of Hierapolis here, as a countermeasure to the nearby Macedonian city of Laodikeia (the meagre ruins of which are signposted off the Pamukkale/Denizli road). The

rivalry between the two cities, whose wealth was based on the wool trade, was so great that they hindered each other's development. Only after integration into the Roman province of Asia did Hierapolis attain greater importance. In the year 60 AD the city was destroyed by an earthquake, but was rebuilt shortly afterwards. From its early years it had a strong Christian community, and during the Byzantine era it even became a bishopric. Following an invasion by the Seljuks, the city was deserted. Carl Human, the discoverer of Pergamon, undertook the first excavations in 1887. Since 1957, systematic work has been carried out by Italian archaeologists in particular.

The travertines at Pamukkale

Accommodation/camping, food and drink, nightlife

The infrastructure at **Pamukkale Köy** is primarily geared to individual travellers. At one time there were over 100 places to stay, but the decline of the travertine terraces (see panel overleaf) also meant the end for many guest houses. Even though the condition of the travertines is improving again, many places are fighting for survival. The money for renovations is lacking, no matter how urgent the need. The accommodation described below offers you a good choice, although some places can be hard to find, since touting is not as pronounced as elsewhere in Turkey. The more luxurious places to stay are on the north side of the Hierapolis ruins, at the edge of **Karahayıt**. By the way: nearly every guest house has a channel bringing water from the springs into its own pool.

Polat Thermal Hotel in Karahayıt has the best sign-posting. This is a five-star hotel with 280 rooms and everything that goes with it: several restaurants, thermal pools, aquapark, Turkish bath, disco, etc. A double room with H/B costs from £57. (2714110, (2714228. An alternative, comfortable hotel is the **Club Hierapolis**, also in Karahayıt: coming from Pamukkale Köy, it's at the beginning of the village, on the right. This is a spa hotel with modern thermal

Once upon a time, there was a white ...

Pamukkale is usually translated as 'cotton castle', but this is not strictly correct. *Pamuk*, the Turkish word for cotton, is used in this context as a synonym for 'white' (just as 'snow' in 'snow-white' might be). So Pamukkale (*kale* = castle) would be better translated as 'cotton-white castle'.

But today you would look in vain for the wonderful Pamukkale white on the terraces — even though it is referred to in tourist brochures as often as Bordeaux red! For decades this natural phenomenon was subject to thoughtless commercial exploitation. Hundreds of thousands of visitors were coached in along a purpose-built road which went right through the centre (today this has been replaced by two new approach roads) and these visitors were then allowed — without taking off their shoes — to trample across this splendid 'white'.

Even more devastating was the construction of luxury hotels on the plateau directly above the terraces, which fed their pools with the hot spring water. Too much precious liquid was taken in this way, so that no more lime was deposited on the terraces. Eventually word got out that Pamukkale was no longer 'worth a visit', since the radiant white had been replaced by a dirty grey. Even then, it took washing-baskets full of letters protesting the situation and pressure from international environmental protection organisations before the authorities began to act. In the year 2000 the last hotel above the terraces was razed to the ground — and now the few modern foundations are mixed with those from antiquity. The entire area has become a UNESCO World Heritage Site. The condition of the travertine terraces has improved substantially since then.

baths, nightclub, etc. Double room with H/B £44. (2714100, www.hierapolishotel.com.
Venüs Hotel is a reader recommendation in Pamukkale Köy. A well-kept, family-run hotel in a quiet position, with unobtrusive service. All rooms (plain but very clean, with carpeting) have balconies, TV and climate control. Pleasant pool area. Double room with breakfast £20. (2722152.
Pansiyon Beyaz Kale, in Pamukkale Köy. The 'White Castle' has a motel-like atmosphere, with 15 simple rooms (some of them with several beds). All rooms with shower/WC and carpeting; newer rooms are on the first floor. Readers have praised the good cooking and the warm-hearted owner; recommended in every guide book under the sun. Cosy pool area, roof terrace. Double rooms with breakfast £17. (2722064, www.geocities.com/weisseburg.
Pansiyon Kervansaray, diagonally opposite the Beyaz Kale, run by Mevlüt Kaya and his family. Rooms are similar to those at the Beyaz Kale (all with shower/WC, balcony, air-conditioning, heating and some with a view to the travertines),

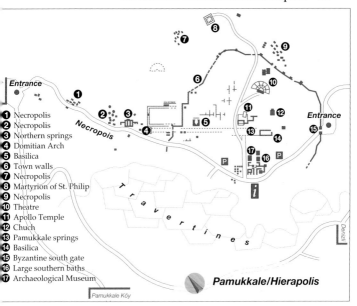

1 Necropolis
2 Necropolis
3 Northern springs
4 Domitian Arch
5 Basilica
6 Town walls
7 Necropolis
8 Martyrion of St. Philip
9 Necropolis
10 Theatre
11 Apollo Temple
12 Chuch
13 Pamukkale springs
14 Basilica
15 Byzantine south gate
16 Large southern baths
17 Archaeological Museum

Pamukkale/Hierapolis

but only a mini-pool. Very clean. Restaurant on the roof. Also in many guides. Double rooms with air-conditioning and breakfast £17. Free pick-up service from the bus station, even from Denizli. ℂ 2722209, www.geocities.com/ kervansaray2tr.

Meltem Guest House, in the centre of Pamukkale Köy near the mosque. Large guest house with an international back-packers' atmosphere. Well-kept rooms with good baths, lovely pool area, own Internet café. Well-organised, unobtrusive service. Dormitories for low-budget travellers. Cycle hire, laundry service. Per person from £6 with breakfast. ℂ 2723134, www. meltemguesthouse.com.

Camping: You can camp in the (often unkempt) gardens of many guest houses, even with camper vans. No particular recommendations are given here, because they change from year to year.

Food and drink: The fact that most visitors only come to Pamukkale once in a lifetime and then mostly by coach and for only two-three hours, doesn't help the catering trade. Annoying touts, sluggish service, small portions, high prices, and food prepared quickly and on the cheap complete the picture. A few simple restaurants are to be found in the centre of Pamukkale Köy close to the mosque — the food will fill you up, but can't be recommended on any other grounds. Check your bill! Readers were pleased enough with the **Restaurant Mustafa** near Pansiyon Kervansary, with its friendly service.

Nightlife: The discos around Pamukkale can all be summed

Bathing in a spring-fed pool;
below: a corner of the huge necropolis
at Hierapolis

up with the word 'pathetic'. The most popular is the **Laila Disco Bar** on Atatürk Cad. in Pamukkale Köy, where you sit on the terrace and watch the action on the street.

Sights

The travertine terraces are *the* sight. They totally cover a slope 120m high and over 5km wide. The spring is as vigorous as ever, and someone is employed to divert the water along the broad channels, so that the central terraces slowly regain their 'cotton-white' appearance. Each terrace is allegedly flushed at least once a week for a whole day. The water is then collected at the bottom of the slope, and supplied first to the guest houses and afterwards to the fields on the plain. Some basins are lit at night. Whether during the day or at night, *before walking over the terraces you must remove your shoes!*

Pamukkale baths: Since bathing in the travertine terraces is now a thing of the past, a bath in the Pamukkale hot spring is today's alternative. The main spring lies in the open inner courtyard of the former Pamukkale Motel. It feeds a beautiful pool studded with palms and ancient columns — hence the name 'Antique Pool'. Bathing in this warm 35°C water is a really pleasant experience — and allegedly helps with stomach ulcers, bronchitis, heart and circulation complaints, intestinal disorders, and much more besides…

Opening times/prices: open daily from 08.00-20.00 (in winter until 17.00); entry £9, children £2.30.

Hierapolis

Almost everything of interest lies scattered over the plateau above the travertines. The ruins of the **large baths** lie just off the road to the hot spring and are impossible to miss. Their massive arches were once faced with marble. Today the building accommodates the small, but beautiful and quite interesting **archaeological museum**, which contains finds from Hierapolis and Laodikeia, particularly richly ornamented sarcophagi, statues and reliefs.

Apollo Temple and Plutonium: A 2.5m-high platform with a small staircase, as well as some sections of capitals scattered among the ruins, allow you to mentally rebuild the Apollo Temple. In front of it lie the imposing ruins of what used to be an enormous fountain built from large rectangular blocks. A few steps further on you come to the Plutonium, a grotto dedicated to Pluto, God of the Underworld. This is where the spring originally gushed forth. Poisonous gases contaminated the large entrance hall, and unauthorised intruders (like birds and even oxen) died. Only the priests could enter unharmed: they crept along the ground holding their breath. The grotto is largely buried, only a chamber with an arch above the door remains. The entrance is blocked, since sulfurous gases are still leaking out.

Theatre: The almost completely excavated theatre (2nd century BC) is still in relatively good condition. With sides measuring over 100m in length, 20 rows of seats in the first tier, 25 rows in the second, and eight staircases, it seated up to 10,000 spectators.

Marble friezes and statues by the carefully restored fly tower give an impression of the former splendour.

Martyrion of St. Philip: St. Philip's mausoleum (signposted as 'San Filip Kilisesi') lies 600m north of the theatre. The grave has never been found, so it is not clear whether the saint was really buried here. This most unusual building was constructed at the beginning of the 5th century and destroyed less than one hundred years later by an earthquake. Sections of the walls are still head-height, while the square layout is also visible. Adjacent to the outside walls are eight rectangular chambers, which are only accessible from the outside, and thought to be lodgings for pilgrims. You will search in vain for an altar, but the semicircular seating for the bishop and community elders is still recognisable.

Necropolis: If you walk along the main street of Hierapolis from the Pamukkale baths, you first pass the foundation walls of a **basilica**, then a **Byzantine city gate** and a **colonnade** dating from the reign of Domitian which terminates at an arch dedicated to him. Once you reach the **northern baths**, which were converted into an enormous **basilica** during the 5th century, you are at the **necropolis**, the largest ancient graveyard in Anatolia, extending for some 2km, with more than 1200 tombs from different epochs — temple tombs, circular barrows which were once crowned with phallic-shaped stones, sarcophagi, etc. … some lying half-sunken in the travertine lime.

8 EXCURSION TO APHRODISIAS

History • Accommodation, food and drink • Circuit of the site

Area code: (0256
Connections: Organised tours
to Aphrodisias are often
coupled with a visit to Pamukkale. In addition, travel
agencies in Pamukkale offer
day trips to Aphrodisias.
If you are going by **private
transport**, coming from Aydın
turn right towards Karacasu
about 16km past Nazilli. From
Karacasu the way is signposted
(it's another 37km). There's a
paid car park at the site (£1.50).

There are good **bus** connections
from Selçuk (1h30min) and
Pamukkale (1h30min) to
Nazilli, from where you can
take a *dolmuş* to Karacasu.
From Karacasu up to 10
dolmuşes a day run to
Aphrodisias in summer (fewer
in winter).
Opening times: The site and
museum are open daily from
09.00-18.00 in summer, 08.00-
17.00 in winter. Entry fee £3.

'**I** magine arriving in a city so rich in archaeological
treasures that sculptures roll in front of your feet, and
marble heads fall from the walls or lie one on top of the
other in the irrigation channels!' Thus enthused the
Turkish archaeologist Kenan T. Erim in the *National
Geographic* magazine, having made research into Aphrodisias his life's work (he died in 1990). Another time he is
quoted at having answered the question 'Why did you
never marry?' with 'Marry? Me? I am married. Where
would I find a better wife than Aphrodite?'

Aphrodisias was one of the main
centres of the Aphrodite cult. The
Goddess of Love, Beauty and
Seduction left her mark on the
city. The cult and its followers
often arranged raucous festivities
for visitors who came to
Aphrodisias from all over the
ancient world. The goddess was
eventually dispelled by the
Christian God, and purged from
the city. The ruins at Aphrodisias
are perhaps somewhat less spectacular than those at Ephesus,
but you can enjoy them without
the crowds. Moreover, its
location in the middle of a
plateau is far more pleasant to
the eye. The most beautiful time
to visit is in spring, when the
flowers bloom between the
ancient monuments, and the

surrounding mountain peaks are
still covered in snow.

History

The nearby Maeander River with
its fertile valley was already
attracting human beings in the
dim and distant past. The first
traces of a stable settlement at
Aphrodisias date from the 7th
century BC. At that time it was a
small Assyrian town called
Ninoe.
In the 2nd century BC Ninoe was
renamed Aphrodisias by decree
of the Roman Empire. The
Roman dictator Sulla, on the
advice of the Oracle in Delphi,
paid homage to the Greek
Goddess of Love, whom the
Romans revered as Venus. From
this time Aphrodisias flourished,

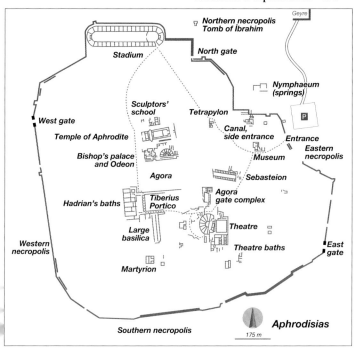

Aphrodisias

experiencing its heyday between the 1st century BC and the 3rd century AD. The city was granted many privileges, was independent, and was considered so holy that it didn't even need a city wall until the 4th century AD. But it was not only the cult of Aphrodite that made the city famous during late antiquity: literary and scientific work also made important contributions, while the fame of the local school of sculpture spread throughout the Empire. The raw material, marble of the finest quality from a nearby quarry, was masterfully worked and exported. Sculptures from Aphrodisias adorned Olympia in Greece and Leptis Magna on the North African coast, as well as many places in Rome. The Aphrodisian sculptors successfully relied upon the city's good reputation, replacing their first names with the ethnic adjective 'Aphrodisieus'.

The splitting of the Roman Empire brought about the fall of Aphrodisias. Under Byzantine rule, the city became a bishopric. In the 7th century the Christians tried to whitewash over the pagan past and baptised the city Stauropolis ('City of the Cross'); later it was called Karia, then Geyre. With the Seljuk conquests of the 11th and 13th centuries, the small town, already in a pitiful state due to earthquakes, sank into obscurity.

Accommodation, food and drink

The few places to stay around Aphrodisias are only of interest if you're desperate, so it's far better to plan your trip ahead and stay elsewhere.

The best place to stay is the **Aphrodisias Hotel** (near Geyre on the main road). Turkish/French management. 25 plain, down-at-heel rooms with outdated equipment, but at least clean. Expensive restaurant (in the garden in summer). Double rooms £20 (very high, for this standard). Camping possible. ☏ 4488132, ☏ 4488422.

As an alternative you can try your luck in one of the guest houses recommended by readers: **Elmas** (coming from Karacasu the first place on the road to Aphrodisias). It's half the price of the hotel, but unfortunately often closed. ☏ 4412637.

As to the option of staying in **Karacasu** (at either the Otogar Moteli at the bus station or the Pansiyon Aphrodisias in the centre) — forget it.

Camping: Almost all restaurants and guest houses between Karacasu and Aphrodisias offer camping in their gardens — usually free, as long as you eat in their restaurants.

Circuit of the site

Visitors are asked to stick to the designated paths. The usual tour runs anti-clockwise and begins behind the museum at the entrance; the museum is then visited at the end.

Tetrapylon: This is probably part of a large ceremonial gate from the 2nd century, which would have been accessible from all four sides. The gate consisted of four rows of four columns, which have been rebuilt as far as

---

The excavations at Aphrodisias

The ruins lie within and around the old village of Geyre, whose inhabitants were resettled in the 1960s, as they stood in the way of the excavations. The first dig — plundering would be a better word — was undertaken in 1904 by the French railway engineer and hobby archaeologist Paul Gaudin. Some of the finds ended up in the museum at Istanbul, others somehow made their way to Boston, Brussels, Berlin and other far-flung corners of the world.

In 1937 excavations were made by Italian archaeologists. Pieces of the most magnificent find — the frieze of the Tiberius Portico decorated with almost life-like faces — are in the museum garden at Aphrodisias.

Starting from 1961, Aphrodisias was researched systematically by a Turkish-American team under Kenan T. Erim. They rebuilt a few columns every year and heaved the fallen capitals back into their original positions. The tomb of the famous archaeologist lies next to the rebuilt tetrapylon. The excavations are continuing today with an international group under the direction of New York University.

---

possible, including the timberwork. The artful spiral fluting of the columns deserves special mention — a masterful piece of work by the local stonemasons. The gate was possibly the entrance to the holy groves around the Aphrodite Temple, whose columns can be seen to the left in the background.

Stadium: This is considered the best-preserved ancient stadium in the whole Mediterranean area and is also the most impressive monument in Aphrodisias. With a capacity of 30,000, it could compete with many Premier League stadiums today. The site is 262m long and 59m wide, with semicircular ends, so that all the spectators had a good view. The entrance tunnel, through which the sportsmen came into the stadium, is also completely intact. The emperor would have taken his place in a box in the centre on the northern side. The holes in the rows of seat held poles supporting canopies to protect the crowd from the sun. Originally a circle of columns towered above the top of the stadium. Mainly athletic games, gladiatorial fights, as well as wrestling and boxing matches took place in the arena.

Temple of Aphrodite: Only 14 columns and the front wall of the cella from the famous Aphrodite Temple (signposted as 'Tapınak') are still standing today. Originally 13 columns ran the length of the cella on either side and eight columns the width. The building was torn down during the Byzantine era, and a Christian church built in its place; only the surrounding colonnade was left untouched. Excavations brought several finds to light, indicating an even earlier sanctuary. North of the temple — appropriately — are the rubble remains of what in antiquity was the sculptors' school.

Bishop's palace and odeon: Southwest of the Aphrodite Temple are the remains of what is called the bishop's palace, a stately house with impressive bluish marble columns. The odeon, still in good condition, was built over the southeast end of the palace in the 2nd century AD. Surviving from the original roofed building are the bottom **nine rows of seats** (the upper rows were made of wood), with lions' feet as a symbol of power, the **orchestra** and the narrow **stage**. The marble facing, mosaic floor and many sculptures from the odeon are in the museum.

Agora: The city's double agora stretches out to the south of the odeon and bishop's palace — two arcaded squares which formed the administrative and commercial centre of Aphrodisias. Excavation of the 202 x 72m large northern agora has so far been only rudimentary; the archaeologists' most recent discovery has been a fountain and the foundations of a possible altar. Coin finds indicate that trade continued here until the 7th century.

Hadrian's baths: The baths are typical of Roman public baths, with a large cold-water bath, warm- and hot-water areas, as well as a sauna. The two marble basins of the **caldarium** (hot-water bath) are worth a mention.

Southern agora: This square measures 212 x 69m and because of the surrounding Tiberius Portico is also known as the Tiberius Agora. **Diocletian's well-known price edict** was discovered on its western side: with inflation in the empire rocketing, the emperor had tried unsuccessfully to get it under control by publicly posting lists with fixed prices everywhere in the realm. After an earthquake in the 4th century, the gateway to the agora was converted into a **nymphaeum**, which, much to the citizens' annoyance, would flood the agora again and again.

Theatre: The hill against which the theatre nestles is a *höyük,* an enormous heap of debris formed by age-old rubble from settlements dating back as far as 5800 BC. Of the theatre (1st century BC) only the **rows of seats** are almost completely intact; the fly tower is in worse condition. Originally Hellenic, the theatre was rebuilt several times by the Romans. The **auditorium**, with its marble seats, was to a large extent dug into the slope. The semicircular **orchestra** was deepened under Markus Aurelius and the lower rows of seats were removed, so that fights between gladiators and animals could be staged without endangering the spectators. After such fights, the orchestra could be flooded with ditch-water and cleaned. By the stage there was also an entrance tunnel, in which the hunters and hunted waited to appear. Only the lower part of the auditorium and half a row of columns have been rebuilt.

Tetrastoon and theatre baths: After an earthquake in the 4th century, the agora was constantly flooded, so the Aphrodisians built a new market by the theatre. This was surrounded on all four sides by a portico *(tetrastoon)* and connected on the south side to an older, basilica-like hall. On its western side are the theatre baths, which were used up until the Byzantine era. In the middle, still in good condition, is the circular, nearly 10m-high caldarium (steam room).

Sebasteion: This once stood at the eastern end of the northern agora; today it's hidden behind the excavation building on the way to the museum. Named after Sebastos, the Greek equivalent of the Latin Augustus, it is dominated by two 80m-long rows of columns along the two longer sides. It was used to pay homage to the emperors of the Julius-Claudius dynasty from Augustus to Nero. In the 4th century, when Christianity won the upper hand, this 'cult' hall was converted into an early 'shopping mall'.

Museum: This is bursting at the seams. Everywhere you look, it becomes clear that Aphrodisias's fame was not based solely on its sculptors' school. Several rooms surround the courtyard:

Emperor's Hall: busts of various emperors, princes and muses. In the next hallway is a relief from the 1st century BC honouring a citizen called Zoilos.

Melpomene Hall: sculptures of the tragic muse Melpomene and a large statue of Apollo.

Odeon Hall: statues of poets and philosophers that were found in the odeon; in the adjacent hallway are incomplete sculptures from the sculptors' studio.

Penthesileia Hall: The central group shows Achilles carrying the dying Amazonian Queen Penthesileia from the battlefield. There are also two versions of a satyr, with the young Dionysus cradled in its arms.

Aphrodite Hall: A copy of the cult statue of Aphrodite (the original was not found) from her temple. More sculptures of important citizens from Aphrodisias.

9 EXCURSION TO EPHESUS

History • Circuit of the site • Sights around Ephesus

Area code: (0232 (Selçuk)
Connections/accommodation: Ephesus is a popular destination for organised tours from both Bodrum and Marmaris. Independent travellers visiting the area usually stay at Selçuk (3km from Ephesus; accessible by **bus** or **train**), a town outside the scope of this guide.
Opening times/prices: The site is open daily from 08.00-18.30 (16.30 in winter); entry fee £4.50. A visit to the hillside houses costs another £4.50 (tickets at the entrance to the houses). It's worth arriving as early as possible, since the excursion coaches don't usually show up until 09.30. Parking costs £1 extra.
Pitfall: In addition to the main entrance near the Kuşadası road, there is a second entrance to Ephesus on the Meryemana road (see page 182). Clever shopkeepers have taken it into their heads to greet tourists at one or other of the entrances and offer to pick them up at the far side, so as to save them having to walk back (about 15 minutes). If you take them up on this kind offer, you are guaranteed to meet a brother or other relative of this Good Samaritan … who just happens to own a carpet shop.

E phesus was a famous city when Athens was still a provincial town and Rome hadn't even been founded. In its heyday the inhabitants of this metropolis numbered a quarter of a million — an almost inconceivable number, given living conditions at that time. Today Ephesus is one of the world's most fascinating ancient sites.

Ephesus was the richest city in Asia Minor and known as the 'bank of Asia'. Its large port was the gateway to the treasures of Anatolia and Persia. But the city didn't only rely on business: Ephesus was the centre of the Artemis cult and was thus an important place of pilgrimage. The Artemision, the enormous Artemis Temple, was ranked among the Seven Wonders of the Ancient World.
Fame and wealth are, however, transitory. The port silted up, and the city declined. Only excavations between 1866 and 1922 brought Ephesus back to life. Few sites in the world offer such an intact city, and in peak times up to 15,000 visit every day.

History

The existence of a settlement in the area goes back to 2000 BC. During that period, the Lelegians established themselves on the hill of the Selçuk citadel, where there was also a sanctuary to the fertility goddess Kybele.
In the 11th century BC, Ionic settlers laid the foundation stone for the city of Ephesus. Their leader was Androklos, who had asked the Oracle at Delphi where the new city was to be based. The answer read: 'A fish and a wild boar will indicate the place'. Equipped with these instructions, the settlers set off. One day, as they tried to cook a not-quite-dead fish over the fire, it jumped from the grill and, knocking the

coals, set some shrubs on fire, out of which jumped a wild boar. The boar took off and only came to a halt at the delta of the now dried-up **Kaystro River**. Here the settlers established their city — at least, so the legend goes.

Ephesus developed quickly into a substantial city due to its port and its favourable location. The Greek cult of Artemis merged with the archaic worship of Kybele into the Ephesian variant of Artemis worship, which found its visible expression in an enormous Artemis Temple: work on it began in the 6th century BC, and it took more than 200 years to complete.

Around 550 BC the city came under attack from the Lydian King, Croesus. Rather than defend themselves, the inhabitants encircled the temples and city with a rope, in order to put themselves symbolically under the protection of the gods. Croesus was impressed: he preserved the unfinished temple and only plundered the city. But scarcely 200 years later the temple was destroyed anyway: in

Artemis of Ephesus

356 BC Herostratos set fire to the finished building in order to immortalise his name (which he obviously succeeded in doing). When Alexander the Great offered in 334 BC to take on all rebuilding costs for the huge temple, the proud Ephesians rejected the offer. They financed the splendid reconstruction themselves and enlarged the temple asylums, in which the use of force was forbidden. Thus the costs of the temple were soon amortised — rich outlaws found sanctuary here and thanked the goddess with their generous donations.

It is thought that starting from 294 BC Lysimachos, one of Alexander the Great's generals and ruler of Pergamon, moved the city, which up until then only extended around the Artemis Temple, to today's location. A new port was dug and the city was surrounded by a 9km-long fortified wall.

In 133 BC Ephesus fell to the Romans and soon thereafter became the capital of the province of Asia. But for a long time Rome was more the inhabitants' enemy than friend, due to the high tax demands. And in 88 BC Ephesus was involved in Mithridates of Pontus's revolt against Roman rule: during the so-called 'Ephesian Vespers', 80,000 traders, tax collectors, and other Roman citizens were killed throughout Asia Minor. The city nevertheless flourished under Roman rule, becoming a metropolis with more than 250,000 inhabitants. Most excavated sights and objects of interest date from this time.

The visit of St. Paul the Apostle, who stayed here in 55-58 AD on his second missionary journey, also came during the time of Roman rule. Paul's lectures had such an effect that the long-established icon-vendors could hardly sell another Artemis. Thereupon a silversmith called Demetrios mobilised the mob against the Christians: gathered in the theatre, they gave voice to the much-quoted saying 'Great is Artemis of the Ephesians!' After the first tumults Paul left the city. Another apostle who is said to have worked in Ephesus was St. John the Evangelist.

In 262 AD the city and temple were destroyed by the Goths, and the following reconstruction was slow. The port silted up, and other commercial centres surpassed Ephesus in rank. In the 7th century they gave up the settlement on the plain and withdrew to the nearby citadel hill (Selçuk). Here, under the protection of the small Christian town of **Hagios Theologos**, the Ephesians survived for several centuries, while the once-great city next door slowly sank into oblivion. In the mid-13th century the Seljuks conquered Hagios Theogolos. In the 14th century, under the new name Ayasoluk, the citadel city experienced a short rebirth as a commercial centre and residence of the Aydınoğulları, which ended with Ottoman conquest in 1423.

In 1866 the British architect and engineer J. T. Wood discovered the Artemision and began excavations. From 1896 work has been carried out by the Austrian Archaeological Institute. Ayasoluk was renamed Selçuk in 1914.

Circuit of the site

Hidden somewhat off the beaten track are the ruins of the **Church of the Virgin Mary**, a former three-nave basilica. It is assumed that it was developed in the 4th century from a market hall, in which the Third Ecumenical Council took place in 431. All that remains, apart from some ruined walls, are columns and a baptismal font. If you would like to see it, turn right along a path between the ticket office and toilets.

Otherwise follow the shady avenue which leads from the entrance straight to the Arcadiane and large theatre. On your right there was once a 200 x 240m-large courtyard surrounded by an arcade — **Verulanus Square**; not a trace of it remains today. After a few metres the ruins of the **theatre gymnasium** emerge on the left.

Arcadiane (Arcadian Way): This long boulevard once led from the theatre to the port, but today ends in a thicket. It was refurbished in 400 AD by Emperor Arcadius, who had columns and arcades built along the entire length (over 500 metres); it was surfaced with marble and was the first road in the world to be illuminated at night. It is still in outstanding condition — resurfaced and with many columns rebuilt. In order to protect it from the masses of visitors, it is no longer possible to walk on the Arcadiane.

The large theatre: Built impressively into the slope, the theatre held 24,000 spectators. Today pop and classical concerts often take place here in the summer. Originally a Hellenistic building

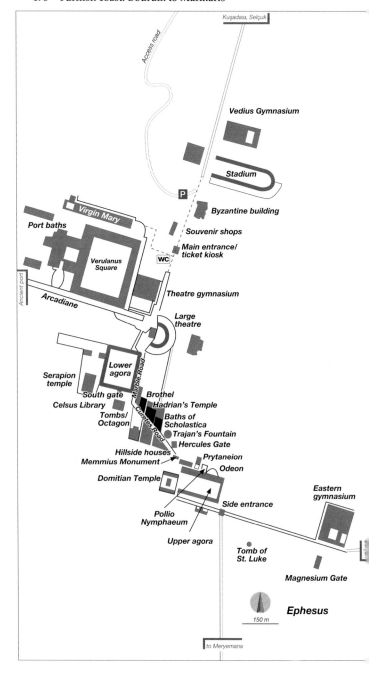

Kuşadası, Selçuk

Access road

Vedius Gymnasium

Stadium

Byzantine building

Souvenir shops

Main entrance/
ticket kiosk

WC

P

Virgin Mary

Port baths

Verulanus
Square

Ancient port

Arcadiane

Theatre gymnasium

Large
theatre

Serapion
temple

Lower
agora

Marble Road

South gate

Celsus Library

Tombs/
Octagon

Brothel

Hadrian's Temple

Baths of
Scholastica

Curetes Road

Trajan's Fountain

Hercules Gate

Hillside houses

Memmius Monument

Prytaneion

Odeon

Domitian Temple

Pollio
Nymphaeum

Side entrance

Upper agora

Tomb of
St. Luke

Eastern
gymnasium

Magnesium Gate

Ephesus

150 m

to Meryemana

from around 270 BC, it owes its current appearance to the structural alterations undertaken by the Roman emperors Claudius and Trajan. The theatre has a diameter of 130m, is 38m high, and has 66 rows of seats divided into three tiers. Only the walls of the first floor still stand from the original three-storey stage (18m), in front of which is the forest of columns in the orchestra. The acoustics are particularly impressive — as is the view of the Arcadiane leading to the silted-up port.

Marble Road: This was once an arcaded avenue similar to the Arcadian Way; it runs from the theatre past a pump-house to the Celsus Library (see below). It owes its name to the heavy marble-slab surfacing, under which is a 2m-high drainage system.

Lower agora: This market place, on the right-hand side of Marble Road, is surrounded by colonnades and measures 110 x 110m. The **south gate** of the agora (next to the Celsus Library, see below) is in fantastic condition, and is called the **Gate of Mazeus and Mithridates** after its donors, two slaves who were once employed by Emperor Augustus who were released and later made their fortunes in Ephesus. Those who approved of this and those who didn't is clear from the bilingual inscription: The Latin version mentions the Romans, the Greek one leaves them out.

Celsus Library: This two-storey library was built in 135 AD at the end of Marble Road by the Consul Gaius Aquila as a heroon in memory of his father Celsus, a governor of the province of Asia.

A gallery ran around the upper floor, from which one could see into the lower reading hall. Since the Austrian archaeologists found no less than 850 of the original building blocks, they succeeded in completely rebuilding the front over a period of eight years starting in 1970; even the statues are once again standing in their original places. They embody, from left to right: education, honesty, virtue and wisdom. Inside the library there are still some ancient notice boards, but no manuscripts — the Goths burned them to heat the baths.

Serapeion: The meagre remains of this temple lie behind the agora. Dating from the 2nd century AD, it must have been enormous. Climbing an external staircase, you come into an entrance hall supported by eight 14m-high Corinthian columns. Each individual column was carved from one piece of marble and weighed several tons. The iron gate to the cella was so heavy that it ran on rollers. The basins and large niches in the cella were used for ritual washing.

Curetes Road: This leads from the library to the upper agora (see below). Arcades border it, and mosaics shine in front of the adjacent public buildings. There was also a drainage system under this road. Just at the beginning, on the left, is what archaeologists have long believed to be a **brothel**, since they found a statue of the God Priapos with an outsize penis, as well as the picture of an exhausted-looking mature woman. A public latrine is next door, with a fountain decorated with columns in the centre and toilet seats against the outside walls. Opposite are three tombs, of which the huge **Octagon** is inscribed. Behind it a futuristic canopy marks the so-called hillside houses.

Hillside houses: The newest attraction at Ephesus was excavated over several years, during which time frescoes and mosaics were found that are in amazingly good condition. To visit you need the extra ticket, but it is spectacular. A tour of these houses gives you a close-up view of how antiquity's 'top 10,000' arranged their mansions, including underfloor heating, hot baths and flowing water.

Hadrian's Temple and the Baths of Scholastica: Continuing along Curetes Road, you come to the impressive, largely reconstructed Temple of Hadrian (130 AD) on the left. The keystone of the architrave shows Tyche, the Goddess of Victory. A frieze depicts the legend of the city's founding.

Next to it lie the ruins of the multi-storey Scholastic Baths. They offered space for up to 1000 visitors, and even had a library and an entertainment area. The statue of the found is still there, except the head. From the baths one could observe the traffic on the road through a glass window.

Trajan's Fountain and Hercules Gate: A few steps further uphill, also on the left-hand side of Curetes Road, is the well-preserved Trajan Fountain — a magnificent nymphaeum which was dedicated to the Emperor Trajan in 114 AD. Twelve statues were once located in the niches, and a large statue of the emperor stood above it; now only his foot is left as a reminder. A few metres further uphill there used to be a triumphal arch. Since a relief of Hercules adorned the side columns, it was also known as Hercules Gate. Today, however, the upper horizontal stones are missing.

Memmius Monument: A few more steps uphill on the left is the Memmius Monument, which was later transformed into a fountain. It was dedicated to Gaius Memmius, a grandchild of the Roman general and dictator Sulla, who plundered the city in 84 BC as punishment for the Ephesian Vespers.

Domitian Temple: Past the **Pollio Nymphaeum**, which was once, like the Trajan Fountain, richly decorated with statues, you come to the massive foundations of the Domitian Temple. Here archaeologists found the head of a monumental statue of the Emperor Domitian, who was murdered in the year 96. History remembers him as an enemy of Christians. There is a kind of 'inscription museum' in the foundations today, where original Latin texts with English translations are placed opposite each stone slab. Unfortunately, it's not always open.

State agora, prytaneion and 'odeon': The 160 x 58m square was the political centre of the city. Somewhat north of it stood the prytaneion, a meeting house. Here the eternal fire of the city burned, guarded by the curetes (priests) and vestal virgins. In this building they found the larger-than-life statue of Artemis which today is housed in the archaeological museum at

Selçuk. From here you can walk through a semicircular hallway to a building which is assumed to be the bouleuterion, the city hall. It is called the 'odeon' because of its shape. The rows of seats are in excellent condition. About 1400 spectators could watch the council meetings from 27 rows of seats. Between the city hall and state agora are the bases of columns which once lined the 160m-long 'Bulls-head Hall', named after their strange capitals.

Sights around Ephesus
Outside the paid-admission area:
The sites near Ephesus with no entrance fees are hardly worth a visit. On the right-hand side of the road past the upper exit is the mis-named **Tomb of St. Luke**, a round mausoleum belonging to an unknown deceased from the 1st century, which was converted into a church during Christian times (for a while it was believed that St. Luke was buried here). A little further along is **Magnesium Gate**, northwest of which are the scant remains of the **eastern gymnasium**, also called the girls' gymnasium on account of the statues found here.

Near the car park by the lower entrance are the ruins of a **Byzantine building**, probably a palace or baths. Further along the Selçuk road lies a 192m-long **stadium**, built under Emperor Nero; a monumental entrance gate still remains, but all the stone grandstands were plundered to built the hilltop citadel. Some 50m further on, surrounded by a fence, is the rubble of the **Vedius Gymnasium**, donated by Publius Vedius Antonius, a rich citizen of

the city. It had, among other things, under-floor heating.

A cave known as the '**Grotto of the Seven Sleepers**' is signposted from the approach road to Ephesus. During the Christian persecutions, seven young men are said to have hidden in these caves. Roman soldiers saw them and bricked up the entrance, whereupon the refugees sank into a sleep lasting 200 years. When they were awoken by an earthquake and broke down the wall, Christianity had long become the state religion, and the persecutions had become history. Emperor Theodosius II later established a pilgrimage church here, in which the bodies of the young men allegedly lay buried. At the time of writing, the cave was in danger of collapse and closed to the public, but the church nave could be seen through the fence.

Artemision: This once-famous temple is half-way along the Ephesus/Selçuk road. Antipater, when compiling his list of the Seven Wonders of the Ancient World, wondered if the Sun God Helios had ever seen anything similar, except at Olympos. Today Helios still looks down on Olympos, but instead of the Artemision he sees almost nothing — just the one column shown on page 55 is still standing.

Opening times: The site is usually freely accessible; occasionally an entry fee is charged.

Selçuk Archaeological Museum: This ranks among the most outstanding museums of its kind in Turkey, with some of the most beautiful finds from Ephesus displayed in seven halls. **Finds**

from the hillside houses (in the first hall on the left) are the first highlights. This multicoloured array of treasures once adorned the wealthy Roman mansions. Among other things, there is a small bronze Eros riding on a dolphin, an Egyptian statuette of a priest from the 7th century BC, a marble fresco of Socrates, and the heads of Venus and Zeus. In the next hall is a **monumental fountain** with a sculpted group of figures from the Pollio Nymphaeum, in which Odysseus and his men prepare to blind the Cyclops Polyphemus. In the **garden** there are a few capitals (and souvenirs for sale); look out here for the large sarcophagus from the Belevi Mausoleum, which was found north of Selçuk. Past the hall containing **objects from tombs**, which illustrates how ancient civilisations buried their dead, one reaches the most beautiful and impressive hall of all — the **Artemis Hall**. Beside an Artemis statue without a head are two Roman marble copies of the cult figure — a 'Great Artemis' about 3m high and a somewhat later 'Beautiful Artemis'. The most prominent part of these statues is the chest, although experts are divided about whether the protrusions represent eggs, breasts or bulls' testicles.

The **ethnological display** merits more than a passing glance — there's a lot more on view than the usual nomadic tent and rural implements. The inner courtyard has a replica of a small market area, including a barber's shop, rose-water maker's and *hamam*. *Address/opening times/prices: in the centre of Selçuk diagonally opposite the Tourist Office. Open daily (except Mon.) from 08.30-12.00 and 13.00-17.00; entry fee £2.20.*

Meryemana: This is the house where the Virgin Mary is believed to have spent the last years of her life. Little is known about the life of Mary after the birth of Jesus, and her burial place is also unclear. Was it Mount Zion in Jerusalem or Aladağ, 9km south of Selçuk, as indicated by the following story?

A German nun, Katharina Emmerich (1774-1824), had a vision of the house where Mary lived and died. Although she had never been to Turkey, in 1891 Lazarist monks from Izmir discovered a house on Aladağ, 7km south of Selçuk, which matched the description and so became a place of pilgrimage. It consists of a dome-covered sturdy stone building in a parkland setting. In the main room, below the apse, is an altar with a black Madonna: this is said to have been Mary's bedroom. Directly below the house is a spring, from where believers can draw holy water. Pilgrims come in droves to Meryemana on Ascension Day, when services are held here. *Getting there/opening times/prices: From the centre of Selçuk take the road towards Aydın and turn right after about 2km (signposted to Meryemana). From here it's another 6km to the house. Open daily from 08.00-19.00. The entrance fee of £3.75 per person is raised by the municipality of Selçuk to maintain this 'Meryemana Cultural Park'.*

Index

Only geographical names are included here; for all other entries, see Contents, page 3. **Bold type** indicates a photograph; *italic type* indicates a map or plan; both may be in addition to a text reference on the same page.

184